United Nations
Department of International Economic and Social Affairs
Statistical Office
Centre for Social Development and Humanitarian Affairs

unicef
United Nations Children's Fund

UNFPA

United Nations Population Fund

UNIFEM
United Nations Development Fund for Women

ST/ESA/STAT/SER.K/8

Social Statistics and Indicators Series K No. 8

The World's Women 1970–1990
Trends and Statistics

United Nations New York, 1991

The designations used and the presentation of material
in this publication do not imply the expression of any opinion
whatsoever on the part of the Secretariat of the United Nations concerning the legal status of any country, territory, city
or area or of its authorities, or concerning the delimitation of
its frontiers or boundaries.

The term "country" as used in this publication also refers, as appropriate, to territories or areas.

The designations "developed regions" and "developing
regions" are intended for statistical convenience and do not
necessarily express a judgement about the stage reached by
a particular country or area in the development process.

ST/ESA/STAT/SER.K/8

United Nations Publication
Sales No. E.90.XVII.3
ISBN 92-1-161313-2

Message from the Secretary-General

Since 1975, when the United Nations observed International Women's Year and proclaimed 1976–1985 as the United Nations Decade for Women: Equality, Development, Peace, the collection and analysis of reliable and comprehensive data on the situation of women has become a top priority in the United Nations system.

This book reflects the work of many parts of the United Nations, not only in collecting statistics on women, but also in presenting and interpreting them in such a way that policy makers and people all over the world can use them to advance the status of women through legislation, development strategies and effective lobbying. The information here should be an invaluable tool for promoting equality and changing attitudes towards women's work, worth and responsibilities.

It is clear from these data and indicators that, although there have been some improvements for women over the past 20 years, the majority still lag far behind men in power, wealth and opportunity. Data are needed to generate awareness of the present situation, to guide policy, to mobilize action and to monitor progress towards improvements.

The data in this book are presented to help achieve all these purposes.

Javier Pérez de Cuéllar
Secretary-General

Foreword

Women are moving to the forefront of the global agenda for social, economic and political development. But moving from agenda to policy to practice takes time, sometimes generations. It also takes numbers—to support the demands for equal status.

For many years, women's advocates have challenged stereotypes depicting women as passive, dependent and inferior to men. But efforts to reinforce their challenges with hard evidence have been undercut by serious limitations in available statistics and analysis, including a male bias in the definition and collection of many statistics and indicators. Women's living conditions—and their contributions to the family, the economy and the household—have generally been invisible. Many statistics have been defined in terms that portray men's conditions and contributions, not women's, or that simply ignore gender.

To remedy such inadequacies, in 1975 the United Nations launched the United Nations Decade for Women: Equality, Development and Peace and called for a pioneering effort in the study of social trends and statistics to collect and compile statistics by gender. This statistical portrait and analysis of the situation of women—a direct outcome of that mandate—presents the most complete depiction so far of women's conditions and contributions across the world. It is only a beginning, however, for improving statistical measures and removing their gender bias is a slow process.

The indicators in this portrait—on health, families, education, economics, public life and human settlements—highlight the fact that men and women indeed function in different worlds. Their responsibilities in and contributions to their family, to the economy and to society are quite different.

One of the most obvious differences between men's and women's worlds is women's child-bearing role and their near-total responsibility for family care and household management. Here, the data show that women have gained more control over their reproductive lives, but not everywhere or to the same extent. And even when women have such control, their responsibility for their family's survival and their own is increasing. In far too many instances, women are the providers of last resort for their families and themselves, often in relentlessly adverse conditions.

The statistics and indicators on economic life point out that women in all parts of the world are finding and exploiting new economic opportunities—and assuming greater economic roles. But their economic employment, generally lodged in subsistence agriculture and services with low productivity, is separate from men's and unequal. And their incomes, seen as supplements to men's, have remained lower. Worse, much of the work women do is still not considered to be of any economic value at all—and is not even measured. Finally, the participation of women in overall economic and political decision-making, although improving slightly, remains extremely low.

Putting this kind of numerical and analytical spotlight on the needs, the efforts and the contributions of women is one of the best ways to speed the process of moving from agenda to policy to practice—to a world of peace, equality and sustained development.

Rafeeudin Ahmed
Under-Secretary-General,
Department of International
Economic and Social Affairs

Dr. Nafis Sadik
Executive Director, United
Nations Population Fund

Margaret J. Anstee
Director-General and Head,
Centre for Social
Development and
Humanitarian Affairs

James Grant
Executive Director, United
Nations Children's Fund

Sharon Capeling-Alakija
Director, United Nations
Development Fund for
Women

Contents

Preface

The idea behind producing *The World's Women 1970–1990* is to provide the numbers and analysis needed to understand how conditions are changing or not changing for women—and to do it in a way that will reach women, the media and women's advocates everywhere. In this approach the report is innovative and experimental for the United Nations. It provides concerned women and men with information they can use to inform people everywhere about how much women contribute to economic life, political life and family life and to support appeals to persuade public and private decision-makers to change policies that are unfair to women.

The direction and the areas covered follow mandates already adopted in the United Nations, including the Convention on the Elimination of All Forms of Discrimination against Women (1979) and the Nairobi Forward-looking Strategies for the Advancement of Women (1985).

The publication is also a statistical sourcebook. Country and area data were assembled on indicators that capture conditions of women and then grouped into regional averages. The regional averages were analysed and interpreted for presentation in text and charts. A wide range of general and ad hoc statistics was assembled but many gaps remain—gaps in coverage of important topics, in timeliness, in comparison with men, in comparisons over time and in country coverage. The publication nevertheless provides a guide for accumulating and interpreting more information in coming years. It also provides the most complete presentation so far of how women fare in different parts of the world.

The World's Women 1970–1990 is a new type of international statistical publication, following the form of publications on "Social Trends and Statistics" developed at the national level in a few countries since the 1960s and 1970s. Sir Claus Moser, as consultant to the participating United Nations organizations, encouraged and assisted in planning this form of statistical publication. It is hoped that this format will be found particularly suited to the presentation of a wide diversity of social and human development indicators which, however important, do not lend themselves to presentation using a few aggregate series as do economic statistics and national accounts.

The World's Women 1970–1990 is a collaborative effort of the many United Nations bodies concerned with promoting women's equality and participation in development. This effort has been led by the United Nations Children's Fund (UNICEF), the United Nations Population Fund (UNFPA), the United Nations Development Fund for Women (UNIFEM) and the Division for the Advancement of Women, Centre for Social Development and Humanitarian Affairs of the United Nations Secretariat, all of which also provided substantial financial support.

The International Research and Training Institute for the Advancement of Women (INSTRAW) and the United Nations Development Programme (UNDP) provided supplementary funding for the wall chart "The Situation of Women 1990—Selected Indicators".[1]

The Statistical Office, Department of International Economic and Social Affairs of the United Nations Secretariat, compiled and organized the statistical material for *The World's Women 1970–1990* and coordinated the overall programme for preparation of the publication. Analysis and policy direction were provided by representatives of UNICEF, UNFPA, UNIFEM and the Centre for Social Development and Humanitarian Affairs of the United Nations Secretariat.

Other United Nations offices and organizations provided statistics and special studies in their own fields of expertise, including the Population Division, Department of International Economic and Social Affairs of the United Nations Secretariat, the International Labour Office (ILO), the Food and Agriculture Organization of the United Nations (FAO), the International Research and Training Institute for the Advancement of Women (INSTRAW), the United Nations Educational, Scientific and Cultural Organization (UNESCO), the World Bank and the World Health Organization (WHO). The Inter-Parliamentary Union, a non-governmental organization, also provided information.

The following individuals and organizations assisted in the preparation of *The World's Women 1970-1990* as consultants to the Secretariat: Gwen Johnson-Ascadi and George Ascadi, Judith Bruce, Ruth Dixon, Randee Falk, Lourdes Urdaneta-Ferrán, Luisella Goldschmidt-Clermont, Andrew Harvey, Abbe Herzig, Carmen McFarlane, Leo Pujadas, Goranna Sipiç and the International Center for Public Enterprises in Developing Countries, Debbie Taylor and Laurent Toulemon. The American Writing Corporation's Valerie Gwinner, Katherine Humphrey, Bruce Ross-Larson and Merrell Tuck-Primdahl, as consultants to the Secretariat, drafted the Overview and provided substantial assistance to the Secretariat in preparing the final manuscript.

Work on *The World's Women 1970–1990* was undertaken under the direction of Robert Johnston and Joann Vanek, assisted by Linda Go, with an advisory panel consisting of Richard Jolly, Gareth Jones and Agnes Aidoo (UNICEF), Catherine S. Pierce, A. Muniem Abu-Nuwar and Alex Marshall (UNFPA), Linda Miranda (UNIFEM); and John Mathiason (Centre for Social Development and Humanitarian Affairs), Tina Jorgensen (Department of Public Information) and Maxim Zhukov (Department of Conference Services) of the United Nations Secretariat.

Note

1   United Nations publication, Sales No. E.90.XVII.3A.

About the chapters

The World's Women 1970–1990 is an experimental publication that uses innovative techniques and formats to highlight the main findings on women's conditions and to present statistics and analyses that non-specialists can readily understand.

Each chapter begins with its main messages—in four or five sentences. And each proceeds with modules of text, charts and sometimes tables to present regional stories drawn from the country tables at the back of the chapter. The intention is not to produce a linear narrative. It is to assemble, for each indicator, some descriptive text and illustrative charts to convey what is generalizable from the data. In some cases, the presentation goes beyond the country tables and draws from their full source, the United Nations Women's Indicators and Statistics Database for microcomputers (Wistat), which pulls together most of the data available on women (and women compared with men), in all parts of the United Nations system. And in some others, the material is drawn from other sources, mainly small-scale studies, which are cited.

The text and tables are accompanied by statements of how the indicators are defined, where the data are from and how they can be interpreted.

Regional and subregional averages

The regional and subregional groupings used are shown in annex III, at the end of the present publication. With few exceptions (each noted) regional and subregional averages are based on unweighted data for the countries and areas for which data are available. The purpose is to show the general picture in the region or subregion, against which the situation of each country or area can be assessed. If country data were weighted by the population in each country, regional and subregional averages would mainly reflect the situation in one or two large countries.

Presentation of data for regions and subregions

Subregional rather than regional averages are shown wherever possible if the basic data show that regional averages would conceal wide differences among countries and that subregional experience is more homogeneous. If series are hetereogeneous even at the subregional level (for example, gross domestic product per capita), country data or small groups of comparable countries are used as the basis of calculation and analysis. If the number of countries or areas for which data are available in a region or subregion is very small, the countries are indicated or the number of countries having data is given.

The basic grouping of countries is by continental region. Because there is no generally accepted standard in the United Nations system for considering a country or area as either developed or developing, these terms are applied only at regional and subregional levels. They are intended for statistical and analytical convenience and do not express a judgement about the stage a country or area has reached in the development process.

For the statistical analysis in this publication, the developed regions consist of Europe and the Union of Soviet Socialist Republics, northern America (United States of America and Canada) and Australia, Japan and New Zealand. The remaining major regions are Africa, Latin America and the Caribbean, and Asia and the Pacific. In Africa and in Asia and the Pacific, subregional averages are used where possible and necessary to identify more homogeneous groups of countries or areas. The subregional groupings are based on the classification developed by the Population Division of the United Nations Secretariat for demographic analysis. In most cases, Africa is divided into northern and sub-Saharan subregions, and Asia and the Pacific into western, eastern, southern and south-eastern subregions and Oceania. In all cases Australia, Japan and New Zealand are excluded from Asia and the Pacific calculations because they are included in the developed regions.

Countries and areas

In general the countries and areas covered are the same as those in the United Nations Women's Indicators and Statistics Database (Wistat). Included are all member States of the United Nations plus non-member States and other entities over 150,000 population in 1985, for a total of 178 countries or areas. These are listed in annex III.

If data are provided for specific countries in text tables (for example, the listing of countries with high maternal mortality), the countries shown are those for which data are available. Such listings in text tables cannot therefore be considered exhaustive. If data are not available for a country in the country tables of indicators at the end of each chapter, two periods (..) indicate the missing data.

The designations employed and the form of presentation of material in *The World's Women 1970–1990* do not imply the expression of any opinion whatsoever on the part of the Secretariat of the United Nations concerning the legal status of any country, territory, city or area or that of its authorities or concerning the delimitation of its frontiers or boundaries.

Through accession of the German Democratic Republic to the Federal Republic of Germany with effect from 3 October 1990, the two German States have united to form one sovereign State. As from the date of unification, the Federal Republic of Germany acts in the United Nations under the designation "Germany". All data shown for Germany pertain to end-June 1990 or earlier and are indicated separately for the Federal Republic of Germany and the former German Democratic Republic.

Sources of data

Statistics and indicators have been compiled for Wistat and *The World's Women 1970–1990* mainly from official national and international sources, as these are more authoritative and comprehensive, more generally available as time series and more comparable among countries. Most of the official national and international sources use data directly from national population and housing censuses and household sample surveys, or are estimates based on these.

Official sources are supplemented by other sources and estimates, where they are widely available, have been subjected to professional scrutiny and debate, and are consistent with other independent sources.

Statistical concepts and sources are highlighted at numerous points in the text and described for each country table in the accompanying notes. For more detailed statistics and description of methods, the original statistical and analytical sources should be consulted. They are cited in the text in brackets and listed at the back of this book.

Statistical abbreviations and conventions

A hyphen (–) between years, for example, 1984–1985, indicates the full period involved, including the beginning and end years; a slash (/) indicates a financial year, school year or crop year, for example 1984/85, or a longer period within which data are available for one time only, for example 1980/85.

The following symbols have been used in the tables:

- A point (.) is used to indicate decimals.
- A minus sign (–) before a number indicates a deficit or decrease, except as indicated.
- Two dots (..) indicate that data are not available or are not separately reported.
- Reference to "dollars" ($) indicates United States dollars, unless otherwise stated.
- Details and percentages in tables do not necessarily add to totals because of rounding.

Overview of the world's women

Words advocating the interests of women, however plausible and persuasive they may be, need numbers to influence policy—and change the world. Numbers are also needed to better inform women of how their lives are changing or not changing—globally, regionally and nationally. That was one of the main conclusions of the World Conference of the International Women's Year, held in Mexico City in 1975, where women's leaders proclaimed 1976–1985 as the United Nations Decade for Women: Equality, Development and Peace, and called on the United Nations statistical services to compile and monitor indicators in several key categories for women:[1]

- *Family life.* How are women's responsibilities in the family changing relative to men's? How are changes in households providing greater opportunities and affecting what women do?
- *Leadership and decision-making.* How many women are represented in government, business and the community? Is their influence on the rise?
- *Health and child-bearing.* Are women living longer, healthier lives? How does the health of women—and girls—compare with men's? What choices do women have in child-bearing? And what are the risks connected with child-bearing world-wide?
- *Education.* Are women better educated today than 20 years ago? How does their education compare with men's?
- *Economic life.* What do women contribute to production—and to development? How is that contribution valued—and measured?

Remarkably there were few indicators available in the early 1970s to answer even the most basic questions. Now there are. This book pieces together what's available to give a more coherent set of indicators and a clearer picture of where women stand.

Consider this: the number of illiterate women rose from 543 million in 1970 to 597 million in 1985, while the number of illiterate men rose from 348 million to 352 million.

And this: women work as much as or more than men everywhere—as much as 13 hours, on average, more each week according to studies in Asia and Africa.

And this: of 8,000 abortions in Bombay after parents learned the sex of the foetus through amniocentesis, only one would have been a boy.[2]

Numbers can thus give words considerable power—the power to change.

Regional trends: 1970–1990*

Over the past 20 years there have been important changes in what women do—out of choice or necessity, depending on the hardships and opportunities they face.

In *Latin America and the Caribbean*, women in urban areas made some significant gains according to indicators of health, child-bearing, education and economic, social and political participation. But there was little change in rural areas, and the serious macroeconomic deterioration of many Latin American countries in the 1980s undercut even the urban gains as the decade progressed.

In *sub-Saharan Africa*, there was some improvement for women in health and education, but indicators in these fields are still far from even minimally acceptable levels in most countries. Fertility remains very high, and there are signs that serious economic decline—coupled with rapid population growth—is undermining even the modest gains in health and education. Women's economic and social participation and contribution is high in sub-Saharan Africa. But given the large differences between men and women in most economic, social and political indicators at the start of the 1970s, the limited progress in narrowing those differences since then and the general economic decline, the situation for women in Africa remains grave.

In *northern Africa and western Asia*, women made gains in health and education. Fertility declined slightly but remains very high—5.5 children in northern Africa and 5.3 in western Asia. Women in these regions continue to lag far behind in their economic participation and in social participation and decision-making.

In *southern Asia*, women's health and education improved somewhat. But as in Africa, indicators are still far from minimally acceptable levels—and are still very far from men's. Nor has economic growth, when it has occurred, helped women—apparently because of their low social, political and economic participation in both urban and rural areas.

Words need numbers to influence policy—and change the world

*For a listing of countries and areas in each region, see annex III.

In much of *eastern and south-eastern Asia*, women's levels of living improved steadily in the 1970s and 1980s. Many of the inequalities between men and women—in health, education and employment—were reduced in both urban and rural areas and fertility also declined considerably. Even so, considerable political and economic inequalities persist in much of the region—because women are confined to the lowest paid and lowest status jobs and sectors and because they are excluded from decision-making.

Throughout the *developed regions*, the health of women is generally good and their fertility is low. But in other fields, indicators of the status of women show mixed results. Women's economic participation is high in eastern Europe and the USSR, northern Europe and northern America—lower in Australia, Japan, New Zealand and southern and western Europe. Everywhere occupational segregation and discrimination in wages and training work very much in favour of men. In political participation and decision-making, women are relatively well represented only in northern Europe and (at least until recently) eastern Europe and the USSR.

Gaps in policy, investment and pay

Resounding throughout the statistics in this book is one consistent message. Major gaps in policy, investment and earnings prevent women from performing to their full potential in social, economic and political life.

Policy gaps

Integration of women in mainstream development policies. The main policy gap is that governments seldom integrate the concerns and interests of women into mainstream policies. Development policies typically emphasize export-oriented growth centred on cash crops, primary commodities and manufactures—largely controlled by men. Those policies typically neglect the informal sector and subsistence agriculture—the usual preserve of women. Even when women are included in mainstream development strategies, it is often in marginal women-in-development activities.

Much of this gap is embodied in laws that deny women equality with men in their rights to own land, borrow money and enter contracts. Even where women now have *de jure* equality, the failures to carry out the law deny equality de facto. Consider Uganda, which has a new constitution guaranteeing full equality for women. One women's leader there had this assessment: "We continue to be second-rate citizens—no, third-rate, since our sons come before us. Even donkeys and tractors sometimes get better treatment."[3]

Counting women's work. A second policy gap is that governments do not consider much of women's work to be economically productive and thus do not count it. If women's unpaid work in subsistence agriculture and housework and family care were fully counted in labour force statistics, their share of the labour force would be equal to or greater than men's. And if their unpaid housework and family care were counted as productive outputs in national accounts, measures of global output would increase 25 to 30 per cent.

Even when governments do consider women's work to be economically productive, they overlook or undervalue it. Until recently, labour force statistics counted production narrowly, excluding such activities as grinding grain and selling home-grown food at the market. The International Labour Organisation widened the definition in 1982 but the application of the new standard is far from universal, and in most countries and regions only a small part of women's production is measured. Without good information about what women really do— and how much they produce—governments have little incentive to respond with economic policies that include women.[4]

Investment gaps

Education. There also are big gaps between what women could produce and the investments they command. Households—and governments— almost always invest less in women and girls than in men and boys. One measure of this is enrolment in school: roughly 60 per cent of rural Indian boys and girls enter primary school, but after five years, only 16 per cent of the girls are still enrolled, compared with 35 per cent of the boys.[5]

The losses from investing less in girls' education are considerable. Studies in Malaysia show that the net return to education at all levels of wages and productivity is consistently 20 per cent higher for girls and young women than for boys and young men.[6] And that does not include the second-round benefits of reduced fertility, improved nutrition and better family care.

One consequence of women's low educational achievement is that it puts them at a disadvantage to their husbands when making major life decisions about the work they do, the number of children they have and the way they invest family income.

Health services. Another investment gap is in health services. Women need, and too seldom receive, maternal health care and family planning services. And families often give lower priority to the health care of girls than boys. Where health services are being cut back, as they so often are under economic austerity programmes, the health needs of women are typically neglected.

Productivity. These gaps in investing in women's development persist in the investments that governments might make to increase their economic productivity. Governments give little or no support to activities in which women predominate—notably, the informal sector and subsistence agriculture. Indeed, government policies typically steer women into less productive endeavours. The infrastructure that might underpin their work is extremely inadequate. And the credit available to them from formal lending institutions is negligible. Often illiterate, usually lacking collateral and almost always discriminated against, women must rely on their husbands or on high-priced money-lenders if they want to invest in more productive ventures.

Pay gaps

Lower pay. There also are big gaps between what women produce and what they are paid. Occupational segregation and discrimination relegate women to low-paying, low-status jobs. And even when women do the same work as men, they typically receive less pay—30 to 40 per cent less on average world-wide. Nor are their prospects for advancement the same as men's, with deeply rooted prejudices blocking them from the top.

No pay. Another pay gap is that much of women's work is not paid and not recognized as economically productive. The work is considered to be of no economic importance and is not counted, which brings the discussion back to policy gaps.

Trends in child-bearing and family life

Giving women the means to regulate their child-bearing enhances their ability to shape their own lives. Modern family planning methods make it far easier for women today to limit their fertility—and as important, to pick the timing and spacing of their births. Almost everywhere, the access to and the use of family planning are increasing, but not as rapidly as they might.

Fertility rates are declining in many developing countries but remain at quite high levels in most countries in Africa, in the southern Asia region and in countries of western Asia. Influencing the falling rates are broader use of effective family planning methods, changing attitudes about desired family size and reductions in infant mortality. With the spread of modern contraception, women are better able to limit their fertility. But safe contraception must be available and accepted by both women and men, and in some societies men often do not allow women to practise family planning.

The child-bearing gap between developed and developing regions remains wide. In Asia and Africa, a woman typically has her first child at about age 19 or even earlier, her last at 37, for a child-bearing span of 18 years. In some countries—such as Bangladesh, Mauritania, Nigeria, the Sudan and Yemen—girls often start having children at age 15. Compare this with developed regions, where a woman typically has her first child at 23 and her last at 30, for a span of only seven years. Women in developed regions have fewer children over a shorter span of years and thus need to devote a smaller part of their lives to child-bearing and parenting.

Family planning and health services have helped women in many ways—improving their overall health status and that of their children and increasing their opportunities to take an expanded role in society.

Child-bearing exposes women to a particular array of health risks. But the broader availability of family planning and maternal health services has reduced some of the risks of pregnancy and childbirth—delaying the first birth, allowing longer spacing between births, and reducing pregnancies among women who have had four or more births and thus face the greatest risk of haemorrhaging after giving birth.[7] Complications from child-bearing nevertheless remain a major (avoidable) cause of death for women in many developing countries—especially where family planning services are poor or hard to reach, where malnutrition is endemic among pregnant women and where births are not attended by trained personnel.

Healthier mothers are more likely to have full-term pregnancies and strong children. With more resources, they are better able to nurture their children. Better educated mothers are more likely to educate their children. The positive outcome: healthier, better educated families.

Poor women generally miss out on this positive cycle. Because they have little or no education, they have little knowledge of health practices and limited economic opportunities. They have no collateral for borrowing to invest in more productive activities. Simply trying to ensure that the family survives takes all their time. The unhappy outcome: sick, poorly educated families—and continuing poverty.

Poor teenage girls, the most vulnerable of mothers, face even greater obstacles. Cultural pressures, scant schooling and inadequate information about and access to family planning make them most likely to have unhealthy or unwanted pregnancies. In developed and developing countries alike, mothers aged 15–19 are twice as likely to die

Family planning helps women to improve their own and their children's health and expand their role in society in childbirth as mothers in their early twenties, and those under 15 are five times as likely.[8] They are less likely to obtain enough education or training to ensure a good future for themselves and their children.

Trends in marriages and households

In developed and developing regions alike, women now spend less time married and fewer years bearing and rearing children. Couples are marrying later and separating or divorcing more, in part because of their increased mobility and migration.

Throughout much of the world—the exceptions are in Asia and the Pacific—households are getting smaller and have fewer children. There are fewer multigenerational households, more single-parent families and more people living alone. Smaller households suggest the gradual decline of the extended family household, most evident in western developed countries, but also beginning to be apparent in developing countries. Also evident is a decline in the strength of kinship and in the importance of family responsibility combined with greater reliance on alternative support systems and greater variations in living arrangements.

Because more women are living (or forced to live) alone or as heads of households with dependents, their responsibility for their family's survival and their own has been increasing since 1970. Motherhood is more often unsupported by marriage and the elderly are more often unsupported by their children—trends that increase the burden on women. And even for women living with men, the man's income is often so inadequate that the woman must take on the double burden of household management and outside work to make ends meet.

Women face another burden that is invisible to the outside world: domestic violence. It is unmeasured but almost certainly very extensive. Domestic violence is masked by secretiveness and poor evidence, and there are social and legal barriers to its active prevention. Men's attacks on women in their homes are thought to be the least reported of crimes—in part because such violence is seen as a social ill, not a crime. Women's economic independence—and the corresponding ability to leave an abusive man—are essential for preventing violence and for fostering self-esteem. And as the awareness of women's rights becomes more universal and enforceable, more women will be opposing domestic violence.

Women's working world differs from men's in type of work, pay and status

Economic life

Economic growth in many of the developed regions has provided new opportunities for women in economic participation, production and income—despite persistent occupational and wage discrimination and the continuing exclusion of women's unpaid housework from economic measurement.

Some countries in Asia and a few in other developing regions were also able to sustain strong economic growth rates, again providing new opportunities for women despite even more pervasive social and economic obstacles to their economic advancement. But in most countries in the developing regions, as well as in eastern Europe and the USSR, the economic outlook was far worse in 1990 than in 1970. And world-wide the population living in the poorest countries increased dramatically. This mixed economic growth has created new obstacles to women's economic participation and their progress towards equality with men—seriously undercutting previous advances. And whether in circumstances of economic growth or decline, women have been called on to bear the greater burdens, and receive the fewest benefits.[9]

Women are the first to be dismissed from the salaried labour force by economic downturns and the contractions under stabilization and adjustment programmes. With essentials less affordable because of rising inflation and falling subsidies, women have little choice but to work harder and longer. And when the demand for workers rises, as in Brazil in the late 1980s, the men find jobs at their old wages while the women must take jobs at even lower pay than before.[10]

Women's working world

Women's working world continues to differ from men's in the type of work, the pay, the status and the pattern of entering and leaving the work force. The biggest difference is that women continue to bear the burden of managing the household and caring for the family—and that men continue to control the resources for production and the income from it. In agriculture, for example, women continue to be left labour-intensive tasks that consume the most time.[11]

Women everywhere contribute to economic production. As officially measured, 46 per cent of the world's women aged 15 and over—828 million—are economically active. At least another 10-20 per cent of the world's women are economically productive but not counted as part of the labour force because of inadequate measurement.

Women are left to provide child care, to provide food and health care, to prepare and process crops, to market goods, to tend gardens and livestock and to weave cloth, carpets and baskets. Much of this work does not benefit from investment, making it very inefficient and forcing women to work very hard for meagre results. In the worst cases, technological investments end up exploiting women—improving their productivity but barring them from any access or control over the profits.

The pattern, then, is that women work as much or more than men. Although women spend less time in activities officially counted as economically productive and make much less money, they spend far more in home production. If a woman spends more time in the labour force, she still bears the main responsibility for home and family care, and sleep and leisure are sacrificed.

Economic participation

Men's participation in the labour force has fallen everywhere. Women's, by contrast, has fallen significantly only in sub-Saharan Africa, where economic crises have been most widespread. Women's share in the total labour force is increasing in most regions.

In many parts of the developed regions, there have been increases in women's economic activity rates over the past two decades. Women's highest shares in wage and salaried employment are in eastern Europe and the Soviet Union, something that could change as new economic policies create widepread unemployment there.

In Africa, most public and wage employees are men, leaving women either in subsistence agriculture or to create whatever opportunities they can in the informal sector.

In Asia and the Pacific, the picture is mixed. Women's economic activity rates (in official statistics) are very low (under 20 per cent) in southern and western Asia, but fairly high (35–40 per cent) in eastern and south-eastern Asia. Women's wage and salary employment rose considerably (from 44 to 57 per cent of the total, excluding southern Asia), reflecting significant expansion of economic opportunities for women.

In Latin America, women's economic participation grew fastest but remained at low levels (31 per cent in urban areas, 14 per cent in rural). The increase reflects greater opportunities in towns and cities as well as greater economic necessities arising from the ongoing economic crisis of the 1980s.

Occupational segregation and wage discrimination

Everywhere in the world the workplace is segregated by sex. Women tend to be in clerical, sales and domestic services and men in manufacturing and transport. Women work in teaching, care-giving and subsistence agriculture and men in management, administration and politics. Looking at job categories in more detail reveals even sharper segregation. For example, in teaching, women predominate in elementary or first level education while men predominate in higher education.

Women hold a mere 10–20 per cent of managerial and administrative jobs world-wide and less than 20 per cent of the manufacturing jobs. In Singapore barely 1 per cent of working women are in managerial work, compared with nearly 10 per cent for a much larger number of working men. Even when women work in male-dominated occupations, they are relegated to the lower echelons. Among all the organizations of the United Nations system, for example, women hold only 3 per cent of the top management jobs and 8 per cent of senior management positions, but 42 per cent of the entry-level civil service slots, suggesting that women are not usually promoted or hired directly into higher levels. Of the top 1,000 corporations in the United States, only two are headed by a woman, a mere 2/10 of 1 per cent.[12]

In every country having data, women's non-agricultural wage rates are substantially lower than men's. In some countries, the gap is around 50 per cent and only in very few is it less than 30 per cent. The average gap is between 30 per cent and 40 per cent and there is no sign that it is substantially narrowing.

Even where women have moved into occupations dominated by men, their income remains lower. Take Canada, where women have made solid inroads into administration, management, engineering, physical sciences, university teaching and law and medicine. Between 1971 and 1981 they accounted for nearly a third of the growth in these professions. Women in these professions earned about 15 per cent more than women in other professional categories but they still lagged 15–20 per cent behind their male counterparts.[13]

The informal sector

One wedge of opportunity for women is the informal sector, including self-employment. Crucial to the survival strategies of many women, the informal sector also opens important long-term opportunities where salaried employment is closed to women, declining or inadequate. Women work in

Everywhere in the world the workplace is segregated by sex

the informal sector because of necessity and convenience. It requires less skill and education. It has fewer biases in favour of men. And it is easier to reconcile with cultural norms that keep women near the home, for there is less conflict between working hours and household tasks. But informal employment is far less secure an employer than the formal workplace and productivity is often low.

Incomes may be lower in the informal sector for several reasons. One is the absence or high cost of credit. Another is lack of government support. A third is exploitation by larger firms controlling raw materials or markets. And although women's participation in the informal sector is increasing, the returns are declining. Studies show that there is greater difference in the earnings of men and women in the informal sector than in the formal.[14]

Women in the informal sector are vulnerable to even slight deteriorations in an economy. Especially in highly indebted countries, informal sector returns have fallen even more than formal sector returns, as more people are pushed into the informal sector. Despite the meagre earnings, the informal sector has been women's only recourse for surviving the economic crises in Africa and Latin America during the 1980s.

Public life and leadership

Women are poorly represented in the ranks of power, policy and decision-making. Women make up less than 5 per cent of the world's heads of State, heads of major corporations and top positions in international organizations. Women are not just behind in political and managerial equity, they are a long way behind. This is in spite of the fact that women are found in large numbers in low-level positions of public administrations, political parties, trade unions and businesses.

The picture barely improves at other decision-making levels. Fifty United Nations member States have no woman in any of their top echelons of government. Although women have made some incursions in the past 20 years in parliaments and at middle management levels, their representation in these areas still averages less than 10 per cent and less than 20 per cent respectively. Their parliamentary representation would have to increase by 35 to 50 percentage points to reach parity with men. The eastern European and USSR parliaments are exceptions. Women have made up about a fourth of the parliamentary bodies there and played an important role. But recent elections show a significant drop in women's representation in these countries, just as parliaments—as a result of political changes—have become more important.

Women continue to be denied equal access to high-status and high-paying positions but there has been some progress since the United Nations Decade for Women began in 1976. Many countries have set up special offices to review complaints of discriminatory practice in political parties, parliaments, unions and professional organizations. Israel, Venezuela and several European countries have quotas to guarantee women more equal participation in the leadership of political parties. Trade unions in Canada, Norway and the United Kingdom have reserved a designated percentage of political seats for women. Women are also defining their own paths in politics. Increasing numbers are entering political life through non-governmental organizations, women's movements and associations of professional women. And women are increasingly active in the politics of their communities and locales.

Community and grass-roots participation have long been an extension of women's traditional place in the community and responsibility for the health and well-being of their families. The past 20 years have seen a burgeoning of groups headed by or heavily made up of women. Discriminatory practices, increasing poverty, violence against women, environmental threats, military build-ups, family and economic imperatives and the negative consequences of economic adjustment and stabilization programmes have all increased women's needs to band together to change conditions or policies. Women in both the developed and the developing regions have discovered that they can translate their efforts to protect themselves into effective political action.

Demands for equal status

International efforts to establish the rights of women culminated in 1979 with the General Assembly's adoption of the Convention on the Elimination of All Forms of Discrimination against Women (see annex II at the end of the book). The Convention confronts stereotypes, customs and norms that give rise to the many legal, political and economic constraints on women. The legal status of women receives the broadest attention—for basic rights of political participation, civil rights and reproductive rights. One hundred two countries have ratified the Convention, legally binding themselves to incorporate the Convention's demands in their policies.

Women are translating their struggle against discrimination into political action

Milestones of advocacy for women's equality

Women, more than ever, are on the global agenda, as a result of 30 years of constant advocacy and pressure.

1946 The United Nations Commission on the Status of Women is formed to monitor the situation of women and promote women's rights around the world.

1952 The Commission initiates the Convention on the Political Rights of Women, the first global mandate to grant women equal political rights under the law—the right to vote, hold office and exercise public functions.

1957 and **1962** Conventions initiated on the equality of married women, guaranteeing them equal rights in marriage and in dissolving marriage.

1967 Declaration on the Elimination of Discrimination against Women.

1975 International Women's Year. The World Conference on Women in Mexico City proclaims 1976–1985 as the United Nations Decade for Women: Equality, Development, Peace. Agencies are asked to collect thorough statistical information on women for the first time.

1979 The United Nations General Assembly adopts the Convention on the Elimination of all Forms of Discrimination against Women.

1980 The World Conference on Women in Copenhagen adopts the Programme of Action for the Second Half of the United Nations Decade for Women: Equality, Development and Peace. Agencies are asked to prepare the most recent data and time-trend analyses on the situation of women.

1985 The Nairobi World Conference reviews progress during the decade for women and adopts the Forward-looking Strategies for the Advancement of Women.

In 1985 the Nairobi Forward-looking Strategies for the Advancement of Women were approved by 157 countries gathered to assess the achievements and failures of the United Nations Decade for Women (see annex I). The Strategies demand that governments:

- Play key roles in ensuring that both men and women enjoy equal rights in such areas as education, training and employment.
- Act to remove negative stereotypes and perceptions of women.
- Disseminate information to women about their rights and entitlements.
- Collect timely and accurate statistics on women and monitor their situation.
- Encourage the sharing and support of domestic responsibilities.

Even with progress in legislation, women—especially poor women—are still a long way from receiving social recognition for what they do. De facto discrimination on the grounds of sex is insidious but widespread. For example, the Bangladesh Constitution guarantees the equal rights of men and women and sanctions affirmative action programmes in favour of women but as the data in the following chapters reveal, the status of women in Bangladesh is among the lowest in the world. It is encouraging, then, that policy makers there have stepped up efforts to implement programmes for women, particularly in health and education.[15]

Many societies deny women independence from family and male control, particularly where girls are married at a very young age to much older men. According to estimates from the World Fertility Survey, almost half the women in Africa, 40 per cent in Asia and 30 per cent in Latin America are married by the age of 18. Men are on average four to eight years older. And a woman's social status is often linked entirely to her reproductive role. Failure to bear children—or even to bear sons—is cause for ostracism, divorce and even brutality in areas of Africa and southern Asia.[16]

The Nairobi Strategies restate demands in the 1957 and 1962 international conventions for equal status of women and men in marriage and in the dissolution of marriage. In addition to such reforms in marriage laws and practices, efforts to improve women's economic status and autonomy—to reflect their economic responsibilities and contributions—can bring them closer to an equal footing with men in and out of the household.

Narrowing the gaps in the 1990s

The numbers throughout this book show the continuing gaps between women and men in policy, investment and pay. What's needed, of course, is equality of opportunity for women—in health, in education, in work and in decision-making at all levels. To get there is going to require extensive changes in policy, in government, in business and in the household, with women and men reworking the conventional assumptions about political, economic and family life. It is also going to require explicit initiatives to advance women's interests, initiatives informed by the analysis of numbers and grounded in the argument that advancing the interests of women benefits everyone.

The cost of these changes, especially when weighed against the benefit, would be small. Many of the policy changes cost nothing. Many of the required investments are small in relation to a country's gross domestic product—and in relation to military spending. True, closing the pay gap will cost something, and men will be the apparent losers. But better pay and incentives for women will increase productivity overall, so that everyone should benefit in the long run.

What's needed is equality of opportunity in health, education, work and decision-making

Many recent publications about women set out the agenda for action: the United Nations Population Fund's *Investing in Women*, the Commonwealth Secretariat's *Engendering Adjustment*, the World Bank's *Women in Development: A Progress Report on the World Bank Initiative*, the UNDP's *Human Development Report 1990*, and UNICEF's *The Invisible Adjustment: Poor Women and the Economic Crisis*, among many others.[17] Each gives its special emphasis to the broad agenda, with the recurring themes described below.

Counting what women do

National statistical services collect little data on women's economic contribution and income. One immediate need is to begin to quantify, and assign an economic value to, unpaid housework. Another is to measure women's paid work better. Also needed are disaggregations of all the main indicators by gender and improved compilation, analysis and dissemination of data already collected.

Putting women beside men at the center of policy

The numbers in this book show how different women's situations are from men's—mainly because of the opportunities they lack. New laws can pave the way to better opportunities for women—in owning and managing productive resources, in entering contracts, in doing many of the things men do in their daily work life. New policies—explicitly accommodating the special requirements of women for basic infrastructure, for access to credit and to markets, for technology and training and for child care—can do the same. This would cost little but require nothing short of a revolution in the way decisions are made in government, in business and in the household.

The agenda for the 1990s is to invest in women to achieve equitable and sustainable development

Investing in women's economic productivity

With the right policies, it will be possible to invest better in women's human capital and in their productive capital.

High maternal death rates are preventable.[18] The nutrition of mothers is also easily improved—with modest resources yielding incalculable benefits in the long term. Ensuring that pregnant women have simple, regular prenatal care and a healthy diet with iron supplements would save hundreds of thousands of lives each year by reducing high-risk pregnancies and increasing the birthweight of newborns. Providing family planning, in addition to conferring considerable benefits on the health of mothers and their children, also has incalculable benefits in the long term, by reducing population growth.

All countries should increase the enrolment—and attendance—of girls at all levels of schooling and give them opportunities in all fields of study. Education does much for a woman's status—in society, in the workplace, in the family. It also enables women to take more control of their lives and to respond better to opportunities. Not least, it puts wives on more equal footing with their husbands in making important decisions about their families' future. Educational systems can also do much to eliminate the cultural and societal barriers that block women's opportunities. Of special concern, however, is dealing with the nearly 600 million illiterate women already missed by educational systems.

Agricultural extension has to be redirected to reach women farmers and respond better to the problems they face. Part of this involves using more women as extension and field workers, and part, developing and delivering technical packages that women can use. The counterpart to extension is rural infrastructure, to make women's efforts more productive and to give them better access to markets.

Credit programmes also need to be redirected to reach women generally. Programmes of small loans, such as those of the Grameen Bank in Bangladesh and of Women's World Banking in every region, are essential for women to respond to the opportunities they see in farming, in small business, in training and in moving up the ladder everywhere.[19] Governments also need to provide other support for women's entrepreneurial endeavors in the informal sector—and in the formal sector. Also of importance is developing and delivering time-saving technology for women's unpaid work.

Reducing the gaps in pay

The requirements here are obvious: put an end to occupational segregation and wage discrimination, and recognize women's unpaid work as economically productive. These are matters for legislators, business leaders, and statistical services. But these are also matters for men and, above all, women. Men are not going to open the doors to their domains. Women are. And equipped with better skills and different views of their role in life, they will.

In sum: the agenda for the 1990s is to invest more in women—and to broaden their opportunities. Investing in wider opportunities for women—in health, in education, in formal and informal work and in decision-making at all levels—is far more than an investment in women, for it is an investment in their families and societies. It is a way to lift people out of poverty. It is a way to slow population growth. It is a way to protect the environment. And it is a way to get onto a path of equitable, sustainable development.

Notes

1   See *Report of the World Conference of the International Women's Year, Mexico City, 19 June–2 July 1975* (United Nations publication, Sales No. E.76.IV.1), chap. II, sect. A, paras. 161–173.

2   Government of India, Department of Women and Child Development, Ministry of Human Resource Development, *The Lesser Child: The Girl in India* (New Delhi, n.d.).

3   Miria Matembe, "Speaking out for women in Abuja", *Africa Recovery,* vol. 3, No. 3 (United Nations publication, 1989).

4   See *Improving Concepts and Methods for Statistics and Indicators on the Situation of Women,* Series F, No. 33 (United Nations publication, Sales No. E.84.XVII.3); *Methods of Measuring Women's Participation and Production in the Informal Sector,* Series F, No. 46 (United Nations publication, Sales No. E.90.XVII.16); and "Development of guidelines on national accounts for women's contribution to development", report of the Secretary-General to the Statistical Commission at its twenty-fifth session (E/CN.3/1989/12).

5   Jee Peng Tan and Michael Haines, "Schooling and demand for children: historical perspectives", World Bank Staff Working Paper, No. 697, Population and Development Series, No. 22 (Washington, D.C., World Bank, 1984).

6   George Psacharopoulos, "Returns to education: a further international update and implication", *Journal of Human Resources,* vol. 20 (Fall 1985).

7   Erica Royston and Sue Armstrong, eds., *Preventing Maternal Deaths* (Geneva, World Health Organization, 1989); and Judith S. McGuire and Barry M. Popkin, "Helping women improve nutrition in the developing world: beating the zero sum game", World Bank Technical Paper, No. 114 (Washington, D.C., World Bank, 1990).

8   Nafis Sadik, *Investing in Women: The Focus of the '90s* (New York, United Nations Population Fund).

9   *Engendering Adjustment for the 1980s: Report of the Commonwealth Expert Group on Women and Structural Adjustment* (London, Commonwealth Secretariat Publications, 1989); Susan Joekes, "Gender and macro-economic policy", Association for Women in Development, Paper No. 4 (Blacksburg, Virginia, 1989); and *The Invisible Adjustment: Poor Women and the Economic Crisis* (Santiago, United Nations Children's Fund, Regional Office for the Americas and the Caribbean, 1989).

10 *The Invisible Adjustment* ....

11 McGuire and Popkin, op. cit.

12 "Chief Executives of the *Business Week* 1000: A Directory", *Business Week,* 19 October 1989.

13 Katherine Marshall, "Women in male-dominated professions", *Canadian Social Trends* (Ottawa, Statistics Canada), Winter 1987.

14 *Engendering Adjustment ...,* p. 39.

15 Rounaq Jahad, "Women and development in Bangladesh: challenges and opportunities" (Dhaka, Ford Foundation, 1989).

16 Odile Frank, "Infertility in sub-Saharan Africa", Center for Policy Studies Working Paper, No. 97 (New York, The Population Council, 1983); and "The epidemiology of infertility—report of a WHO scientific group", Technical Report Series 582 (Geneva, World Health Organization, 1975).

17 *Investing in Women ...; Engendering Adjustment ...; Women in Development...,* World Bank (Washington, D.C., 1990); *Human Development...,* United Nations Development Programme (New York and Oxford; Oxford University Press, 1990); *The Invisible Adjustment* ....

18 Royston and Armstrong, eds., op. cit.

19 See Andreas Fuglesand and Dale Chandler, "Participation as process: what we can learn about Grameen Bank, Bangladesh" (Oslo, Norwegian Ministry of Development Cooperation, 1986); and "Women's World Banking: Background Paper 1980" (New York, Women's World Banking, Inc., 1980).

1
Women, families and households

Major changes in households and family life over the past 20 years in many parts of the world have given women greater opportunities but made their struggle to balance family, household and economic responsibilities more complex and often more difficult.

Marriage patterns differ for men and women—with women marrying at an earlier age and, since their life expectancy is longer, surviving their husbands in most regions by about 10 years. Women are less likely to remarry after divorce than men and are more likely to be widowed.

Across all regions, fewer women marry today than in 1970, and those who do spend less of their lives married and fewer years having children.

More women today live alone or as heads of households because of wars, male migration, longer life expectancy than men and changing patterns of marriage and divorce. Globally, about 30 per cent of all women heading households are elderly (aged 60 or older).

The world's women

That women live longer than men is widely known. Less widely known is that there are not as many women as men. Of the world's 5.3 billion people in 1990, fewer than half (2.63 billion) were women. Indeed, in many countries there are fewer than 95 women for every 100 men (list 1.1). [23]*

In most regions, women do outnumber men. More boys are born in the world than girls, but females generally have lower mortality rates than males at all ages. The biggest difference is in the developed regions—where the ratio of women to men is 106 to 100. In Latin America and the Caribbean there are 100 women for every 100 men—and in Africa, 101 women (chart 1.2).

In many areas, social and cultural factors deny girls and women the same nutrition, health care and other support that males receive. In a few countries widow burning and dowry deaths persist, and female infanticide is still suspected in some rural areas (see the section and table below on domestic violence). A new phenomenon—abortion on the basis of male preference—is also now known to occur. In these circumstances, women have higher death rates than men, especially at early child-bearing ages and sometimes throughout their child-bearing years.[1] The result: only 95 women for every 100 men in Asia and the Pacific—enough to offset the world balance in favour of men.

Where women live

In 1970 more than half the world's 1.8 billion women lived in the developing regions of Asia and the Pacific, fewer than a third in the developed regions. A tenth lived in Africa, one twelfth in Latin America and the Caribbean.

By 1990 the proportion of women in Africa, Asia and Latin America and the Caribbean had increased, while that in the developed regions had declined. Fifty-five per cent of the world's women now live in Asia (chart 1.3).

Between 1965–1970 and 1985–1990 the annual rate of growth of the world's women declined in all regions but Africa, where it rose from 2.7 per cent to 3 per cent. In the developed regions, the annual growth rate of the female population fell from 0.9 per cent to 0.5 per cent. [15]

1.1
Where there are fewer than 95 women per 100 men
Women per 100 men

Developed regions
Albania (94.3)

Africa
Libyan Arab Jamahiriya (90.8)

Asia and Pacific
Eastern Asia
China (94.3)
Hong Kong (93.9)
South-eastern Asia
Brunei Darussalam (93.8)
Southern Asia
Afghanistan (94.5)
Bangladesh (94.1)
Bhutan (93.3)
India (93.5)
Nepal (94.8)
Pakistan (92.1)
Western Asia
Bahrain (68.8) [a]
Jordan (94.8)
Kuwait (75.2) [a]
Oman (90.6) [a]
Qatar (59.8) [a]
Saudi Arabia (84.0) [a]
Turkey (94.8)
United Arab Emirates (48.3) [a]
Oceania
Papua New Guinea (92.8)
Vanuatu (91.7)

Source: Statistical Office and Population Division of the United Nations Secretariat.

a   Oil-producing countries which also have large male immigrant populations.

*Numbers within brackets refer to the numbered entries in the list of statistical sources at the end of this book.

Population

Total population figures are usually estimates of persons resident in the country or area at mid-year. They are usually based on population census data adjusted to the specified year, taking account of birth, death and international migration rates as determined from population surveys and registers and other national sources as available. Short-term residents and visitors in the country or area for less than one year are usually excluded.

Ages of women

Reductions in child-bearing rates and mortality rates are changing the age distribution of populations everywhere, with men and women moving towards an older average (or median) age. The median age in developed regions is much higher than in developing regions. In developed regions, more than half the women are over age 35, up from 32 years in 1970. In Latin America and the Caribbean women's median age rose by 3 years between 1970 and 1990—from about 19 to 22. And in Asia and the Pacific it rose by about 4 years, from 19 to 23. The median age of women is declining only in Africa, down from 17.9 in 1970 to 17.6 in 1990, because very high birth rates are offsetting increases in life expectancy (chart 1.4).

The percentages of females under age 15 and over age 59 vary widely. These differences reflect differences in fertility and mortality rates and affect family structures and the labour market. The growing numbers of children in Africa and of the elderly in most other parts of the world mean that the number of family members likely to be dependent on women is rising.

1.2
Women now outlive men almost everywhere, but they are still in the minority in many developing regions because of higher female mortality in the past

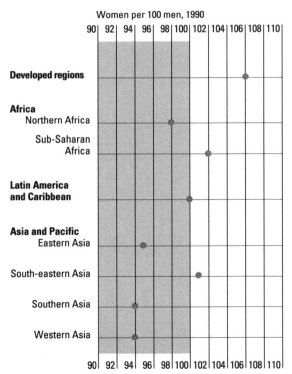

Women per 100 men, 1990

Note: Based on the total population of each sex in each region.

Source: *Global Estimates and Projections of Population by Sex and Age: The 1988 Revision* (United Nations publication, ST/ESA/SER.R/93).

1.3
More than three-quarters of the world's women live in the developing regions

Distribution of the world's women, 1990 (%)

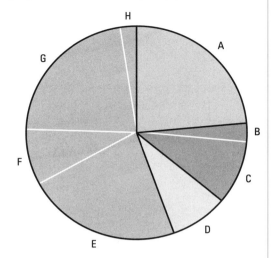

Developed regions		**Asia and Pacific**	
A	All developed regions (23.6)	E	Eastern Asia (22.4)
Africa		F	South-eastern Asia (8.4)
B	Northern Africa (2.7)	G	Southern Asia (22.2)
C	Sub-Saharan Africa (9.7)	H	Western Asia (2.4)
Latin America and Caribbean			Oceania (0.1)
D	All Latin America and Caribbean (8.5)		

Note: For a listing of countries and areas included in each region, see annex III.

Source: *Global Estimates and Projections of Population by Sex and Age: The 1988 Revision* (United Nations publication, ST/ESA/SER.R/93).

Between 1970 and 1990 the proportion of women under age 15 dropped to one fifth in developed regions and about one third in Latin America and the Caribbean and in Asia and the Pacific. But in Africa 45 per cent of the women are still under 15, because child-bearing rates there are still high—averaging five to six births a woman.

Everywhere in the world except Africa, the proportion of women aged 60 and over is rising because of longer life expectancy and lower child-bearing rates (list 1.5). This trend is particularly important for women because elderly women outnumber elderly men everywhere. For every 100 elderly men, there are 152 elderly women in the developed regions, 116 in Africa and in Latin America and the Caribbean, and 107 in Asia and the Pacific (chart 1.6).

1.4
The median age of women is rising rapidly everywhere except Africa

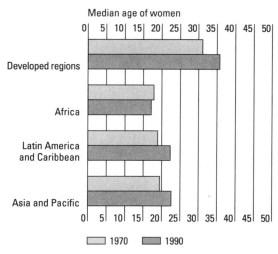

Median age of women

— 1970   — 1990

Note: Based on the total female population in each region.

Source: Prepared by the Statistical Office of the United Nations Secretariat from *Global Estimates and Projections of Population by Sex and Age: The 1988 Revision* (United Nations publication, ST/ESA/SER.R/93).

Families

Differences in women's and men's marriage patterns

Women in many developing areas marry when they are very young (list 1.7): almost 50 per cent of African women, 40 per cent of Asian women and 30 per cent of Latin American women are married by the age of 18. Men tend to marry at older ages. In Bangladesh and the Sudan men entering their first marriage are on average more than seven years older than women marrying for the first time, and in Colombia and Cuba, four years older. [14]

This age gap increases a woman's chances of being less experienced and more dependent on her husband even when she contributes to the family's economic survival. The gap also means that women are far more likely than men to be widowed. Unless a woman can rely on government assistance or her own property, investments or savings, she depends entirely on her husband and children in her old age.

Most women in the developed regions marry between the ages of 20 and 27—on average at age 23—and very early marriages are exceptional.

The average age at marriage for women in Latin America and the Caribbean is 22. Except for several Caribbean countries where the age at marriage is unusually high, this average is fairly consistent across the region.

In Asia, by contrast, the average age at first marriage (21 years) hides wide subregional variations. Most women in eastern Asia marry between 22 and 25 years of age, while those in southern Asia often marry in their teens. A survey of women in Bangladesh found that 73 per cent had married by age 15—and 82 per cent by age 16.

1.6
There are more elderly women than men almost everywhere

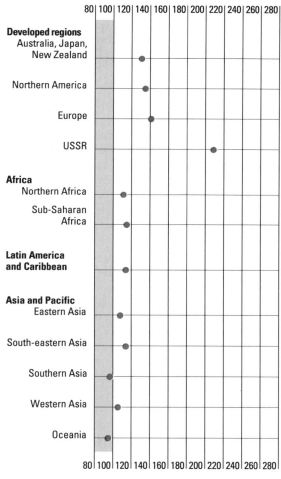

Women per 100 men in the population aged 60 and over, 1990

Note: Based on the total population of each sex aged 60 years and above in each region.

Source: *Global Estimates and Projections of Population by Sex and Age: The 1988 Revision* (United Nations publication, ST/ESA/SER.R/93).

1.5
Where women aged 60 and over make up 19 per cent or more of the female population
Percentage of women aged 60 and over

Austria (24)
Belgium (23)
Bulgaria (21)
Czechoslovakia (19)
Denmark (23)
Finland (22)
France (22)
Germany:
Fed. Rep. of Germany (25)
former German Dem. Rep. (23)
Greece (21)
Hungary (22)
Italy (22)
Japan (19)
Luxembourg (22)
Netherlands (20)
Norway (24)
Portugal (20)
Spain (21)
Sweden (26)
Switzerland (23)
United Kingdom (23)
United States (19)
USSR (19)

Source: Population Division of the United Nations Secretariat.

Caring for the sick, disabled and elderly

As life expectancies have increased the number of elderly needing care has risen. But women—who have been primarily responsible for such care—are finding it more difficult to fill that role as they enter the work force in greater numbers. Other changes affecting care for the elderly are rates of marriage, divorce and persons living alone. Care is increasingly provided by persons outside the household, but as many governments are cutting spending for programmes to help the elderly, options for care outside the home are narrowing.

Studies of informal care for the elderly in Norway have found that 4 per cent of women and 3 per cent of men said they cared for sick or elderly household members and 13 per cent of women and 10 per cent of men gave care to persons outside the households. In the United Kingdom, 15 per cent of women and 12 per cent of men provided informal care. But both studies also indicated that women spend much more time caring for elderly relatives. In the amount of care, women's role was substantially higher.

In Norway, women provided 67 per cent of all hours spent on care. For those caring for household members, 64 per cent of women and 36 per cent of men spent two or more hours a day. For those caring for persons outside the household, 56 per cent of women and 46 per cent of men spent at least 10 hours during the previous month.

The Norway study also found that women have less access to informal care, particularly in old age. One-third of the 67–74 year-olds had no one, in the household or outside, to ask for help.

Populations in developing countries are also aging rapidly, which will make the problem of dealing with the elderly that much more difficult, particularly for older rural women left alone due to migration, longer life expectancy and simple disintegration of the family nucleus.

Sources: Susan Lingson, *Informal Care of Sick and Elderly*, Norwegian Central Bureau of Statistics, Study No. 57 (Oslo, 1985); and Hazel Green, *Informal Carers:* General Household Survey 1985, No. 15, Supplement A (London, Office of Population Censuses and Surveys, Social Survey Division, and Her Majesty's Stationery Office, 1988).

In Africa the average age for first marriage of women is 20 years, but there are striking differences between the northern and sub-Saharan regions. All five northern African countries with recent data had average ages of first marriage for women of 21 years or more. But 15 of 24 sub-Saharan countries had averages under 20.

Among 20–24 year olds, twice as many women are married as men. In most of Asia and the Pacific and in Africa, at least half the women in this age group are married, but less than a third of the men. Significant proportions of women aged 15–19 are married, but less than 5 per cent of men the same age (chart 1.8). Women thus bear the responsibility of managing a family and rearing children at younger ages than men. Because they begin working as homemakers at such young ages, few women finish secondary school or work outside the home.

Differences in the marital status of women and men diminish in the 25–44 age group. The proportions who are married are particularly similar, although more men are single, whereas more women are widowed or divorced.

Changing marriage patterns [10]

Between 1970 and the early 1980s the proportion of people who have never married rose and that of currently married people fell—a trend especially marked for women aged 20–24 in all regions but Asia. In Africa the proportion of never-married women in this age group increased from 25 to 33 per cent. Less pronounced increases also occurred among teenage women, men aged 20–24, and women and men aged 25–44. These changes show the trend towards later marriage and perhaps towards a decline in marriage as well.

Even if marriage is less common, however, this does not mean an overall movement away from life as a couple. Many people in the developed regions and in Latin America and the Caribbean are not married but living in consensual unions and as couples.

The proportion of women divorced has increased in all regions, especially in the developed regions. Among men, the proportion divorced has increased everywhere except in Africa. The increasing fragility of marriage has meant a new substage in the lives of many—a period when people who were once married are no longer part of a couple. Experiences following marital separations vary considerably. Some live alone and others with children. Some people enter new long-term partnerships and others do not. Women in developing regions are less likely than men to live alone (because they must care for children and the elderly) and are also somewhat less likely to enter another relationship.

As men and women age, more differences appear in their marriage patterns. The proportion of women who are married peaks in the age group 25–44. For women aged 60 years and over, more are widowed than married. By contrast, the proportion of married men is highest in the age group 45–59 years. Among those aged 60 and older, more than 75 per cent of all men are married, compared with only 40 per cent of women (chart 1.8). These differences in later life are the result of women's longer life expectancy and male-female differences in age at first marriage. The differences also reflect cultural factors which make remarriage less likely for women than men in some regions.

The ratio of widows to widowers is high everywhere—about 4 to 1—and does not appear to have changed appreciably over the past two decades. Overall, more than 50 per cent of elderly women are not currently married. Africa and Asia have higher proportions of widows than the other regions. (The figures for widowers show much less inter-regional diversity.) Indeed, more than 30 per cent of women aged 45 and over in Africa and in

Asia and the Pacific are widows, largely because women there marry earlier and marriage is more prevalent.

Trends in the developed regions

Detailed data on changes in marriage and in the composition of families available for the developed regions reveal major changes in household and family life. [11] Fewer women aged 15 and over are currently married (56 per cent in 1985 compared with 61 per cent in 1970). Slightly more are single (24 per cent in 1985, up from 23 per cent in 1970). The percentage widowed has stayed about the same at 14 per cent, and the percentage divorced has risen from 2.8 per cent in 1970 to 6.4 per cent in 1985.

In the United States of America, where marriage and divorce rates are higher than in other countries in the developed regions, marriage rates continue to be high, and divorce rates have risen since 1970. Although most people in the United States marry, many marriages do not last a lifetime. The situation differs in northern Europe, where

Marital status

Marital status is the personal status of each individual in relation to the marriage laws or customs of the country. The categories of marital status recommended by the United Nations for statistical purposes include: (a) single (corresponding to never married), (b) married (corresponding to currently married), (c) married but separated (legally or de facto), (d) widowed and not remarried, and (e) divorced and not remarried. Persons cohabiting may be considered as married or as living in de facto (consensual) unions and therefore considered married according to the laws and customs of each country, but such couples are imprecisely defined and often undercounted.

1.8

Many more women than men under age 45 are married, but for those 45 and over it is mainly men who remain currently married
Percentage currently married, around 1980

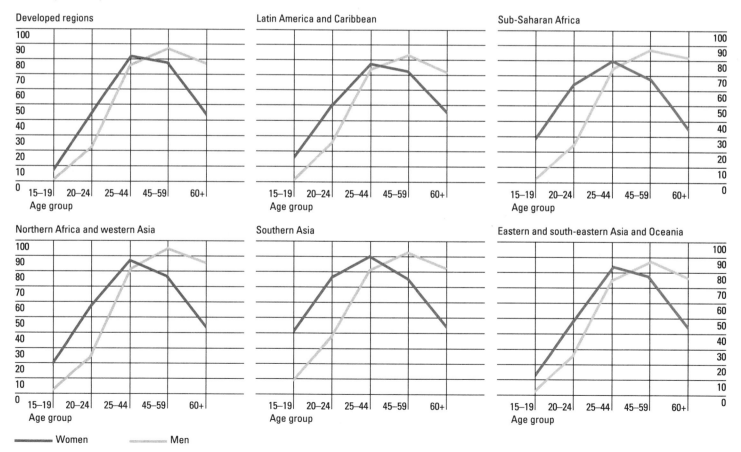

Women ⸺   Men ⸺

Sources: Prepared by the Statistical Office of the United Nations Secretariat from *Demographic Yearbook 1982* and *1987* (United Nations publications, Sales Nos. E/F.83.XIII.1 and E/F.88.XIII.1).

Households and families

In most population statistics, a household is defined as one or more persons who make common provision for food or other essentials for living. In multi-person households, household members may be related or unrelated or a combination. Persons residing in collective living quarters of institutions, as in military installations, correctional institutions, hospitals and the like, are not considered to be living in households. Persons who make independent provision for food or other essentials for living comprise one-person households.

marriages are half as frequent and twice as stable. But marriages there declined from 1970 to 1985 while divorces rose. The pattern in western Europe is similar to that in northern Europe. In southern Europe, although divorce remained uncommon, marriages declined. In eastern Europe and in Japan, declines in marriage and increases in divorce were discernible but less pronounced.

The percentage of singles (persons never married), the number of unmarried couples and the number of births outside marriage all increased in the developed regions between 1970 and 1985—but with substantial variation across countries.

The percentage of younger people who have never married is increasing. This rise does not, however, mean an increase in people living alone because, parallelling the decline in married couples in Europe, there is an increase in unmarried couples who are living together. In France, for example, it appears that the increase in unmarried couples living together in the 1970s offset the decline in marriage.

The proportion of births outside of marriage, after steadily becoming rarer from the beginning of the century until 1960–1970, has since increased significantly in many countries (table 1.9). In Denmark it quadrupled between 1970 and 1985. In other northern European countries, the United States of America, Australia, New Zealand and some western European countries, it doubled or tripled. The mothers were women of all ages—from young single women to divorced women who had not remarried.

The proportion of births outside marriage varies considerably within developed regions. (It also varies among regions. In Japan, 1 per cent of the births in 1985 were outside marriage compared with rates over 40 per cent in several African, Caribbean and northern European countries). However, the statistics from the developed regions generally show that although marriage has declined, cohabitation has increased.

In 1970, 62 per cent of single women in France who became pregnant and had a child had married before giving birth; in 1980, fewer than 40 per cent had done so. However, most of the births outside marriage were to unmarried couples. In 1985, as in 1970, births to French women living alone constituted only 2–3 per cent of all births. The situation in France is probably similar to other countries of western Europe. The proportion of single-parent families in European countries has not greatly increased in recent decades (falling mortality for the parental age group partly offset the rise in divorces). In the United States, however, births outside marriage are more frequent among women who are not living as part of a couple. In the United States and the United Kingdom, high proportions of births outside marriage are to teenagers—33 and 29 per cent, respectively.[2]

1.9

The proportion of births to unmarried women is rising rapidly in many countries and regions

	Percentage of births to unmarried women	
	1970	1985
Developed regions		
Australia	8	16
Austria	13	22
Bulgaria	9	11
Denmark	11	43
Finland	6	16
Germany		
former German Dem. Rep.	13	34
France	7	20
New Zealand	13	25
Norway	7	26
Portugal	7	12
Sweden	18	46
United Kingdom	8	19
United States	10	21
Africa		
Mauritius	3	26
Reunion	24	44
Seychelles	45	70
Latin America and Caribbean		
Argentina	26	33
Bahamas	29	62
Belize	44	54
Chile	20	32
Costa Rica	29	37
French Guiana	63	76
Guadeloupe	43	57
Martinique	51	64
Puerto Rico	19	27
Asia and Pacific		
Guam	9	30
Hong Kong	3	6
Philippines	3	6

Note: Years are approximate.

Source: Prepared by the Statistical Office of the United Nations Secretariat from *Demographic Yearbook 1975* and *1986* (United Nations publications, Sales Nos. E/F.76.XIII.1 and E/F.87.XIII.1).

Households [10, 11]

On a regional basis, on average from 8 to 23 per cent of households are one-person households, so that at least three quarters of households consist of two or more persons. In general, 1 to 2 per cent of the population lives in communal or institutional living quarters.

1.10
Average household size is decreasing in most regions

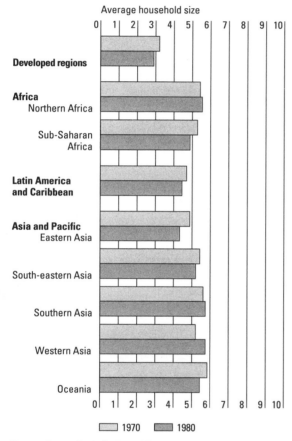

Average household size

Developed regions

Africa
Northern Africa

Sub-Saharan Africa

Latin America and Caribbean

Asia and Pacific
Eastern Asia

South-eastern Asia

Southern Asia

Western Asia

Oceania

☐ 1970 ■ 1980

Sources: Prepared by the Statistical Office of the United Nations Secretariat from the United Nations Women's Indicators and Statistics Database (Wistat) and *Demographic Yearbook* (United Nations publication, various years).

Regional variations

Average household size varies significantly, from 2.9 persons in the developed regions to 5.4 persons in Asia and the Pacific. As the number of one-person households increases, the average household size decreases. For instance, in Asia and the Pacific, one-person households account for only 8 per cent of the total, and in the developed regions, 23 per cent.

In all regions but northern Africa and western and southern Asia, household size declined from 1970 to 1980 (chart 1.10). The declines were between 0.2 and 0.6 persons per household—small but significant. In the developed regions, the average number of persons per household decreased between 1960 and 1980 (except New Zealand). The two countries with the largest households—Canada and Japan—had the steepest declines, because of the increase in divorce, the later age of marriage, the decline in fertility and the shift towards nuclear or unrelated households. In the developed regions, the percentage of one-person and two-person households rose while the percentage of households with four or more fell. By 1980 one-person and two-person households accounted for at least half the households in northern and western Europe and for almost 40 per cent in Japan and southern and eastern Europe. Many one-person households are elderly women.

Households in developing regions are much more likely to have children than those in the developed world.

Women-headed households

Women-headed households, a growing worldwide phenomenon, make up over 20 per cent of all households in Africa, the developed regions and Latin America and the Caribbean (chart 1.11). Many are elderly women living alone, while others are single mothers and their families. Asia has the lowest proportions of women-headed households (14 per cent) and one-person households.

Although men in all regions head a large majority of households, women head a substantial percentage, except in Asia and the Pacific. There are also marked intraregional variations: women head 38 per cent of households in Norway and 16 per cent in Spain (list 1.12).

Women-headed households

Given prevailing cultural assumptions and methods of data collection in most countries, women are not usually enumerated as heads of households unless they are either living alone (that is, in one-person households) or there is no adult male in the household. Since it is usually assumed that household heads have primary authority and responsibility for household affairs and in most cases are its chief economic support, available statistics on men and women heads of households considerably understate women's household responsibilities. Statistics on women heads of households do, however, give a useful indication of the number of households where women have sole responsibility for supporting the household.

1.12
Where more than 20 per cent of households are headed by women
Percentage of households headed by women, early 1980s

Developed regions
Australia (25)
Austria (31)
Belgium (21)
Canada (25)
Czechoslovakia (23)
France (22)
Luxembourg (23)
New Zealand (24)
Norway (38)
Poland (27)
Sweden (25)
Switzerland (25)
United Kingdom (25)
United States (31)

Africa
Botswana (45)
Congo (21)
Ghana (27)
Malawi (29)
Reunion (25)
Rwanda (25)
Sudan (22)
Zambia (28)

Latin America and Caribbean
Barbados (44)
Chile (22)
Cuba (28)
Dominica (38)
El Salvador (22)
French Guiana (31)
Grenada (45)
Guadeloupe (34)
Guyana (24)
Honduras (22)
Jamaica (34)
Martinique (35)
Netherlands Antilles (30)
Panama (22)
Peru (23)
Puerto Rico (25)
St. Kitts and Nevis (46)
St. Lucia (39)
St. Vincent/Grenadines (42)
Trinidad and Tobago (25)
Uruguay (21)
Venezuela (22)

Asia and Pacific
Hong Kong (24)

Source: Statistical Office of the United Nations Secretariat.

Women-headed households differ in many ways from households headed by men. Far fewer include spouses. In the developed regions a majority of women-headed households consist of women living alone, while in the developing regions a majority, while lacking a spouse, include children.

Households headed by women are generally poorer than those headed by men. In multi-person households headed by women, there often is one working age provider rather than two, and elderly women living alone usually have no earnings at all. In addition, women heads in multi-person households have to support their children or other dependents—a responsibility that persists in later life. In developing regions, more than half the women who are heads of household do not have a spouse but do have other household members. Because of this and since women aged 60 and over usually are not earning money, a disproportionate number of women-headed households are living in poverty.

In developing regions, the vast majority of women-headed households have two or more members. In the developed regions, households headed by women are more closely divided between one-person households and those of two or more people.

For Asia and the Pacific the proportion of one-person households is only 8.2 per cent, with 45 per cent of these women and 55 per cent men. And a much lower proportion of households of two or more are headed by women—just 10 per cent, compared with 90 per cent headed by men.

A large proportion of elderly household heads are women. In the developed regions and in Latin America and the Caribbean, women make up nearly 40 per cent of all the household heads aged 60 years or older, more than 30 per cent in Africa, and more than 25 per cent in Asia and the Pacific.

Women heads of household also tend to be younger in Africa and in Latin America and the Caribbean (see chapter 5 on male migration in Africa and female migration in Latin America). More fall in the 25–44 year age group than in any other age group. Thus, whereas women who head households in the developed regions are more likely to be elderly, those in Africa and Latin America and the Caribbean are more likely to be in their child-bearing years.

About half the women heads of household are widowed in Africa, the developed regions and Asia and the Pacific. In Latin America and the Caribbean, only 28 per cent are widowed while 36 per cent are single. In all regions, women heads of households are more likely to be married or single than divorced. The proportions of women household heads who are divorced are particularly low for Asia and the Pacific (6 per cent) compared with Latin America and the Caribbean (13 per cent), Africa (14 per cent) and the developed regions (16 per cent).

1.11
Up to 30 per cent of households are now headed by women. Nearly half the women heading households in developed regions and at least a quarter in other regions are elderly

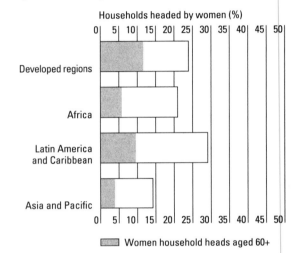

Households headed by women (%)

Women household heads aged 60+

Note: Data mainly refer to early 1980s.

Source: Prepared by the Statistical Office of the United Nations Secretariat from the United Nations Women's Statistics and Indicators Database (Wistat) and the *Demographic Yearbook 1987* (United Nations publication, Sales No. E/F.88.XIII.1).

Domestic violence

Domestic violence, the dark side of family life, is inflicted on a family's weakest members—women, children, the very old and the disabled. It manifests itself in habitual physical abuse, psychological torture, deprivation of basic needs and sexual molestation. Secrecy, insufficient evidence and social and legal barriers continue to make it difficult to acquire accurate data on domestic violence against women, which many criminologists believe to be the most underreported crime. Most data on violence against women are compiled from small studies, giving only a glimpse of what is assumed to be a world-wide phenomenon. They can not be used to provide precise indicators on the extent of violence against women, but they do show that violence in the home is common and that women are most frequently the victims.

Domestic violence against women exists in all regions, classes and cultures. The United Nations Secretariat's Division for the Advancement of Women compiled available information on domestic violence in 36 countries in the mid-1980s:

- In Austria in 1985, domestic violence against the wife was cited as a contributing factor to the breakdown of the marriage in 59 per cent of 1,500 divorce cases. Of those instances, 38 per cent of working-class wives called the police in response to battering, while only 13 per cent of middle-class women and 4 per cent of upper-class women did.
- In Colombia during 1982 and 1983, the Forensic Institute of Bogotá found that of 1,170 cases of bodily injuries, one of five was due to conjugal violence—and 94 per cent of those hospitalized were battered women.
- India had 999 registered cases of dowry deaths in 1985, 1,319 in 1986 and 1,786 in 1987.
- Of 153 Kuwaiti women asked if they had ever been assaulted, a third answered yes. Asked if they knew of friends or relatives who had been victims of such violence, 80 per cent responded yes.
- In Thailand, 25 per cent of the malnourished children at a Bangkok rehabilitation centre treated during the first half of 1985 were from families where the mother was regularly beaten by her spouse. More than 50 per cent of married women studied from Bangkok's biggest slum and construction sites were beaten regularly by their husbands.

1.13

Many countries are now recognizing that there is significant violence against women both in and out of the family

A.   Type of violence against women reported

	Domestic violence	Incest	Homicide in family	Sexual assault and rape	Sexual harass-ment
Developed regions					
Australia	X		X		
Austria	X		X		
Belgium	X	X		X	X
Canada	X		X	X	X
Finland	X	X		X	X
France				X	
Germany					
Fed. Rep. of Germany	X	X	X		X
Greece	X		X	X	
Italy		X		X	
New Zealand	X		X		
Poland	X				
Portugal				X	
Spain					X
United Kingdom	X			X	X
United States	X	X	X	X	X
Africa					
Kenya	X		X		
Nigeria	X				
Uganda	X				
Latin America and Caribbean					
Argentina	X				
Brazil	X			X	
Chile	X	X	X		
Colombia	X	X		X	
Dominican Republic			X		
Ecuador	X				
Jamaica	X	X		X	
Peru	X				
Puerto Rico	X		X		
Trinidad and Tobago	X	X		X	
Venezuela				X	
Asia and Pacific					
Bangladesh	X		X		
China			X		
India	X		X	X	X
Israel	X				
Kuwait	X				
Malaysia	X			X	
Philippines				X	
Thailand	X		X		

[cont.]

1.13
Many countries are now recognizing that there is significant violence against women both in and out of the family [cont.]

B.   Immediate protective measure taken to assist abused women

	Police	Shelters	Non-governm'tal orgs.	Legal aid	Financial assistance	Housing assistance
Developed regions						
Australia	X	X	X	X	X	X
Austria	X	X				
Belgium	X	X	X	X		
Canada	X	X	X		X	
Finland		X	X			
Germany						
Fed. Rep. of Germany	X	X	X	X		
Greece		X	X	X		
Poland			X	X		
United Kingdom		X			X	X
United States	X	X	X			
Africa						
Egypt		X				
Nigeria					X	
Uganda			X			
Latin America and Caribbean						
Brazil	X		X			
Colombia	X		X			
Jamaica		X	X		X	
Trinidad and Tobago		X	X			
Asia and Pacific						
Bangladesh		X	X	X	X	
China			X			
India	X			X		
Kuwait	X					
Malaysia			X	X		X
Thailand	X	X		X	X	

Source: Compiled by the Division for the Advancement of Women, Centre for Social Development and Humanitarian Affairs of the United Nations Secretariat, from national reports to the United Nations in 1988.

■ In the United States of America in 1984, 2,928 people were killed by a family member. Of female homicide victims alone, nearly a third died at the hands of a husband or partner. Husbands were responsible for 20 per cent of women killed in 1984, while boyfriends were the offenders in 10 per cent of the cases.

To compile information more systematically, the Committee on the Elimination of Discrimination against Women asked countries to report on laws they have enacted to protect women from violence and to provide statistics on the incidence of violence against women (table 1.13).

Indicators
Female population and age groups

Table 1 presents statistics on the total female population in 178 countries and areas of the world, girls under 15 years of age and women aged 60 and over, ratios of women to men and annual growth rates of the female population.

These data have been compiled from two main sources: estimates and projections of population by age group and sex for countries and areas with a population of over 300,000 prepared by the Population Division of the United Nations Secretariat and published every two years, and national statistics compiled by the Statistical Office of the United Nations Secretariat in the *Demographic Yearbook*. [10]

The general definition of population is given on page 12 above. Data sources for preparing current population estimates and projections include population censuses, demographic surveys, population registers and other national sources as available. The latest estimates and projections use statistics available as of 1988. [15] For countries and areas not included in the Population Division estimates, data have been compiled from statistics of population by age group and sex contained in the *Demographic Yearbook*. [10: various years] Because, in the absence of a well-functioning population register, national statistics on population by age must be based largely on data from population censuses, these data from the *Demographic Yearbook* are available only for census years and in some cases the latest available data may thus be quite old. In addition, population census data from the *Demographic Yearbook* have not been adjusted to take age-reporting problems and other deficiencies and inconsistencies in population data into account, as discussed in the *Demographic Yearbook* (see, for example, the 1982 issue, pp. 6–12).

Throughout the present publication, annual rates of change in various population categories are computed as average annual percentage changes using mid-year population estimates and the following formula:

$$r = \left(\sqrt[t]{\frac{P_t}{P_o}} - 1 \right) \times 100$$

where P_o is population in the base year, P_t is the population in the final year, t is the number of intervening years and r is the annual percentage rate of change.

Households and families;
marriage and marital status

Table 2 presents selected indicators on households and families, age at first marriage and marital status of women, and fertility.

The series on households and marital status are based on population census results provided by national statistical services to the Statistical Office of the United Nations Secretariat for the *Demographic Yearbook* and the *Compendium of Human Settlements Statistics*. [10 and 7] The data on women heads of households are mainly from the *Demographic Yearbook 1987*, supplemented in a few cases with data compiled by the United States Bureau of the Census from national census publications. [33]

The definition of household recommended by the United Nations for use in population and housing censuses is described on page 16 above. In most censuses, persons not resident in a given household cannot be considered members of that household. However, some national population censuses may include some categories of absent household members. In most cases, each household occupies one housing unit. However, it is possible for more than one household to occupy one housing unit, for one household to occupy more than one housing unit or for a household to be homeless or occupy temporary, makeshift or collective living quarters such as camps. The determining criterion is considered to be the housekeeping arrangement to provide for food or other essentials for living.

In population censuses in most countries, the head of the household is defined as that person in the household or the family who is acknowledged as such by the other members. However, it is important to recognize that the procedures followed in applying the concept may distort the true picture, particularly in regard to women heads of households. In the most biased cases, it is assumed that no woman can be the head of any household that also contains an adult male. In some cases, instructions to enumerators may explicitly state that a woman can be entered as head only in the absence of any male above a specified age. In other cases, even where there are no such instructions, enumerators and even respondents may simply take some such assumption for granted. This common sex-biased stereotype often reflects circumstances that may have been true in the past but are no longer true, as the household and economic roles of women are changing. For these reasons, the concept of household head (or reference person), as shown in the table, has become a matter of controversy in many developed countries because of the priority usually given to males in assigning headship. In many other countries the application of the concept can be ambiguous in other ways. None the less, for most countries this is the only practical way of identifying households for which, in general, women are responsible for a household with no spouse present.

The series on average age at first marriage has been prepared by the Population Division, Department of International Economic and Social Affairs, of the United Nations Secretariat from a world-wide review of the available information on patterns of first marriage. [14] This indicator is calculated on the basis of a single census or survey according to procedures described by Hajnal.[3]

The United Nations recommendation concerning the definition of marital status for statistical purposes is described on page 15 above. For countries or areas where consensual unions are taken into account in the population census, the concept "currently married" includes persons reported as living in such unions.

Estimates and projections of fertility are prepared every two years by the Population Division of the United Nations Secretariat. [23] The total fertility rate refers to the average number of children that would be born to each woman if the fertility patterns of a given period were to stay unchanged. This measure gives the approximate total number of children an average woman will bear in her lifetime, assuming no mortality.

Notes

1   Terence H. Hull, "Recent trends in sex ratios in China", *Population and Development Review* (New York), vol. 16, No. 1 (March 1990); Government of India, Department of Women and Child Development, Ministry of Human Resource Development, *The Lesser Child: The Girl in India* (New Delhi, n.d.); "Women's survival as a development problem", *Bulletin of the American Academy of Arts and Sciences,* vol. XLIII, No. 2 (November 1989), cited in *The Girl Child—An Investment in the Future* (New York, United Nations Children's Fund, 1990); and Holly Johnson, "Wife abuse", *Canadian Social Trends* (Ottawa, Statistics Canada), Spring, 1988.

2   Constance Sorrentino, "The changing family in international perspective", *Monthly Labor Review* (Washington, D.C.), March 1990.

3   J. Hajnal, "Age at marriage and proportion marrying", *Population Studies,* vol. 7, No. 2 (1953).

Table 1
Female population and age groups

Country or area	Female population						Younger women and elderly women					
	Number (000s)		Per 100 males		% change per annum		% under age 15		% 60 years and over		60 and over: f per 100 m	
	1970	1990	1970	1990	1965-70	1985-90	1970	1990	1970	1990	1970	1990
Developed regions												
Albania	1058	1575	98	94	2.7	1.9	42	32	7	9	112	115
Australia	6227	8391	98	100	2.0	1.2	28	22	14	17	126	126
Austria	3952	3908	113	109	0.4	-0.1	23	16	23	24	155	168
Belgium	4930	5080	104	105	0.5	0.0	23	17	21	23	135	139
Bulgaria	4246	4546	100	102	0.7	0.2	22	19	16	21	114	119
Canada	10639	13393	100	102	1.7	0.9	30	20	12	18	115	129
Czechoslovakia	7350	8032	105	105	0.3	0.2	22	22	19	19	137	147
Denmark	2483	2600	101	103	0.7	0.0	23	16	19	23	122	132
Finland	2381	2561	107	106	0.2	0.3	23	18	17	22	154	161
France	25980	28748	105	105	0.8	0.3	24	19	21	22	147	142
Germany[a]												
Federal Rep. of Germany	31784	31436	110	108	0.5	-0.3	22	14	22	25	151	170
former German Dem. Rep.	9212	8689	117	109	-0.1	-0.2	21	18	25	23	158	184
Greece	4501	5098	105	103	0.5	0.2	24	19	17	21	121	122
Hungary	5334	5463	106	107	0.3	-0.2	20	19	19	22	133	151
Iceland	101	126	98	99	1.2	1.0	32	25	13	16	113	118
Ireland	1469	1853	99	99	0.5	0.9	31	27	17	16	111	123
Italy	27497	29453	104	106	0.7	0.1	23	16	18	22	130	137
Japan	53126	62758	104	103	1.1	0.4	23	18	12	19	122	134
Luxembourg	173	188	104	105	0.5	0.0	21	16	20	22	130	148
Malta	170	179	109	103	0.4	0.4	26	22	14	16	121	130
Netherlands	6528	7455	100	102	1.2	0.4	27	17	16	20	123	138
New Zealand	1410	1705	100	102	1.5	0.8	31	22	14	17	125	126
Norway	1949	2131	101	102	0.9	0.3	24	18	20	24	123	131
Poland	16730	19661	106	105	0.6	0.6	26	24	15	17	143	152
Portugal	4754	5320	111	107	-0.1	0.2	27	20	15	20	143	138
Romania	10361	11781	104	103	1.3	0.5	25	23	15	17	127	130
Spain	17290	19964	105	103	1.0	0.3	27	20	16	21	134	132
Sweden	4027	4226	100	103	0.8	0.0	20	16	21	26	118	127
Switzerland	3152	3338	101	105	1.0	0.1	23	16	19	23	137	138
USSR	130887	151660	117	111	0.9	0.6	26	24	14	19	197	211
United Kingdom	28568	29148	106	105	0.4	0.1	23	18	21	23	145	139
United States	104697	127668	104	105	1.2	0.8	27	20	16	19	131	138
Yugoslavia	10370	12051	104	102	0.9	0.6	26	22	13	16	125	141
Africa												
Algeria	7025	12678	105	100	3.4	3.1	46	44	7	6	119	123
Angola	2847	5084	104	103	1.5	2.7	42	44	5	5	125	121
Benin	1380	2407	104	103	2.1	3.2	44	47	7	5	118	116
Botswana	339	671	119	109	2.3	3.5	48	47	4	5	144	123
Burkina Faso	2828	4546	102	102	2.1	2.7	43	43	5	5	120	122
Burundi	1787	2780	107	104	1.4	2.8	41	45	6	6	134	128
Cameroon	3452	5701	104	103	2.1	2.6	41	43	7	7	131	122
Cape Verde	142	201	110	112	2.9	2.6	45	39	9	7	145	140
Central African Rep.	977	1495	109	106	1.6	2.4	39	42	7	7	127	129
Chad	1859	2878	104	103	1.8	2.5	41	42	6	6	125	122
Comoros	137	262	103	102	2.3	3.1	44	46	5	5	118	118
Congo	611	1010	104	103	2.2	2.7	42	43	6	6	123	120
Côte d'Ivoire	2734	6211	98	97	4.0	4.2	48	50	4	4	113	97
Djibouti	82	202	97	98	7.5	3.1	44	46	4	4	116	104
Egypt	16323	26617	98	97	2.3	2.6	41	40	7	7	117	119
Equatorial Guinea	149	224	105	103	1.5	2.3	39	41	7	7	119	121
Ethiopia	15379	23550	101	102	2.4	2.1	44	45	5	5	123	89

Table 1. Female population and age groups [*cont.*]

Country or area	Female population						Younger women and elderly women					
	Number (000s)		Per 100 males		% change per annum		% under age 15		% 60 years and over		60 and over: f per 100 m	
	1970	1990	1970	1990	1965-70	1985-90	1970	1990	1970	1990	1970	1990
Gabon	257	594	104	103	0.3	3.4	32	32	10	10	123	125
Gambia	235	435	103	103	2.8	2.9	42	43	5	5	119	115
Ghana	4347	7564	102	101	1.9	3.2	45	45	5	5	119	117
Guinea	2212	3479	102	102	2.0	2.5	42	43	5	5	119	116
Guinea-Bissau	272	507	107	105	0.1	2.1	38	40	7	7	123	120
Kenya	5748	12555	100	100	3.4	4.3	48	52	6	5	119	114
Lesotho	557	921	110	108	1.9	2.9	40	42	7	6	158	139
Liberia	679	1263	98	98	2.8	3.3	44	46	5	5	115	105
Libyan Arab Jamahiriya	945	2163	91	91	3.9	3.8	46	47	4	4	89	87
Madagascar	3426	6049	103	102	2.3	3.2	43	45	5	5	117	119
Malawi	2345	4279	108	103	2.6	3.3	46	45	4	5	127	123
Mali	2948	4809	108	106	2.1	2.9	44	45	5	5	127	128
Mauritania	619	1024	103	102	2.2	2.8	42	44	5	5	122	119
Mauritius	424	558	100	102	1.8	1.3	43	28	5	8	144	139
Morocco	7638	12556	100	100	2.8	2.6	46	40	6	6	93	106
Mozambique	4787	7937	104	103	2.4	2.7	42	43	5	6	124	121
Namibia	527	942	103	101	2.4	3.2	43	45	6	6	118	118
Niger	2096	3585	102	102	2.1	3.0	43	47	8	5	120	122
Nigeria	28988	57009	103	102	3.3	3.5	46	48	4	4	121	119
Reunion	216	307	96	106	2.6	1.7	45	30	5	9	81	144
Rwanda	1888	3657	103	102	3.2	3.4	47	49	4	4	120	118
Sao Tome and Principe	..	..	..	..	..	..	..	..	..	..	..	..
Senegal	2023	3722	102	102	3.0	2.7	43	44	5	5	119	115
Seychelles[b c]	26	33	101	101	..	..	43	35	10	11	133	157
Sierra Leone	1356	2112	104	104	1.8	2.5	41	44	6	6	126	123
Somalia	1856	3952	102	110	2.3	3.3	43	46	6	4	120	123
South Africa	11242	17731	100	101	2.5	2.2	40	36	7	7	137	130
Sudan	6927	12540	100	99	2.3	2.9	44	45	5	5	115	114
Swaziland	214	400	104	103	2.5	3.4	45	47	5	5	124	121
Togo	1028	1747	104	102	4.4	3.1	43	45	5	5	121	120
Tunisia	2590	4036	102	98	2.7	2.4	45	37	7	6	115	94
Uganda	4961	9295	102	102	4.0	3.5	47	48	4	4	117	117
United Rep. Tanzania	6885	13816	104	102	3.1	3.7	47	48	4	4	131	121
Western Sahara	32	..	74	..	..	..	42	..	5	..	68	..
Zaire	10008	18188	106	102	2.0	3.2	43	45	5	5	146	130
Zambia	2113	4285	102	103	3.0	3.8	45	48	4	4	118	94
Zimbabwe	2654	4903	101	102	3.3	3.2	49	44	5	5	118	114

Latin America and Caribbean

Country or area	1970	1990	1970	1990	1965-70	1985-90	1970	1990	1970	1990	1970	1990
Antigua and Barbuda	34	..	112	..	..	..	42	..	10	..	168	..
Argentina	11944	16320	99	102	1.6	1.3	29	29	11	15	110	128
Bahamas[d]	85	119	102	106	..	..	43	33	6	7	141	134
Barbados	127	136	113	109	0.0	0.6	35	24	14	16	159	152
Belize	60	..	100	..	..	..	49	..	7	..	106	..
Bolivia	2191	3709	103	103	2.4	2.8	42	43	6	5	117	116
Brazil	47863	75376	100	101	2.6	2.1	42	35	6	7	111	109
Chile	4814	6668	103	102	2.1	1.7	38	30	9	10	126	136
Colombia	10423	15840	100	99	2.8	2.1	45	36	5	7	121	120
Costa Rica	858	1491	98	98	3.1	2.7	46	36	5	7	110	112
Cuba	4177	5076	95	97	1.9	0.8	37	22	8	12	86	101
Dominica	..	..	..	..	..	..	..	..	..	..	..	..
Dominican Republic	2178	3526	97	97	3.0	2.2	47	38	5	6	100	101
Ecuador	3014	5358	99	99	3.2	2.8	45	40	6	6	116	111
El Salvador	1784	2677	99	104	3.6	2.1	46	43	5	6	115	120

Table 1. Female population and age groups [*cont.*]

Country or area	Female population Number (000s) 1970	1990	Per 100 males 1970	1990	% change per annum 1965-70	1985-90	Younger women and elderly women % under age 15 1970	1990	% 60 years and over 1970	1990	60 and over: f per 100 m 1970	1990
French Guiana [e]	20	..	84	..	..	..	41	..	9	..	106	..
Grenada	..	..	..	..	..	..	..	..	..	..	..	..
Guadeloupe	163	174	104	105	1.3	0.4	41	25	8	14	119	129
Guatemala	2588	4550	97	98	2.8	2.9	46	45	5	5	105	105
Guyana	357	518	101	99	2.0	1.7	47	34	6	7	115	112
Haiti	2297	3312	104	104	2.1	1.9	41	38	6	6	122	118
Honduras	1307	2546	99	98	2.8	3.2	47	44	5	5	115	106
Jamaica	957	1268	105	101	0.8	1.5	46	34	9	9	119	125
Martinique	166	170	104	106	0.6	0.2	40	23	9	15	128	128
Mexico	26328	44393	100	100	3.3	2.3	46	36	6	6	116	119
Netherlands Antilles [b][f]	112	..	105	..	..	..	36	..	9	..	134	..
Nicaragua	1030	1931	101	100	3.2	3.4	48	45	4	5	121	116
Panama	749	1188	96	97	2.9	2.1	44	35	6	7	98	100
Paraguay	1176	2111	100	97	2.7	3.0	46	40	6	6	118	120
Peru	6544	11083	98	99	2.8	2.5	44	39	6	6	114	115
Puerto Rico	1384	1903	104	105	0.9	1.5	36	27	10	13	105	121
St. Kitts and Nevis [f]	24	..	113	..	..	..	46	..	13	..	159	..
St. Lucia [c]	53	72	112	106	..	..	47	43	9	9	156	143
St. Vincent/Grenadines	..	..	..	..	..	..	..	..	..	..	..	..
Suriname	187	204	100	102	2.3	1.5	48	34	6	7	112	109
Trinidad and Tobago	484	643	103	101	1.5	1.6	41	31	7	9	118	118
Uruguay	1412	1590	101	103	0.9	0.8	27	25	14	18	118	128
US Virgin Islands	31	..	100	..	..	..	36	..	6	..	127	..
Venezuela	5239	9781	98	98	3.5	2.7	45	38	5	6	110	114

Asia and Pacific

Country or area	1970	1990	1970	1990	1965-70	1985-90	1970	1990	1970	1990	1970	1990
Afghanistan	6627	8042	95	94	2.5	2.7	43	42	4	5	109	105
Bahrain	102	210	86	69	1.4	3.6	49	39	4	4	89	107
Bangladesh	32085	56033	93	94	2.8	2.7	46	44	6	4	80	87
Bhutan	512	732	96	93	1.8	2.1	40	40	6	6	117	109
Brunei Darussalam [b][c]	63	110	87	94	..	..	46	38	5	4	85	88
Cambodia	3465	4138	100	101	2.5	2.5	43	35	5	5	121	126
China	403327	551124	94	94	2.6	1.4	40	26	8	10	123	109
Cyprus	311	352	102	101	0.9	1.0	30	25	15	15	113	122
East Timor	297	363	96	97	1.9	2.3	42	36	5	5	112	110
Fiji	256	373	97	99	2.4	1.6	43	36	4	6	89	106
French Polynesia [b]	55	..	95	..	..	..	46	..	4	..	86	..
Guam	38	..	79	..	..	..	43	..	3	..	105	..
Hong Kong	1937	2828	97	94	1.3	1.3	36	22	9	14	184	116
India	267905	412328	93	93	2.3	2.1	40	37	6	7	95	100
Indonesia	60722	90517	102	101	2.3	1.6	42	34	5	7	114	111
Iran (Islamic Rep. of)	14076	27801	98	97	3.3	3.5	46	43	5	5	111	107
Iraq	4597	9278	97	96	3.2	3.5	46	46	4	5	110	110
Israel	1475	2292	98	100	3.1	1.6	32	30	11	13	99	121
Jordan	1118	2078	95	95	3.3	4.1	46	48	5	4	101	103
Kiribati [g][h]	27	..	103	..	..	..	43	..	7	..	122	..
Korea, D. People's R.	7080	11539	104	101	2.7	2.3	43	36	6	7	129	157
Korea, Republic of	15865	21742	99	100	2.2	1.2	41	26	6	9	143	156
Kuwait	322	897	76	75	12.0	4.0	49	45	3	3	102	77
Lao People's Dem. Rep.	1343	2025	98	99	2.3	2.5	42	42	5	5	109	114
Lebanon	1227	1525	99	106	2.8	2.0	43	34	8	8	112	114
Macau	121	..	95	..	..	..	37	..	8	..	130	..
Malaysia	5375	8602	98	98	2.8	2.3	45	35	5	6	95	114
Maldives [e]	48	..	88	..	..	..	46	..	3	..	51	..
Mongolia	625	1110	100	99	3.2	3.1	44	41	6	6	119	114

Table 1. Female population and age groups [*cont.*]

Country or area	Female population Number (000s) 1970	1990	Per 100 males 1970	1990	% change per annum 1965-70	1985-90	Younger women and elderly women % under age 15 1970	1990	% 60 years and over 1970	1990	60 and over: f per 100 m 1970	1990
Myanmar	13558	20942	100	101	2.3	2.1	41	36	7	7	121	114
Nepal	5672	9318	98	95	2.1	2.5	41	42	6	5	108	92
New Caledonia [i]	48	..	91	..	..	..	41	..	6	..	102	..
Oman	323	698	98	91	2.8	3.6	44	47	5	5	112	102
Pacific Islands	44	..	96	..	..	..	46	..	5	..	92	..
Pakistan	31699	58798	93	92	2.9	3.6	47	46	5	4	84	95
Papua New Guinea	1158	1930	92	93	2.5	2.8	43	42	5	5	97	96
Philippines	18629	31046	99	99	3.2	2.5	45	39	4	6	107	112
Qatar	39	138	55	60	7.6	4.6	50	46	4	3	82	47
Samoa [b]	71	..	93	..	..	..	50	..	5	..	110	..
Saudi Arabia	2790	6450	94	84	3.5	4.1	45	49	5	5	109	102
Singapore	1013	1328	95	97	2.1	1.1	39	22	6	9	113	115
Solomon Islands	76	..	89	..	..	..	45	..	4	..	59	..
Sri Lanka	6011	8575	92	99	2.3	1.5	43	32	5	8	79	96
Syrian Arab Republic	3049	6176	95	98	3.3	3.7	48	48	6	4	101	108
Thailand	17945	27751	101	99	3.2	1.5	45	32	5	7	120	120
Tonga [j]	38	..	94	..	..	..	46	..	5	..	106	..
Turkey	17435	27072	97	95	2.7	2.1	41	35	7	7	105	106
United Arab Emirates	84	518	61	48	7.0	4.1	44	46	6	3	111	55
Vanuatu [e k]	36	67	89	92	..	..	47	46	4	4	61	96
Viet Nam	21964	34265	106	104	2.2	2.2	42	38	7	7	130	136
Yemen	3218	5447	103	108	2.2	3.0	43	45	5	5	110	117

Sources:

Global Estimates and Projections of Population by Sex and Age: The 1988 Revision (United Nations publication, ST/ESA/SER.R/93); and *Demographic Yearbook* (United Nations publication, various years).

a   Through the accession of the German Democratic Republic to the Federal Republic of Germany with effect from 3 October 1990, the two German States have united to form one sovereign State. As from the date of unification, the Federal Republic of Germany acts in the United Nations under the designation "Germany". All data shown for Germany pertain to end-June 1990 or earlier and are indicated separately for the Federal Republic of Germany and the former German Democratic Republic.

b   Data under 1970 refer to year 1971.
c   Data under 1990 refer to year 1986.
d   Data under 1990 refer to year 1985.
e   Data under 1970 refer to year 1967.
f   Data exclude adjustment for underenumeration.
g   Data under 1970 refer to year 1968.
h   Including Tuvalu.
i   Data under 1970 refer to year 1969.
j   Data under 1970 refer to year 1966.
k   Data under 1990 refer to year 1987.

Table 2
Indicators on families and households

Country or area	Households and families					Marriage and marital status							
	Average household size		Women-headed			Average age at first marriage (years)		Total fertility rate (births per woman)		Women currently married (%)		% women 60+ not currently married	% women 25–44 currently divorced
	1970	latest	% of total	% with children, no spouse	% women living alone	f	m	1970	1990	aged 15–19	aged 25+		
Developed regions													
Albania	..	..	..	..	..	..	..	5.1	3.0	..	..	..	..
Australia	3.3	3.0	25	23	..	23.5	25.7	2.9	1.9	4.2	62	53	6.0
Austria	2.9	2.7	31	..	20	23.5	26.9	2.5	1.5	4.4[a]	52[a]	68[b]	6.5[b]
Belgium	2.9	2.7	21	24	15	22.4	24.8	2.3	1.6	5.3	62	57	4.1
Bulgaria	3.2	2.9	..	..	..	20.8[c]	24.5[c]	2.2	1.9	17.2[c]	73[c]	44[c]	3.6[c]
Canada	..	2.8[d]	25	25	12	23.1	25.2	2.5	1.7	4.6[d]	62[d]	51[d]	5.4[d]
Czechoslovakia	3.1	2.8	23	32	15	21.6	24.7	2.1	2.0	7.5	62	61	7.7
Denmark	2.8	2.4	..	..	..	26.1	28.9	2.2	1.5	0.8	51	57	10.4
Finland	3.0	2.6	..	..	..	24.6	27.1	2.1	1.7	1.2	51	63	8.1
France	3.1	2.7	22	17	16	24.3	26.4	2.6	1.9	1.3	55	57	7.5
Germany[e]													
Federal Rep. of Germany	2.7	2.4	..	..	..	23.6	27.9	2.3	1.4	1.7	54	63	6.4
former German Dem. Rep.	2.6	2.5	..	..	..	21.5	25.2	2.3	1.7	2.6	57	66	10.9
Greece	3.3	3.1	16	..	..	22.5	27.6	2.4	1.7	13.6	66	51	1.8
Hungary	3.0	2.8	20	..	..	21.0	24.8	2.0	1.8	10.8	61	63	9.5
Iceland	..	..	..	..	..	..	..	3.2	2.1	1.9	53	58	5.2
Ireland	3.9	3.7	..	..	..	23.4	24.4	3.9	2.5	1.2[a]	54[a]	63[b]	2.3[b]
Italy	3.3	3.0	20	..	12	23.2	27.1	2.5	1.5	4.6	61	58	0.4
Japan	..	3.1	15	..	9	25.1	28.6	2.0	1.7	0.9[a]	63[a]	54[b]	3.4[b]
Luxembourg	3.1	2.8	23	..	..	23.1	26.2	2.2	1.5	4.4	60	62	3.9
Malta	4.0	3.2	..	..	..	..	..	2.2	1.9	..	..	..	..
Netherlands	..	..	..	..	..	23.2	26.2	2.7	1.5	1.2	57	54	7.1
New Zealand	3.7	2.9	24	32	11	22.7	24.9	3.2	1.9	1.7	62	51	6.3
Norway	2.9	2.7	38	18	17	24.0	26.3	2.7	1.7	1.0	55	54	7.2
Poland	3.4	3.1[c]	27[c]	..	12[c]	22.5[c]	25.6[c]	2.3	2.2	4.5	64	62	4.0
Portugal	..	2.9	18	..	..	22.1	24.7	2.9	1.8	8.9	64	52	1.0
Romania	3.2	..	..	..	..	21.1[c]	24.9[c]	3.1	2.2	14.2[a c]	67[a c]	55[b c]	4.3[b c]
Spain	3.8	3.5	16	40	7	23.1	26.0	2.9	1.7	5.3	60	57	1.4
Sweden	..	2.2	27	..	19	27.6	30.0	2.1	1.7	0.3	47	55	10.2
Switzerland	2.9	2.5	25	17	18	25.0	27.9	2.3	1.6	1.0	55	56	7.0
USSR	3.7	4.0[c]	..	..	..	21.8	24.2	2.4	2.4	9.2[a c]	57[a c]	71[b c]	9.1[b c]
United Kingdom	2.9[f]	2.7	25[q]	32	..	23.1[f]	25.4[f]	2.5	1.8	2.7[g]	57[g]	56[g]	8.8[g]
United States	3.1	2.7	31	..	15	23.3	25.2	2.6	1.8	5.2	57	59	11.4
Yugoslavia	3.8	3.6	..	..	..	22.2	26.2	2.5	2.0	10.9	64	58	3.7
Africa													
Algeria	..	7.2[c h]	..	..	..	21.0[c]	25.3[c]	7.5	6.1	..	..	..	..
Angola	..	..	..	..	..	..	..	6.4	6.4	..	..	..	..
Benin	..	5.4[c]	..	..	..	18.2	..	6.9	7.0	..	76	..	..
Botswana	..	5.4	45	..	4	26.4	30.8	6.9	6.3	7.0[a]	41[a]	67[b]	4.0[b]
Burkina Faso	..	5.7[c]	5[c]	..	..	17.4[c]	27.0[c]	6.7	6.5	53.4[c]	79[c]	57[c]	0.5[c]
Burundi	..	4.5[c]	..	..	..	20.8[c]	24.4[c]	5.8	6.3	19.2	64	60	6.0
Cameroon	..	5.2[c]	14[c]	..	..	17.5[c]	..	5.8	5.8	44.3[a c]	66[a c]	73[b c]	3.7[b c]
Cape Verde	..	..	..	..	..	..	..	6.0	5.2	4.4[a]	41[a]	64[b]	2.6[b]
Central African Rep.	..	5.1[c]	..	..	..	..	..	5.7	5.9	45.5[c]	71[c]	66[c]	8.8[c i]
Chad	..	..	..	..	..	..	..	6.1	5.9	..	..	..	..
Comoros	..	5.3	..	..	..	19.5	25.8	6.3	6.2	26.0	60	71	10.8
Congo	..	5.3	21	53	6	..	..	5.9	6.0	15.7	53	60	7.7
Côte d'Ivoire	..	8.6	..	..	..	17.8	..	7.4	7.4	52.5[a c]	72[a c]	73[b c]	4.4[b c]
Djibouti	..	..	..	..	..	..	..	6.6	6.6	..	..	..	..
Egypt	..	5.2[c]	..	..	..	21.3	..	6.6	4.8	21.1[c i]	63[c i]	70[c i]	1.5[c i]
Equatorial Guinea	..	..	..	..	..	..	..	5.7	5.7	..	..	..	..
Ethiopia	..	4.3[c]	..	..	..	17.7	25.5	6.7	6.2	53.2	70	74	7.7

Table 2. Indicators on families and households [*cont.*]

	Households and families					Marriage and marital status							
	Average household size		Women-headed		% wo-men living alone	Average age at first marriage (years)		Total fertility rate (births per woman)		Women currently married (%)		% women 60+ not currently married	% women 25–44 currently divorced
Country or area	1970	latest	% of total	% with children, no spouse		f	m	1970	1990	aged 15–19	aged 25+		
Gabon	..	..	..	..	..	..	..	4.2	5.0	..	..	..	..
Gambia	8.3	..	..	..	..	..	..	6.5	6.4	..	..	..	..
Ghana	..	..	27 c	..	..	19.3	..	6.8	6.4	..	..	..	..
Guinea	..	6.7	..	..	..	..	..	6.4	6.2	..	..	..	..
Guinea-Bissau	..	4.7 c	..	..	..	..	..	5.2	5.4	..	..	..	..
Kenya	5.6	5.1 c	..	..	..	20.4 c	25.8 c	8.1	8.1	..	..	..	..
Lesotho	..	5.0 c	..	..	..	19.6 c	..	5.7	5.8	..	..	..	..
Liberia	..	..	15 c	..	..	..	..	6.4	6.5	..	..	..	..
Libyan Arab Jamahiriya	5.8	..	..	..	..	..	..	..	6.9	..	..	..	..
Madagascar	..	4.5 c	15 c	..	..	20.3 c	23.5 c	6.6	6.6	34.3 c	71 c	45 c	0.0 c
Malawi	..	3.0 c	29 c	..	..	17.8 c	22.9 c	6.9	7.0	47.0 a c	73 a c	55 b c	8.4 b c
Mali	..	5.1 c	15 c	..	4 c	18.1 c	28.2 c	6.6	6.7	48.9 c	72 c	66 c	1.9 c
Mauritania	..	5.5 c	..	..	..	19.2	..	6.5	6.5	36.9 c	56 c	84 c	13.6 c
Mauritius	5.3	4.8	19	..	..	21.7	24.7	4.3	1.9	10.9	57	67	0.7
Morocco	5.4	5.9	17 c	..	..	21.3	..	7.1	4.8	16.9	59	69	4.7
Mozambique	..	4.3	..	..	..	17.6	22.7	6.5	6.4	47.7	69	65	7.2
Namibia	..	..	..	..	..	..	..	6.1	6.1	..	..	..	..
Niger	..	..	..	..	..	..	..	7.1	7.1	..	..	..	..
Nigeria	..	5.8	..	..	..	18.7	..	7.1	7.0	..	..	..	..
Reunion	4.9	4.2	25	57	6	25.8	28.1	4.8	2.4	2.8	45	65	2.9
Rwanda	..	4.6 c	25 c	..	5 c	21.2	..	8.0	8.3	15.0 c	63 c	63 c	3.2 c
Sao Tome and Principe	..	3.8	..	..	..	..	..	..	..	24.4	52	71	0.2
Senegal	..	..	..	..	..	17.7 c	..	6.7	6.4	33.3 c	54 c	58 c	2.9 c
Seychelles	4.7	4.8 c	..	..	..	..	..	6.1	3.3	8.6	48	66	4.5
Sierra Leone	..	..	..	..	..	..	..	6.4	6.5	..	..	..	..
Somalia	..	..	..	..	..	20.1	26.5	6.6	6.6	..	..	..	..
South Africa	..	..	..	..	..	..	..	5.9	4.5	5.1	49	57	3.7
Sudan	..	5.8 c	22 c k	..	..	21.3 c	..	6.7	6.4	..	..	..	..
Swaziland	..	..	..	..	..	..	..	6.5	6.5	..	..	..	..
Togo	5.7	5.9	..	..	..	..	..	6.2	6.1	..	..	..	..
Tunisia	5.1	5.5	10 c	..	..	24.3	28.1	6.8	4.1	6.5	58	56	1.3
Uganda	..	..	..	..	..	..	..	6.9	6.9	..	..	..	..
United Rep. Tanzania	4.4	4.8 c	..	..	..	..	..	6.9	7.1	35.7 c	70 c	59 c	5.9 c
Western Sahara	..	..	..	..	..	..	..	..	..	..	..	..	..
Zaire	..	4.3 c	..	..	..	20.1 c	25.4 c	6.0	6.1	..	..	..	..
Zambia	4.6	5.0	28	..	6	19.4	25.1	6.7	7.2	29.4 a	65 a	53 b	8.7 b
Zimbabwe	4.2	..	..	..	..	20.4	25.4	7.5	5.8	24.5	65	57	5.8

Latin America and Caribbean

Antigua and Barbuda	4.3	..	..	..	..	..	..	..	..	..	..	..	..
Argentina	3.8	3.9	19	..	..	22.9	25.3	3.1	3.0	10.1 a	58 a	58 b	3.4 b
Bahamas	4.1	4.3	..	..	..	..	..	3.5	2.5	4.5	48	58	2.1
Barbados	4.0	3.6	44	..	10	..	..	3.5	2.0	0.6	31	63	1.9
Belize	5.2	5.3	..	..	..	..	..	6.3	..	8.9	42	58	0.6
Bolivia	..	4.3 c	..	..	..	22.1 c	24.5 c	6.6	6.1	15.6 c	59 c	55 c	2.6 c
Brazil	3.8	4.4 l	14 l	63 l	3 l	22.6	25.9	5.3	3.5	14.6 l	59 l	55 l	0.0 l
Chile	5.2	4.5	22	..	3	23.6	25.7	4.4	2.7	10.4	58	57	0.0
Colombia	5.9	5.2	..	..	..	20.4	24.0	6.0	3.6	..	..	..	..
Costa Rica	5.6	4.7	18	..	..	22.7 c	..	5.8	3.3	15.4	58	52	2.2
Cuba	4.5	4.1	28	..	..	19.9	23.5	4.3	1.7	26.9	66	49	9.8
Dominica	..	4.3	38	..	..	..	..	..	..	0.4	29	59	0.8
Dominican Republic	5.3	5.4 c	..	..	..	20.5 c	..	6.7	3.8	..	..	..	..
Ecuador	..	5.1 m	..	..	..	22.1 c	..	6.7	4.7	17.8 m	61 m	46 m	1.2 m
El Salvador	..	5.0 c	22 c	..	..	..	..	6.6	4.9	..	..	..	..

Table 2. Indicators on families and households [cont.]

Country or area	Households and families					Marriage and marital status							
	Average household size		Women-headed			Average age at first marriage (years)		Total fertility rate (births per woman)		Women currently married (%)		% women 60+ not currently married	% women 25–44 currently divorced
	1970	latest	% of total	% with children, no spouse	% women living alone	f	m	1970	1990	aged 15–19	aged 25+		
French Guiana	3.4	3.3	31	41	9	..	..	3.8	..	2.1	32	69	3.0
Grenada	..	4.2	45	..	..	..	..	..	..	0.5	26	69	0.8
Guadeloupe	4.4	3.8	34	52	10	26.6	29.6	5.2	2.2	1.4	37	64	4.0
Guatemala	5.2	5.2	..	..	..	20.5	23.5	6.6	5.8	26.4	63	58	4.2
Guyana	5.4	5.1	24	..	3	20.7[n]	26.0[o]	5.3	2.8	11.6	48	64	2.8
Haiti	..	4.9[c]	..	..	..	23.8	27.3	6.2	4.7	8.0	61	39	0.2
Honduras	..	..	22[c]	..	..	..	..	7.4	5.6	..	..	..	..
Jamaica	4.3	4.2	34[c]	..	..	25.2[p]	30.5[o]	5.4	2.9	0.5	24	56	0.8
Martinique	4.4	3.8	35	53	9	28.8	30.1	5.0	2.1	0.5	33	65	4.4
Mexico	4.9	5.5	..	..	..	20.6	23.6	6.7	3.6	20.1	63	47	1.0
Netherlands Antilles	5.1	4.1	30	66	6	..	..	3.1	..	..	..	..	..
Nicaragua	..	..	..	..	..	..	..	7.1	5.5	..	..	..	..
Panama	4.9[q]	4.6[q]	22[q]	..	3[q]	21.2	25.0	5.6	3.1	20.1[q]	32[q]	47[q]	1.5[q]
Paraguay	..	5.2	..	..	..	22.1[c]	..	6.4	4.6	14.1	57	52	0.0
Peru	4.8[l]	4.9[l]	23[c]	..	..	22.7	25.7	6.6	4.5	14.2[l]	59[l]	51[l]	0.6[l]
Puerto Rico	..	3.7	25	..	..	22.3	24.1	3.4	2.4	13.6	56	54	9.5
St. Kitts and Nevis	4.0	3.8	46	..	9	..	..	..	..	0.5	26	66	1.9
St. Lucia	4.6	4.6	39	..	6	..	..	..	3.8	0.7	30	60	0.5
St. Vincent/Grenadines	4.0	4.8	42	..	..	..	..	..	..	1.3	25	70	0.8
Suriname	..	..	..	..	..	..	..	5.9	3.0	..	..	..	..
Trinidad and Tobago	4.8	4.5	25	..	5	22.3[n]	27.9[o]	3.9	2.7	11.3[r]	48[r]	60[r]	1.9[r]
Uruguay	..	3.3	21[c]	..	..	22.4[c]	25.4[c]	2.8	2.6	12.2[c]	59[c]	59[c]	2.9[c]
US Virgin Islands	..	3.4	..	..	..	..	..	5.3	..	5.9	49	60	12.4
Venezuela	5.8	5.3[e]	22	..	..	21.2	24.8	5.9	3.8	18.4[l]	57[l]	55[l]	2.5[l]
Asia and Pacific													
Afghanistan	6.2	5.9[ch]	..	..	..	17.8[c]	25.3[c]	7.1	6.9	53.3[ch]	79[ch]	62[ch]	0.1[ch]
Bahrain	6.4	6.6	..	..	..	..	..	7.0	4.1	14.5	60	49	2.8
Bangladesh	5.6	5.7	17	82	2	16.7	23.9	6.9	5.5	65.4	77	67	1.1
Bhutan	..	..	..	..	..	..	..	5.9	5.5	..	..	..	..
Brunei Darussalam	5.8	5.8	..	..	..	..	..	6.0	3.5	8.0	57	45	1.6
Cambodia	..	..	..	..	..	..	..	6.2	4.7	..	..	..	..
China	..	4.4[s]	..	..	..	22.4	25.1	6.0	2.4	4.3[s]	66[s]	59[s]	0.3[s]
Cyprus	3.9	..	..	..	..	24.2[c]	26.3[c]	2.8	2.3	4.5[ac]	65[ac]	46[bc]	1.4[bc]
East Timor	..	..	..	..	..	..	..	6.2	5.4	..	..	..	..
Fiji	..	6.0[c]	..	..	..	21.6[c]	24.5[c]	4.6	3.2	12.8	64	56	3.1
French Polynesia	..	5.0	15	..	3	..	..	..	..	..	..	..	..
Guam	..	4.1	..	..	..	..	..	4.8	..	9.7	65	51	5.2
Hong Kong	..	3.7	24[c]	..	..	25.3	28.7	4.0	1.7	2.0[a]	57[a]	57[b]	1.2[b]
India	5.6	5.5[t]	..	..	..	18.7	23.4	5.7	4.3	43.5[at]	74[at]	65[bt]	0.8[bt]
Indonesia	4.6	4.9	14	..	..	20.0	24.1	5.6	3.3	17.3	63	75	4.5
Iran (Islamic Rep. of)	5.0	4.9[c]	7[c]	..	3[c]	19.7[c]	24.2[c]	7.0	5.6	33.9[c]	72[c]	61[c]	0.8[c]
Iraq	6.0	6.3[c]	..	..	..	20.8[c]	25.2[c]	7.2	6.4	31.5[ac]	67[ac]	56[bc]	1.3[bc]
Israel	3.8	3.5[u]	18[u]	..	12[u]	23.5	26.1	3.8	2.9	5.9[u]	62[u]	53[u]	4.2[u]
Jordan	..	6.6[cv]	..	..	..	22.6	26.8	8.0	7.2	20.1[c]	64[c]	59[c]	1.1[c]
Kiribati	6.1	6.1[c]	..	..	..	..	..	..	..	20.8[cw]	59[cw]	66[cw]	8.5[cw]
Korea, D. People's R.	..	..	..	..	..	..	..	5.7	3.6	..	..	..	..
Korea, Republic of	5.2	4.5	15	..	..	24.1	27.3	4.5	2.0	0.9	59	64	1.1
Kuwait	..	6.5	5	..	0	22.9	26.3	7.5	4.8	14.3	64	70	1.8
Lao People's Dem. Rep.	..	..	..	..	..	..	..	6.2	5.7	..	..	..	..
Lebanon	..	..	..	..	..	..	..	6.1	3.4	..	..	..	..
Macau	5.0	..	..	..	..	..	..	2.0	..	1.6	51	56	0.2
Malaysia	5.1	5.2	..	..	..	23.5	26.6	5.9	3.5	8.2[ax]	57[ax]	64[bx]	1.6[bx]
Maldives	5.4	6.1[c]	..	..	..	..	..	..	..	43.1[c]	68[c]	66[c]	10.3[c]
Mongolia	4.6	..	..	..	..	..	..	5.9	5.4	..	..	..	..

Table 2. Indicators on families and households [*cont.*]

Country or area	Households and families					Marriage and marital status							
	Average household size		Women-headed			Average age at first marriage (years)		Total fertility rate (births per woman)		Women currently married (%)		% women 60+ not currently married	% women 25–44 currently divorced
	1970	latest	% of total	% with children no spouse	% women living alone	f	m	1970	1990	aged 15–19	aged 25+		
Myanmar	..	5.2 ʸ	16 ʸ	..	..	22.4	24.6	5.7	4.0	16.0 ʸ	59 ʸ	61 ʸ	2.7 ʸ
Nepal	5.5	5.8	..	..	..	17.9	21.5	6.2	5.9	50.1 ᵃ	81 ᵃ	39 ᵇ	0.4 ᵇ
New Caledonia	..	4.1	18	36	6	..	..	..	..	9.1 ᶜ	57 ᶜ	64 ᶜ	2.9 ᶜ
Oman	..	..	..	..	..	..	..	7.2	7.2	..	..	..	..
Pacific Islands	..	6.7	..	..	..	..	..	5.7	..	19.8	62	49	3.3
Pakistan	5.7	6.7 ᶻ	4 ᶻ	63 ᶻ	1 ᶻ	19.8	24.9	7.0	6.5	29.1 ᶻ	73 ᶻ	50 ᶻ	0.5 ᶻ
Papua New Guinea	..	4.5	..	..	..	..	..	6.2	5.7	16.7	71	48	4.8 ⁱ
Philippines	5.9	5.6	11 ᶜ	..	..	22.4	25.3	6.0	4.3	14.0	61	48	0.0
Qatar	..	..	..	..	..	..	..	7.0	5.6	16.1	68	44	2.4
Samoa	6.2	5.9 ᶜ	..	..	..	..	..	5.8	..	5.6 ᵃ	54 ᵃ	54 ᵇ	5.8 ᵇ
Saudi Arabia	..	..	..	..	..	..	..	7.3	7.2	..	..	..	..
Singapore	5.3	4.7	18	..	3	26.2	28.4	3.5	1.7	2.3 ᵃ	52 ᵃ	63 ᵇ	1.7 ᵇ
Solomon Islands	5.1	5.6 ᶜ	..	..	..	..	..	..	..	25.9 ᶜ	66 ᶜ	56 ᶜ	0.6 ᶜ
Sri Lanka	5.6	5.2	17	..	..	24.4	27.9	4.7	2.7	9.7	59	47	0.5
Syrian Arab Republic	5.9	6.2	13 ᶜ	..	..	22.1 ᶜ	..	7.8	6.8	24.6 ᵃᵃ	66 ᵃᵃ	50 ᵃᵃ	0.8 ᵃᵃ
Thailand	5.8	5.2	16	..	..	22.7	24.7	6.1	2.6	15.6 ᵃ	59 ᵃ	56 ᵇ	3.5 ᵇ
Tonga	..	6.5 ᶜ	..	..	..	..	..	..	..	4.6 ᵃᶜ	55 ᵃᶜ	56 ᵇᶜ	3.1 ᵇᶜ
Turkey	5.1	5.2	10 ᶜ	..	..	20.6	23.6	5.6	3.6	20.8	70	52	0.9
United Arab Emirates	..	5.2 ᶜ	..	..	..	18.0 ᶜ	25.9 ᶜ	6.8	4.8	55.0 ᶜ	76 ᶜ	71 ᶜ	2.5 ᶜ
Vanuatu	..	5.0 ᶜ	..	..	..	..	..	..	..	13.7 ᵃᶜ	61 ᵃᶜ	53 ᵇᶜ	1.1 ᵇᶜ
Viet Nam	..	5.3 ᶜ	..	..	..	..	..	5.9	4.1	..	..	..	..
Yemen	..	5.0 ᶜ ᵇᵇ	..	..	..	17.8 ᵇᵇ	22.2 ᵇᵇ	7.0	6.9	..	..	..	..

Sources:

Demographic Yearbook (United Nations publication, various years); *Fertility Behaviour in the Context of Development: Evidence from the World Fertility Survey,* Population Studies No. 100 (United Nations publication, Sales No. E.86.XIII.5); *First Marriage: Patterns and Determinants* (United Nations publication, ST/ESA/SER.R/76); *Population and Vital Statistics Report, 1984 Special Supplement* (United Nations publication, Sales No. E/F.84.III.2); *World Population Prospects 1988,* Population Studies No. 106 (United Nations publication, Sales No. E.88.XIII.7); United States Department of Commerce, Bureau of the Census, *Women of the World* (Washington, D.C., 1984/85); and unpublished data compiled by the Economic Commission for Europe and Population Division of the United Nations Secretariat from national sources.

a   Excluding separated.
b   Including separated.
c   Data refer to late 1970s.
d   Excluding persons living in Indian reserves and settlements.
e   Through the accession of the German Democratic Republic to the Federal Republic of Germany with effect from 3 October 1990, the two German States have united to form one sovereign State. As from the date of unification, the Federal Republic of Germany acts in the United Nations under the designation "Germany". All data shown for Germany pertain to end-June 1990 or earlier and are indicated separately for the Federal Republic of Germany and the former German Democratic Republic.
f   England and Wales only.
g   Excluding Northern Ireland.
h   Excluding nomads.

i   Including widowed.
j   For Egyptian nationals only.
k   Refers to the settled population only.
l   Excluding Indian jungle population.
m   Excluding nomadic Indian tribes.
n   Including legal and consensual and visiting unions.
o   Legal unions only.
p   Including legal and consensual unions.
q   Excluding indigenous areas and the former Canal Zone.
r   Excluding students still attending school.
s   Covering only the civilian population of 29 provinces, municipalities and autonomous regions, except Tibet.
t   Including data for the Indian-held part of Jammu and Kashmir, the final status of which has not yet been determined.
u   Including data for East Jerusalem and Israeli residents in certain other territories under occupation by Israeli military forces since June 1967.
v   Excluding data for Jordanian territory under occupation since June 1967 by Israeli military force.
w   For indigenous population only.
x   Peninsular Malaysia only.
y   Excluding people from areas restricted for security reasons.
z   Excluding data for Jammu and Kashmir, the final status of which has not yet been determined, Junagardh, Manavadar, Gilgit and Baltistan.
aa   Including Palestinian refugees.
bb   Data refer to the former Yemen Arab Republic only.

2
Public life and leadership

Some of the disparities between women and men in public life and leadership have narrowed, but wide gaps remain. Women still play a very minor role in high-level political and economic decision-making in most countries.

Women almost everywhere have the right to vote, they make up more than half of most electorates and many more women work in the public sector than ever before. Yet women rarely achieve elective office or have equal access to political careers. They are blocked from top positions in trade unions, political parties, government, interest associations and business.

Women have long been leaders in the community and at the grass roots—and they are strong advocates for environmental protection and for peace.

Top positions

Of the 159 United Nations member States, only six (3.8 per cent) were headed by women at the end of 1990: Iceland, Ireland, Nicaragua, Norway, Dominica and the Philippines. Women also are poorly represented in the top echelons of government. Only 3.5 per cent of the world's cabinet ministers are women, and women hold no ministerial positions in 93 countries of the world. [4]

Most women in government leadership are in such ministries as education, culture, social welfare and women's affairs. In some regions they are also making inroads in justice and legal affairs. But even in the "social" fields, women average only 12 to 14 per cent of the positions in developed regions, excluding eastern Europe and the USSR, 9 per cent in sub-Saharan Africa and 6 per cent or less in the rest of the world. Overall, women are least represented in executive, economic, political and legal ministries in Africa and in Asia and the Pacific. Men maintain a stronghold on such key areas as defence, economic policy and political affairs in all regions.

Women are shut out of all the decision-making jobs at the four highest levels of government in 49 countries: 21 in Africa, 16 in Asia and the Pacific, 8 in Latin America and the Caribbean and 4 in Europe and northern America. In only three countries do women hold more than 20 per cent of ministerial-level government positions: Bhutan, Dominica and Norway.

In a few countries—the Bahamas, Barbados, Dominica, Finland and Norway—there are enough women in decision-making positions to have a strong influence. But where women have been confined to traditional roles—as in northern Africa, eastern Asia, and western Asia—their representation and influence in decision-making are negligible (list 2.1).

Decision-making positions in Government

Decision-making positions in Government are defined as ministers or equivalent, deputy or assistant ministers or equivalent, secretaries of state or permanent secretaries or equivalent, and deputy of state or director of Government or equivalent.

In nearly 100 countries, women held no positions at the ministerial level in 1987–1988. In the developed regions these were Belgium, Czechoslovakia, France, Japan, Luxembourg, Malta, Spain, the USSR and Yugoslavia. In Africa there were 31 countries where women held no ministerial-level position in 1987–1988, in Latin America and the Caribbean 24 countries and in Asia and the Pacific 30 countries.

Source: Division for the Advancement of Women, Centre for Social Development and Humanitarian Affairs of the United Nations Secretariat, and United States National Standards Association.

2.1
Where women have achieved at least 10 per cent of ministerial-level positions

Percentage of ministerial-level positions held by women, 1987–1988

Developed regions
Austria (11)
Canada (13)
Denmark (14)
Finland (12)
Germany:
Fed. Rep. of Germany (10)
former German Dem. Rep. (10)
Norway (37)
Romania (12)
Sweden (17)
Switzerland (11)

Africa
Burkina Faso (12)
Burundi (10)
Senegal (13)
United Rep. of Tanzania (16)

Latin America and Caribbean
Dominica (22)
Guatemala (12)
Uruguay (13)

Asia and Pacific
Bhutan (25)
Philippines (11)

Source: Division for the Advancement of Women, Centre for Social Development and Humanitarian Affairs of the United Nations Secretariat and United States National Standards Association.

Women Heads of Government in the twentieth century

Presidents

Corazón Aquino*	Philippines
Vigdís Finnbogadóttir*	Iceland
Violeta Chamorro*	Nicaragua
Ertha Pascal-Trouillot	Haiti
Lidia Geiler	Bolivia
Isabela Perón	Argentina
Mary Robinson*	Ireland

Prime Ministers

Margaret Thatcher	United Kingdom
Maria Liberia-Peters	Netherlands Antilles
Eugenia Charles*	Dominica
Gro Harlem Brundtland*	Norway
Indira Gandhi	India
Siramavo Bandaranaike	Sri Lanka
Golda Meir	Israel
María de Lourdes Pintasilgo	Portugal
Benazir Bhutto	Pakistan

*In office 31 December 1990

Women have the right to vote, and they do, but the proportion of women in parliaments is not high (chart 2.2). [3] In 1987 only 10 per cent of countries' parliamentarians on average were women. The strength of parliamentary representation by women varies by political system and historical period (lists 2.4 and 2.5). In 1987 the highest representation of women in parliaments was in eastern Europe and the USSR—nearly 28 per cent—but recent political restructuring in these regions has given women a weaker role. In the most recent elections, the percentage of women in eastern Europe's parliaments dropped significantly (table 2.3).

The highest consistent parliamentary representation by women has been in the Nordic countries, where they have been politically prominent for some time. But on average, women's representation in parliaments improved in every region from 1975 to 1987. The largest increases were in the developed regions outside eastern Europe and the USSR and in sub-Saharan Africa—and recent elections suggest continuing increases (chart 2.2).

Political participation

Two paths traditionally lead to decision-making positions in government—political candidacy and a career in the civil service. Both paths present difficulties for women as well as opportunities. Political candidates are often recruited from political parties, labour unions and interest associations, and women's access to leadership in these institutions depends on the degree of equality within a society.

Women make up a sizeable proportion of the membership of labour unions in western Europe—roughly 30 per cent of the membership of unions affiliated with the International Federation of Free Trade Unions. But they are rarely elected to union decision-making bodies. Their proportion of union membership ranges from more than 50 per cent in Denmark, Finland and Sweden to 30–33 per cent in

2.2
Women's parliamentary representation, though improved, is still very low in most regions

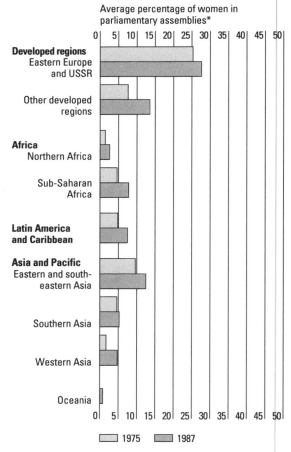

Average percentage of women in parliamentary assemblies*

☐ 1975   ▧ 1987

*Unicameral assembly or lower chamber of bicameral assembly.

Source: Prepared by the Statistical Office of the United Nations Secretariat from Inter-Parliamentary Union, "Distribution of seats between men and women in national assemblies", Reports and Documents, No. 14 (Geneva, 1987).

Austria, Belgium, Ireland, Italy and the United Kingdom, 22 per cent in the Federal Republic of Germany (prior to unification) and 10–15 per cent in Luxembourg and the Netherlands. Women also figure heavily in the membership of political parties in many countries. In several western European countries, for example, they make up from 25 to 45 per cent of the membership of the major political parties. But again, they are grossly under-represented in the leadership of these parties.[1]

Community and grass-roots leadership

Although women have been systematically cut off from men's traditional routes to political leadership, they have been able to develop their involvement in non-governmental and community-based organizations (NGOs and CBOs) as a means to power. For many women, community and grass-roots participation come as an extension of their traditional roles as community members responsible for their families' health and well-being. And there are many examples of movements—such as those for the environment and for peace—led primarily by women around issues that affect these roles.

2.3
Women's parliamentary representation is now rapidly falling in eastern Europe and the USSR

	Women in parliament (%)	
	1987	1990
Bulgaria	21	9
Czechoslovakia	30	6
Germany		
former German Dem. Rep.	32	21
Hungary	21	7
Poland		
Senate	..	6
Lower House	20	4
Romania	34	4
USSR		
Congress of Peoples' Deputies	..	16
Soviet of Nationalities	31	14
Supreme Soviet	35	14

Source: Compiled by the Division for the Advancement of Women, Centre for Social Development and Humanitarian Affairs of the United Nations Secretariat, from national reports to the United Nations.

Women are usually more successful in winning places on local representative bodies than in national parliaments. In reports presented to the Committee on the Elimination of Discrimination against Women, the percentage of women in local bodies was higher than in national bodies in 12 of 14 countries—the exceptions were Austria and Japan.[2]

Some women environmental leaders

Gro Harlem Brundtland, Prime Minister of Norway, Chairman of the World Commission on Environment and Development, which produced the global report on the environment, *Our Common Future* (1987).

María V. Cherkasova, zoologist. Secretary of the Union of Soviet Socialist Republics' Socio-Ecological Union, which coordinates 200 environmental groups from 11 Soviet republics.

Christine Kwabea Debra, commissioned officer in the Ghana Army Nursing Corps. Executive Chairman of the Environmental Protection Council of Ghana.

Lois Gibbs, housewife. Organized the Love Canal grass-roots movement and founded the Citizens Clearinghouse for Hazardous Wastes in the United States.

Janet Gibson, biologist. Led the successful fight to protect Belize's barrier reef.

Chee Yoke Ling, secretary-general of Malaysia's Friends of the Earth. Launched movements—primarily involving women—protesting poisonous pesticides and radioactive wastes.

Wangari Maathai, founder and head of Kenya's Green Belt Movement. Regularly confronts the Government of Kenya to preserve forests and other natural resources.

Sithembiso Nyoni, co-ordinator of the Organization of Rural Associations for Progress, a grass-roots environment and development group, in Matabeleland, Zimbabwe.

María Luisa Robleto, head of the Nicaraguan Environmental Movement. At forefront of women's battle to control pesticide use.

Vandana Shiva, physicist and philosopher of science. Director of the Research Foundation for Science, Technology and Natural Resource Policy, Delhi, India. Involved in the Chipko Andolan reafforestation movement.

2.4
Where women make up less than 4 per cent of parliamentary representation
Percentage women in parliament, 1987

Developed regions
Japan (1.4)
Malta (2.9)

Africa
Algeria (2.4)
Comoros (0.0)
Djibouti (0.0)
Egypt (3.9)
Equatorial Guinea (3.3)
Kenya (1.7)
Madagascar (1.5)
Mali (3.7)
Morocco (0.0)
South Africa (3.5)
Sudan (0.7)
Swaziland (2.0)
Zaire (3.5)
Zambia (2.9)

Latin America and Caribbean
Antigua and Barbuda (0.0)
Barbados (3.7)
Belize (3.6)
Bolivia (3.8)
Ecuador (1.4)
El Salvador (3.3)
Paraguay (1.7)
Uruguay (0.0)
Venezuela (3.9)

Asia and Pacific
Bhutan (1.3)
Cyprus (1.8)
Iran (Islamic Rep. of) (1.5)
Jordan (0.0)
Korea, Republic of (2.5)
Lebanon (0.0)
Papua New Guinea (0.0)
Singapore (3.8)
Solomon Islands (0.0)
Thailand (3.5)
Tonga (0.0)
Turkey (3.0)
United Arab Emirates (0.0)
Vanuatu (0.0)
Yemen (0.0)

Source: Inter-Parliamentary Union (Geneva).

2.5
**Women make up
more than 15 per cent
of parliamentary
representation in fewer
than 25 countries**
Percentage women
in parliament, 1987

Developed regions
Albania (29)
Bulgaria (21)
Czechoslovakia (30)
Denmark (29)
Finland (32)
Germany:
former German Dem. Rep. (32)
Hungary (21)
Iceland (21)
Netherlands (20)
Norway (34)
Poland (20)
Romania (34)
Sweden (29)
USSR (35)
Yugoslavia (19)

Africa
Mozambique (16)
Seychelles (24)

**Latin America
and Caribbean**
Cuba (34)
Trinidad and Tobago (17)

Asia and Pacific
China (21)
Korea, Dem. People's Rep. (21)
Mongolia (25)
Viet Nam (18)

Source: Inter-Parliamentary Union
(Geneva).

Women in many parts of the world are leading efforts to build awareness of environmental issues, ranging from movements to educate children about the environment in the USSR to acts of civil disobedience protesting the use of hazardous wastes and poisonous pesticides in Malaysia. Women far removed from decision-making in both developed and developing regions have found that their efforts to survive can be the basis for effective political action.

Grass-roots women's groups and women field workers have been gaining momentum. Reforestation movements—like the Green Belt Movement in rural Kenya and the Chipko Andolan movement in India—begin with a few poor, rural women saving a few trees and eventually become influential interest groups.[3] Working class housewives successfully campaigned the United States Government to clean up hazardous waste sites affecting residential housing at Love Canal.[4]

Many environmental leaders are women but few are recognized. The United Nations Environment Programme has distributed 750 environmental awards—12 to women.

Women in the public sector

Educated women work in the public sector because it often offers them white-collar conditions, employment security, benefits and possibly some opportunity to advance (table 2.6). Numerous countries in developed and developing regions—Finland, Denmark, Mexico, the Philippines and Sweden among them—show that public administrations are taking the lead in employing women. Public enterprises have made less progress. In Argentina, for example, women are much less represented in public enterprises than in public administration, and those who hold positions are generally better educated than their male counterparts.[5]

Although statistics on women in bureaucratic careers are not generally available, one pattern seems to dominate. Many women work at the lowest echelons, but their representation dwindles rapidly as the pay, status and levels increase.

This pattern is mirrored in the United Nations system. Highly visible throughout the world, the United Nations organizations should set an example in personnel practices. But as with national civil services, the proportion of women in top management

Women awards recipients of the United Nations Environment Programme

Barbara d'Achille, journalist. Campaigned for environmental protection and sustainable development in Peru for 18 years.

Mary Zanoni Allegretti. Working since 1980 with Brazil's National Council of Rubber Tappers to pro-tect the Amazonian forest and its people.

Roula Angelakis-Malakis, journalist. Influences public opinion about environmental issues and their effects.

Kathryn S. Fuller, head of the World Wildlife Fund, USA. Promotes debt-for-nature initiatives in developing countries, with debt repayments eased in exchange for environmental protection funds.

Niki Goulandris, artist, naturalist, museum director, former minister of social services. Founded Goulandris Natural History Museum in Kifssia, Greece.

Elizabeth May, environmental lawyer. Executive Director of Cultural Survival in Canada, which protects forests and indigenous cultures in Canada and Brazil.

Anna H. Merz, financed and created a rhino sanctuary in Kenya.

Christine Milne, school teacher and Green Independent member of the Tasmanian Parliament. Successfully lobbied government and industry to protect forests from non-sustainable exploitation by industry.

Fiona Reynolds, environmental campaigner and lobbyist. Secretary of the Council for National Parks, then Assistant Director for Policy of the Council for the Protection of Rural England. Campaigned successfully for environmental improvements in planning and water legislation.

Margaret Thatcher, former British prime minister. Advocates international action against global warming and the greenhouse effect.

María Aída Velásquez, chemist and Benedictine nun. Since 1966, has initiated public awareness and training activities on environmental issues and against nuclear power in the Philippines.

W.M.U. Wanigasundara, journalist. Pioneered environmental magazine in Sri Lanka and contributes to the international press on environmental topics.

2.6
Women are finding more jobs in the public sector

	Public sector employees who are women (%)
Developed regions	
Denmark	67
Finland	50 [a]
Sweden	68
Yugoslavia	36
Latin America and Caribbean	
Argentina	28 [a]
	12 [b]
Mexico	24 [b]
Asia and Pacific	
India	7 [b]
Indonesia	18 [a]
Iraq	21
Philippines	50
Thailand	28

Source: Data compiled by the Statistical Office of the United Nations Secretariat and the International Center for Public Enterprises (Ljubljana, Yugoslovia) from national reports and studies for various years from 1976 to 1985.

a   Public administration only.
b   Public enterprises only.

positions with the United Nations system is extremely low—3.6 per cent (chart 2.7). Below the senior levels of decision making, the representation of women is much higher. But women are well represented only at the most junior professional levels, the only levels at which staff are recruited on the basis of competitive examinations. [9]

Women in economic decision-making

Rarely found in high positions in finance ministries, central banks or foreign trade departments, women are grossly underrepresented in economic decision-making.

Administrative and managerial workers—including legislative officials, government administrators and managers—make up an elite of 2 to 3 per cent of all workers. [2] The Latin America and Caribbean region had the highest proportion of women in these administrative and managerial jobs in the 1980s, at about 20 per cent. That proportion averaged 18 per cent in the developed regions, 13 per cent in Africa and 10 per cent in Asia and the Pacific. Although these shares are low, the gains since 1970 are significant. The proportion of

women in administrative and managerial positions more than doubled in Africa during this period, nearly doubled in Asia and the Pacific, and rose 6–7 percentage points in the developed regions and in Latin America and the Caribbean (chart 2.8).

In the private sector, women constitute a small and growing pool of middle managers, the level from which top executives are drawn, but men maintain a stronghold on top executive positions. There are no international surveys on women at the highest decision-making level in private business, but a recent study of the 1,000 most valuable publicly held companies in the United States in 1989 showed only two women among the chief executive officers (up from one in 1988), far below the representation of women among national presidents, prime ministers and ministers. These companies had annual sales of $3.3 trillion, underscoring the miniscule influence of women in big business. [6]

2.7
Women in public administration work mainly at the lowest levels

Women among professional staff in United Nations system (%) [a]

Legend: 1975 / 1988

Categories: Senior management, Senior professional, Mid-level professional, Junior professional

Sources: Compiled from "Composition of the Secretariat", annual reports of the Secretary-General to the General Assembly.

a   Excluding World Bank and International Monetary Fund, since their system of grades differs from that of the United Nations common system of salaries and allowances.

Public sector

In economic statistics and national accounts, the public sector is defined to include both (a) all public administration and government services which are not usually sold to the public and (b) public enterprises. Public enterprises are enterprises publicly owned and/or controlled which sell the goods or services they produce. Statistics on the government sector usually cover public administration only as the boundary between public and private enterprises in the enterprise sector is ambiguous and subject to frequent changes in definition and practice of public ownership and/or control.

Peace

The casualties from wars increasingly are civilians, and a growing proportion are women and children. Rather than merely be passive victims, women have been leaders and mainstays of nongovernmental peace movements. But as with environmental leaders, few women have been recognized for their contributions to peace.

Although there are no wide-scale statistics on women's involvement in disarmament movements, it is clear that they are affected by decisions regarding military policies and expenditures. When defense is a priority expenditure, domestic social programmes usually suffer. And cuts in education, food subsidies and health and family programmes tend to affect women disproportionately. Women are generally responsible for the family's health and nutrition and rely more heavily on food and health services. They also rely on educational programmes to redress long-standing inequities in their access to training and employment opportunities.

Since 1970 military expenditures, according to best estimates, increased more than 40 per cent in developed regions (from $497 billion to $716 billion) and nearly 130 per cent in developing regions (from $62 billion to $143 billion). In 1986 defence budgets exceeded the combined health and education budgets of one developed country and 27 developing countries (table 2.10). [5]

2.8
Women's overall representation as managers in the public and private sectors is rising in all regions

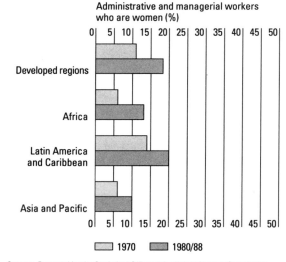

Administrative and managerial workers who are women (%)

☐ 1970   ■ 1980/88

Source: Prepared by the Statistical Office of the United Nations Secretariat from International Labour Office, *Year Book of Labour Statistics* (Geneva, various years).

2.9
Military spending per capita is highest by far in western Asia

Military expenditures per capita, 1986 (US dollars)

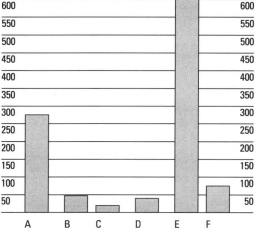

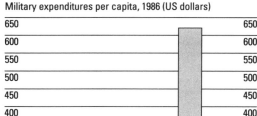

Developed regions
A   All developed regions
Africa
B   Northern Africa [a]
C   Sub-Saharan Africa

Latin America and Caribbean
D   All Latin America and Caribbean
Asia and Pacific
E   Western Asia
F   Other Asia and Pacific [b]

Source: Compiled by the Statistical Office of the United Nations Secretariat from R. L. Sivard, *World Military and Social Expenditures 1989,* 13th edition (Washington, D.C., 1989).

a   Excluding Libyan Arab Jamahiriya ($US 635).
b   Excluding Brunei Darussalam ($US1099).

Indicators

Table 3 presents indicators on women's participation in public life: their representation in national legislative bodies in 1975 and 1987, the year they obtained the right to vote in each country, and their representation in top-level decision-making posts in government.

The definition of "decision-making positions in government" is given on page 31 above. Indicators on women in parliment are based on data provided to the Inter-Parliamentary Union by national authorities and published periodically, most recently in 1988. [3] Information on the year women obtained the right to vote was compiled by the Inter-Parliamentary Union.

Data on women in decision-making positions in Government are based on reports by individual governments and published in the *World-wide Government Directory of 1987–88.* [4] The indicators shown here have been compiled from this source and analysed by the Division for the Advancement of Women, Centre for Social Development and Humanitarian Affairs of the United Nations Secretariat. The category "executive offices; economic, political and legal affairs" comprises the offices of

2.10

Where countries spent more for the military than for health and education combined in 1960 and 1986

1960	1986
Developed regions	
Greece	
United States	
France	
Yugoslavia	
Portugal	
USSR	USSR
Africa	
	Angola
	Burundi
	Chad
Egypt	Egypt
Ethiopia	Ethiopia
	Sudan
	Uganda
	Zaire
Latin America and Caribbean	
Bolivia	
Dominican Republic	
Ecuador	
	El Salvador
Nicaragua	Nicaragua
	Peru
Asia and Pacific	
	Brunei Darussalam
Cambodia	
China	China
Indonesia	
Iran (Islamic Rep. of)	Iran (Islamic Rep. of)
Iraq	Iraq
	Israel
Jordan	Jordan
Korea, Republic of	Korea, Republic of
Myanmar	Myanmar
	Oman
Pakistan	Pakistan
Saudi Arabia	Saudi Arabia
	Sri Lanka
Syrian Arab Republic	Syrian Arab Republic
Turkey	Turkey
	United Arab Emirates
	Yemen

Source: Compiled by the Statistical Office of the United Nations Secretariat from R. L. Sivard, *World Military and Social Expenditures 1989,* 13th edition (Washington,D.C., 1989).

the president or prime minister, and ministries such as finance, trade, industry and agriculture (economic); foreign affairs, interior and defence (political); and law and justice (legal). The category "social affairs" comprises ministries such as health, education, housing and welfare. The indicator on women criminal justice prosecutors has been compiled by the Crime Prevention and Criminal Justice Branch, Centre for Social Development and Humanitarian Affairs of the United Nations Secretariat, from national responses to questionnaires in the Second United Nations Surveys of Crime Trends, Operations of Criminal Justice Systems and Crime Prevention Strategies. [20] The term "prosecutor" refers to a government official whose duty is to initiate and maintain criminal proceedings on behalf of the State against persons accused of committing a criminal offence.

Women peace prize recipients

Nobel Peace Prize Laureates, 1901–1987
Bertha von Suttner, 1905
Jane Addams, 1931
Emily Greene Balch, 1946
Mairead Corrigan, 1976
Betty Williams, 1976
Mother Teresa, 1979
Alva Reimer Myrdal, 1982

87 prizes given, with 8 per cent to women

Laureates of the UNESCO Prize for Peace Education, 1981–1989
Helena Kekkonen, Finland, World Organization of the Scout Movement, 1981
Laurence Deonna, Switzerland, Servicio Páz y Justicia en América Latina, 1987
Elise Boulding, USA, International Peace Research Association, 1989

9 prizes given, with 33 per cent to women

Peace Messenger Awards, 1987–1989
All Pakistan Women's Association
Finnish Women for Peace
Greek Women's Anti-Nuclear Movement
International Alliance of Women—Equal Rights, Equal Responsibilities
International Council of Jewish Women
International Council of Women
International Federation of Business and Professional Women
International Federation of University Women
Lesotho Alliance of Women
National Association of Negro Business and Professional Women's Clubs, USA
National Council for Women's Rights, Mexico
Pakistan Federation of Business and Professional Women
Romanian National Women's Council

Soroptimist International
Soviet Women's Committee
Union of Women, Central African Republic
Women for Peace, Switzerland
Women's Christian Association
Women's International Democratic Federation
Women's International League for Peace and Freedom
Women's International League for Peace and Freedom, Australia
World Association of Girl Guides and Girl Scouts
World Union of Catholic Women's Organizations
World Women's Organization against Nuclear, Chemical, and Bacterial Weapons
World Young Women's Christian Association
Young Women's Christian Association, Jamaica

375 prizes given, with 7 per cent to women's organizations

Notes

1   *The Situation of Women in the Political Process in
     Europe,* Part II: *Women in the Political World in
     Europe,* vol. II (Strasbourg, Council of Europe,
     1984). See also *Participation of Women in Deci-
     sion-making for Peace: Case Study on Sweden*
     (United Nations publication, Sales No. E.89.IV.7).

2   "Full participation of women in the construction of
     their countries and in the creation of just social and
     political systems", report of the Secretary-General
     to the Commission on the Status of Women at its
     thirty-third session (E/CN.6/1989/7).

3   Anil Agarwal and Sunita Narain, "Strategies for
     the involvement of the landless and women in affor-
     estation: five case studies from India" (Geneva,
     International Labour Office, World Employment
     Programme, forthcoming), cited in *Linking Energy
     with Survival—A Guide to Energy, Environment
     and Rural Women's Work* (Geneva, International
     Labour Office, Rural Employment Policies Branch,
     1987).

4   *Everyone's Backyard* (Falls Church, Virginia,
     Citizens' Clearinghouse for Hazardous Waste),
     Summer 1983.

5   Unpublished studies of the International Center for
     Public Enterprises in Developing Countries
     (Ljubljana, Yugoslavia).

6   "Chief Executives of the *Business Week* 1000: A
     Directory", *Business Week,* 19 October 1989.

Table 3
Indicators on women in public life

	Political participation			Women decision-makers in government, 1987											
	Parliamentary seats occupied by women (%)		Year of women's right	Executive offices; economic, political and legal affairs		Social affairs		All ministries		Ministerial level		Criminal justice prosecutors, 1980	
Country or area	1975	1987	to vote	no.	%	no.	%	no.	%	no.	%	no.	%
Developed regions													
Albania	33.2	28.8	1945	1	5.0	0	0.0	1	4.5	1	5.6	..	..
Australia	0.0	6.1	1901[a]	1	1.0	1	4.2	2	1.7	1	3.3	..	..
Austria	7.7	11.5	1918	3	5.5	2	6.9	5	5.4	2	11.8	..	..
Belgium	6.6	7.5	1948[b]	3	4.6	0	0.0	3	3.6	0	0.0	..	..
Bulgaria	18.8	21.0	1944	3	2.8	1	3.0	4	2.8	1	5.3	..	..
Canada	3.4	9.6	1918[c]	12	6.2	2	5.9	14	6.2	6	17.1	..	..
Czechoslovakia	26.0	29.5	1920	0	0.0	1	20.0	1	0.7	0	0.0	60	54.1
Denmark	15.6	29.1	1915	4	4.1	6	16.2	10	8.0	3	13.6	..	..
Finland	23.0	31.5	1906	3	11.1	4	44.4	7	19.4	4	23.5	15	4.1
France	1.6	6.4	1944	1	3.4	3	25.0	4	9.8	0	0.0	..	..
Germany[d]													
Federal Rep. of Germany	5.8	15.4	1919	3	4.9	3	30.0	6	8.3	2	11.8	432	10.0
former German Dem. Rep.	31.8	32.2	1919	8	4.1	1	5.0	4	1.6	4	10.3	..	..
Greece	2.0	4.3	1952[e]	0	0.0	6	33.3	7	9.9	1	4.2	2	0.6
Hungary	28.7	21.0[f]	1945	2	3.3	0	0.0	2	3.0	1	4.0	..	..
Iceland	5.0	20.6	1915	2	4.9	1	8.3	3	5.7	2	33.3	..	..
Ireland	2.8	8.4	1918	1	3.7	1	7.1	2	4.9	1	5.6	..	..
Italy	3.8	12.9	1945	0	0.0	1	16.7	1	3.3	1	4.5	6	8.5
Japan	1.4	1.4	1945	0	0.0	0	0.0	0	0.0	0	0.0	30	1.5
Luxembourg	5.1	14.1	1919	0	0.0	0	0.0	0	0.0	0	0.0	..	..
Malta	3.6	2.9[g]	1947	0	0.0	0	0.0	0	0.0	0	0.0	..	..
Netherlands	9.3	20.0	1919	4	9.5	1	5.0	5	8.1	1	6.3	..	..
New Zealand	4.6	14.4	1893	0	0.0	4	20.0	5	5.3	3	9.4	4	4.4
Norway	15.5	34.4	1913	10	18.5	3	25.0	13	20.3	6	33.3	..	..
Poland	15.9	20.2	1918	0	0.0	1	14.3	1	2.6	1	3.4	..	..
Portugal	8.0	7.6	1931[h]	2	5.0	3	37.5	5	10.4	1	7.1	..	..
Romania	15.2	34.4	1946[i]	17	12.5	5	22.7	22	13.9	5	11.6	..	..
Spain	..	6.4	1931	0	0.0	0	0.0	0	0.0	0	0.0	5	1.7
Sweden	21.4	28.5	1921[j]	3	8.8	1	8.3	4	8.7	4	18.2	89	14.6
Switzerland	7.5	14.0	1971	1	2.9	..	..	1	2.9	1	12.5	..	..
USSR	32.1	34.5	1917	2	0.3	6	6.6	8	1.0	0	0.0	..	..
United Kingdom	4.3	6.3	1918[k]	3	4.1	3	21.4	7	7.9	2	8.0	..	..
United States	3.7	5.3	1920	21	11.5	4	11.8	27	11.7	1	5.6	..	..
Yugoslavia	15.0	18.8[g]	1946	5	3.4	0	0.0	5	3.2	0	0.0	..	..
Africa													
Algeria	..	2.4	1962	0	0.0	1	6.7	1	1.3	1	3.3	..	..
Angola	..	14.5[l]	1975	1	5.6	0	0.0	1	4.8	1	4.8	..	..
Benin	..	4.1	1956	0	0.0	0	0.0	0	0.0	0	0.0	..	..
Botswana	0.0	5.1	1965	2	3.8	1	11.1	3	4.9	0	0.0	..	..
Burkina Faso	..	..	..	6	4.8	19	27.5	25	13.0	3	11.5	..	..
Burundi	..	9.2[g]	1961	0	0.0	2	33.3	2	9.1	2	10.0	..	..
Cameroon	5.8	14.2	1946	1	3.1	4	30.8	5	11.1	2	6.5	..	..
Cape Verde	1.8	14.5[l]	1975	0	0.0	0	0.0	0	0.0	0	0.0	..	..
Central African Rep.	..	..	..	0	0.0	0	0.0	0	0.0	0	0.0	..	..
Chad	..	..	..	0	0.0	1	14.3	1	2.7	1	4.2	..	..
Comoros	..	0.0	1956	0	0.0	0	0.0	0	0.0	0	0.0	..	..
Congo	..	9.8	1963	0	0.0	0	0.0	0	0.0	0	0.0	..	..
Côte d'Ivoire	9.2	5.7	1956	2	3.1	3	16.7	5	6.0	4	9.5	..	..
Djibouti	..	0.0	1946	0	0.0	0	0.0	0	0.0	0	0.0	..	..
Egypt	1.9	3.9[g]	1956	0	0.0	0	0.0	0	0.0	0	0.0	..	..
Equatorial Guinea	5.7	3.3	1963	0	0.0	1	20.0	1	5.0	0	0.0	..	..
Ethiopia	..	..	..	0	0.0	0	0.0	0	0.0	0	0.0	..	..

Table 3. Indicators on women in public life [*cont.*]

	Political participation			Women decision-makers in government, 1987										
	Parliamentary seats occupied by women (%)		Year of women's right to vote	Executive offices; economic, political and legal affairs		Social affairs		All ministries		Ministerial level		Criminal justice prosecutors, 1980	
Country or area	1975	1987		no.	%	no.	%	no.	%	no.	%	no.	%
Gabon	4.3	13.4[f]	1960	2	4.0	2	12.5	4	6.1	1	2.0	..	..
Gambia	0.0	..	..	2	3.9	2	25.0	4	6.8	1	5.9	..	..
Ghana	..	..	..	2	5.7	3	23.1	5	10.4	0	0.0	..	..
Guinea	..	..	..	0	0.0	0	0.0	0	0.0	0	0.0	..	..
Guinea-Bissau	..	14.7	1977	0	0.0	1	16.7	1	2.9	1	4.5	..	..
Kenya	3.5[g]	1.7[g]	1963[m]	0	0.0	0	0.0	0	0.0	0	0.0	..	..
Lesotho	..	..	..	1	1.8	0	0.0	2	2.7	1	3.2	..	..
Liberia	..	6.3	1946	1	5.6	1	25.0	2	9.1	2	10.5	..	..
Libyan Arab Jamahiriya	..	..	..	0	0.0	0	0.0	0	0.0	0	0.0	..	..
Madagascar	..	1.5	1959	1	1.0	4	9.8	6	4.1	1	4.5	26	28.9
Malawi	6.7	..	..	0	0.0	0	0.0	0	0.0	0	0.0	..	..
Mali	..	3.7	1956	0	0.0	1	16.7	1	5.6	1	6.3	..	..
Mauritania	..	..	..	0	0.0	0	0.0	0	0.0	0	0.0	..	..
Mauritius	..	5.7	1956	0	0.0	1	5.0	1	2.0	1	4.2	..	..
Morocco	0.0	0.0	1963	0	0.0	0	0.0	0	0.0	0	0.0	15	32.6
Mozambique	..	16.0	..	0	0.0	0	0.0	0	0.0	0	0.0	..	..
Namibia	..	..	..	..	..	..	..	..	..	..	..	..	..
Niger	..	..	..	0	0.0	2	6.1	2	1.8	0	0.0	..	..
Nigeria	..	..	..	3	5.9	1	7.1	4	4.3	0	0.0	..	..
Reunion	..	..	..	..	..	..	..	..	..	..	..	..	..
Rwanda	..	12.9	1961	0	0.0	0	0.0	0	0.0	0	0.0	..	..
Sao Tome and Principe	..	11.8	..	0	0.0	0	0.0	0	0.0	0	0.0	..	..
Senegal	4.0	11.7	1945	1	6.7	2	22.2	3	12.0	3	12.0	3	23.1
Seychelles	..	24.0[g]	..	5	16.1	1	10.0	6	14.6	1	9.1	..	..
Sierra Leone	1.0	..	..	2	3.2	1	5.3	3	3.7	0	0.0	..	..
Somalia	0.0	4.0[g]	1956	0	0.0	2	15.4	2	3.3	0	0.0	..	..
South Africa	..	3.5[n]	1979[o]	0	0.0	0	0.0	0	0.0	0	0.0	..	..
Sudan	..	0.7	1953	0	0.0	0	0.0	0	0.0	0	0.0	..	..
Swaziland	..	2.0[g]	..	0	0.0	1	12.5	0	0.0	0	0.0	..	..
Togo	..	5.2	1956	0	0.0	1	20.0	1	4.3	0	0.0	..	..
Tunisia	2.7	5.6	1956	1	2.3	2	20.0	3	5.4	1	4.2	..	..
Uganda	..	..	..	1	2.7	1	7.1	2	3.9	0	0.0	..	..
United Rep. Tanzania	8.3	..	1959	5	10.0	3	33.3	8	13.6	4	16.0	..	..
Western Sahara	..	..	..	..	..	..	..	..	..	..	..	..	..
Zaire	11.1	3.5	1960	0	0.0	0	0.0	0	0.0	0	0.0	..	..
Zambia	5.1	2.9	..	2	3.2	0	0.0	2	2.4	0	0.0	1	1.0
Zimbabwe	..	9.0	1957[p]	4	7.0	0	0.0	4	5.9	1	4.0	..	..

Latin America and Caribbean

	1975	1987		no.	%	no.	%	no.	%	no.	%	no.	%
Antigua and Barbuda	..	0.0	..	0	0.0	0	0.0	0	0.0	0	0.0	..	..
Argentina	8.6	4.7	1952	2	2.1	1	5.0	3	2.6	0	0.0	3	13.0
Bahamas	..	..	..	8	25.0	4	22.2	12	24.0	0	0.0	..	..
Barbados	8.3	3.7	..	8	16.3	2	28.6	10	17.9	0	0.0	..	..
Belize	..	3.6	..	2	6.9	0	0.0	2	5.0	0	0.0	..	..
Bolivia	..	3.8	1952[q]	0	0.0	2	16.7	2	3.3	0	0.0	..	..
Brazil	0.3	5.3	1934	3	5.0	0	0.0	3	3.8	1	3.4	..	..
Chile	..	..	..	0	0.0	1	14.3	1	2.1	0	0.0	..	..
Colombia	..	..	1957	0	0.0	1	16.7	1	3.2	1	6.7	..	..
Costa Rica	5.3	10.5	1949	2	7.1	1	7.7	3	7.3	0	0.0	..	..
Cuba	..	33.9	1934	1	2.8	0	0.0	1	2.4	1	2.9	..	..
Dominica	..	12.9[g]	1951	6	18.8	5	45.5	11	25.6	2	22.2	..	..
Dominican Republic	..	5.0	..	0	0.0	0	0.0	0	0.0	0	0.0	..	..
Ecuador	..	1.4	1928	0	0.0	0	0.0	0	0.0	0	0.0	..	..
El Salvador	..	3.3	..	0	0.0	0	0.0	0	0.0	0	0.0	..	..

Table 3. Indicators on women in public life [*cont.*]

| | Political participation | | | Women decision-makers in government, 1987 | | | | | | | | | |
| | Parliamentary seats occupied by women (%) | | Year of women's right to vote | Executive offices; economic, political and legal affairs | | Social affairs | | All ministries | | Ministerial level | | Criminal justice prosecutors, 1980 | |
Country or area	1975	1987		no.	%	no.	%	no.	%	no.	%	no.	%
French Guiana	..	..	..	..	..	..	..	..	..	..	..	..	..
Grenada	..	12.5	..	2	8.0	3	33.3	5	14.7	0	0.0	..	..
Guadeloupe	..	..	..	..	..	..	..	..	..	..	..	..	..
Guatemala	..	7.0	1945	0	0.0	2	22.2	3	10.0	2	14.3	..	..
Guyana	11.9	..	..	1	3.1	3	50.0	4	10.3	1	7.1	..	..
Haiti	..	..	..	1	4.2	0	0.0	1	3.4	0	0.0	..	..
Honduras	..	5.2	1957	0	0.0	2	20.0	2	5.0	0	0.0	1	2.6
Jamaica	3.8	11.7	..	4	8.9	2	12.5	5	8.1	0	0.0	..	..
Martinique	..	..	..	..	..	..	..	..	..	..	..	..	..
Mexico	5.0	10.8	1953	0	0.0	1	7.1	1	1.4	0	0.0	..	..
Netherlands Antilles	..	..	..	..	..	..	..	..	..	..	..	..	..
Nicaragua	..	13.5	1955 [r]	1	1.5	2	14.3	3	3.8	1	5.0	..	..
Panama	..	6.0	1941	1	5.3	0	0.0	1	3.7	0	0.0	..	..
Paraguay	..	1.7	1962	0	0.0	0	0.0	0	0.0	0	0.0	..	..
Peru	..	5.6	..	1	1.8	0	0.0	1	1.7	0	0.0	..	..
Puerto Rico	..	..	..	..	..	..	..	..	..	..	..	..	..
St. Kitts and Nevis	..	6.7 [q]	..	0	0.0	1	50.0	0	0.0	0	0.0	..	..
St. Lucia	..	..	..	1	4.8	1	14.3	2	7.1	0	0.0	..	..
St. Vincent/Grenadines	..	5.3 [q]	..	0	0.0	0	0.0	0	0.0	0	0.0	..	..
Suriname	5.1	12.9 [s]	1948	0	0.0	0	0.0	0	0.0	0	0.0	..	..
Trinidad and Tobago	2.8	16.7	..	5	13.2	2	22.2	7	14.9	2	9.5	..	..
Uruguay	0.0 [l]	0.0 [l]	1932	1	4.5	0	0.0	2	7.1	2	13.3	14	50.0
US Virgin Islands	..	..	..	..	..	..	..	..	..	..	..	..	..
Venezuela	2.7	3.9	1947	1	4.5	0	0.0	1	3.7	0	0.0	..	..

Asia and Pacific

Afghanistan	..	..	..	0	0.0	0	0.0	0	0.0	0	0.0	..	..
Bahrain	..	..	..	3	3.9	1	2.2	4	3.3	0	0.0	0	0.0
Bangladesh	4.8 [t]	9.1 [u]	1947	0	0.0	1	7.1	1	1.4	1	2.8	0	0.0
Bhutan	..	1.3	1953	2	7.4	..	..	2	7.4	2	28.6	..	..
Brunei Darussalam	..	..	..	0	0.0	0	0.0	0	0.0	0	0.0	..	..
Cambodia	..	..	..	..	..	..	..	..	..	..	..	..	..
China	22.6	21.2	1949	3	1.4	4	6.1	7	2.5	0	0.0	..	..
Cyprus	0.0 [f]	1.8 [f]	1960	1	3.3	0	0.0	1	2.8	1	6.7	1	3.7
East Timor	..	..	..	..	..	..	..	..	..	..	..	..	..
Fiji	..	..	..	5	7.5	0	0.0	5	6.8	0	0.0	..	..
French Polynesia	..	..	..	..	..	..	..	..	..	..	..	..	..
Guam	..	..	..	..	..	..	..	..	..	..	..	..	..
Hong Kong	..	..	..	..	..	..	..	..	..	..	..	..	..
India	4.3	8.3 [f]	1950	3	3.7	1	5.9	4	4.0	0	0.0	1	1.8
Indonesia	7.2	..	1945 [v]	0	0.0	2	3.6	2	1.3	2	4.9	497	10.7
Iran (Islamic Rep. of)	..	1.5	1963	0	0.0	0	0.0	0	0.0	0	0.0	..	..
Iraq	..	13.2	1980	0	0.0	0	0.0	0	0.0	0	0.0	..	..
Israel	6.7	8.3	1948	12	8.8	4	14.3	16	9.8	1	3.2	..	..
Jordan	0.0	0.0	1973	0	0.0	0	0.0	0	0.0	0	0.0	..	..
Kiribati	..	..	..	..	..	..	..	..	..	..	..	..	..
Korea, D. People's R.	20.9	21.1	1946									..	..
Korea, Republic of	5.5	2.5 [f]	1948									0	0.0
Kuwait	..	..	..	2	1.6	3	6.8	5	2.9	0	0.0	..	..
Lao People's Dem. Rep.	..	..	..	1	1.1	0	0.0	1	1.0	0	0.0	..	..
Lebanon	0.0	0.0	..	0	0.0	0	0.0	0	0.0	0	0.0	..	..
Macau	..	..	..	..	..	..	..	..	..	..	..	..	..
Malaysia	3.2	5.1	1957	0	0.0	1	5.3	1	1.5	0	0.0	..	..
Maldives	..	..	1932	9	9.5	4	12.1	13	10.1	0	0.0	..	..
Mongolia	22.9	24.9	1923	0	0.0	0	0.0	0	0.0	0	0.0	..	..

Table 3. Indicators on women in public life [cont.]

Country or area	Political participation			Women decision-makers in government, 1987										
	Parliamentary seats occupied by women (%)		Year of women's right to vote	Executive offices; economic, political and legal affairs		Social affairs		All ministries		Ministerial level		Criminal justice prosecutors, 1980	
	1975	1987		no.	%	no.	%	no.	%	no.	%	no.	%
Myanmar	2.0	..	..	0	0.0	0	0.0	0	0.0	0	0.0	..	..
Nepal	..	5.8[f]	1951	1	1.5	1	10.0	2	2.6	0	0.0	..	..
New Caledonia	..	..	..	..	..	..	..	..	..	..	..	..	..
Oman	..	..	..	0	0.0	1	2.5	1	0.8	0	0.0	..	..
Pacific Islands	..	..	..	..	..	..	..	..	..	..	..	..	..
Pakistan	4.1	8.9[w]	1947	2	2.2	1	7.1	3	2.9	0	0.0	..	..
Papua New Guinea	..	0.0	..	3	4.3	1	9.1	4	4.9	1	2.9	..	..
Philippines	..	..	1939	4	7.5	4	30.8	8	11.1	2	10.0	106	9.5
Qatar	..	..	..	0	0.0	0	0.0	0	0.0	0	0.0	0	0.0
Samoa	..	4.3	..	..	..	..	..	..	..	..	..	..	..
Saudi Arabia	..	..	..	1	1.1	0	0.0	1	0.7	0	0.0	..	..
Singapore	0.0	3.8	1948	0	0.0	0	0.0	0	0.0	0	0.0	0	0.0
Solomon Islands	..	0.0	1945	0	0.0	0	0.0	0	0.0	0	0.0	..	..
Sri Lanka	..	4.8	1931	1	1.1	2	7.4	3	2.5	2	5.1	..	..
Syrian Arab Republic	2.7	9.2	1949	0	0.0	0	0.0	0	0.0	0	0.0	..	..
Thailand	1.1	3.5	1932	2	3.8	0	0.0	2	3.3	0	0.0	26	2.6
Tonga	..	0.0	..	..	..	..	..	..	..	..	..	0	0.0
Turkey	..	3.0	1934	0	0.0	0	0.0	0	0.0	0	0.0	..	..
United Arab Emirates	..	0.0[x]	..[y]	0	0.0	0	0.0	0	0.0	0	0.0	0	0.0
Vanuatu	..	0.0	1980	..	..	..	..	..	..	..	..	..	..
Viet Nam	..	17.7	1946	0	0.0	0	0.0	0	0.0	0	0.0	..	..
Yemen	..	0.0[z]	1970[aa]	0	0.0	0	0.0	0	0.0	0	0.0	..	..

Sources:
Inter-Parliamentary Union, "Distribution of seats between men and women in national assemblies", Reports and Documents No. 14 (Geneva, 1987); Second United Nations Survey of Crime Trends, Operations of Criminal Justice Systems and Crime Prevention Strategies, Crime Prevention and Criminal Justice Branch, Centre for Social Development and Humanitarian Affairs of the United Nations Secretariat, unpublished data; and National Standards Association, *World-wide Government Directory of 1987–1988* (Bethesda, Maryland, 1987).

a The Constitution of 1901 contained certain provisions which disallowed all "aboriginal natives" from voting (men and women). These provisions were altered by referendum in 1967. Since that time, subject to certain qualifications, principally age, all men and women in Australia have had an equal right under the law to vote and to stand for election.
b The Law of 9 May 1919 gave the right to vote in national elections to the widows or mothers of servicemen killed during the war and of citizens shot or killed by the enemy and to women political prisoners. In 1921, women were given the right to stand for election at the level of the commune and of the province and in Parliament. The Law of 27 March 1948 then gave all women the right to vote.
c In 1917, women who were serving in the military or who had a close male relative serving in the military (i.e. father, husband or son) were granted the right to vote at the federal level. Women were given the right to stand for election at the federal level in 1920.
d Through the accession of the German Democratic Republic to the Federal Republic of Germany with effect from 3 October 1990, the two German States have united to form one sovereign State. As from the date of unification, the Federal Republic of Germany acts in the United Nations under the designation "Germany". All data shown for Germany pertain to end-June 1990 or earlier and are indicated separately for the Federal Republic of Germany and the former German Democratic Republic.
e The Constitution of 1927 provides that all Greek citizens are equal in law and that "political rights can be conferred to women by law". On 2 January 1930, the Council of State expressed the view that women could have the right to vote in municipal and communal elections. In April 1949, Law

No. 959 gave women the right to vote and to stand for office in municipal and communal elections. The Constitution of 1 January 1952 then established the right to vote and to stand for election at the national level.
f As a percentage of total occupied seats, thus excluding vacancies.
g Includes both elected and appointed members.
h Decree No. 19694 of 5 May 1931 formally gave women the right to vote and to stand for election, albeit with some restrictions: it was necessary for women to have completed secondary or higher studies, while men only had to know how to read and write. In 1968, Law No 2137 established equal political rights for men and women but maintained some restrictions on elections to certain local administrative bodies (which were already in the preceding Law). Total equality was only achieved in the Constitution of 1976.
i Women had restricted electoral rights as from 1929. They were given full electoral rights, under the same conditions as men, in July 1946.
j Between 1918 and 1921 women were given the right to vote for various representative bodies but not for Parliament.
k 1918 for women over 30 years of age; 1928 for full voting equality with men (over 21—now 18 for both sexes).
l Not including substitute members.
m The rights to vote and to stand for election were given to European women in 1919; in 1956 they were given to African men and women under certain conditions, educational level or property; in 1963, all Kenyans were given the rights to vote and to stand for election.
n Refers to elections to the House of Representatives of the Tricameral Parliament.
o In 1930, whites only; in 1979, Coloured and Indians.
p Up to 1957, only men and British women could vote. In 1957, the right to vote was extended to black married women. A wife was deemed to have the same means of qualifications as her husband but, in the case of a polygamous marriage, this privilege only applied to the first wife. Wives were required to be literate in English and to have educational qualifications in their own right. In order to be registered as a general voter, a person had to have one of four alternative qualifications: (i) income of 720 pounds per annum or ownership of immovable property valued at 1,500

pounds; (ii) income of 3,480 pounds per annum or ownership of immovable property valued at l,000 pounds plus the completion of a primary course of education of prescribed standard; (iii) being a minister of religion, who had undergone certain stipulated training and periods of service in the ministry and who followed no other profession, trade or gainful occupation; (iv) being a chief as defined in the Act.

q   Literate women were given the right to vote in 1938; this right was given to all women in 1952.

r   The Constitutions of 1939, 1948 and 1950 indicated that a law would determine when women would be given the right to vote. That right was established by the Electoral Law of 1950 and enshrined in the Constitution of 1955.

s   All appointed.

t   Fifteen seats reserved for women elected by the Parliament itself.

u   Thirty seats reserved for women.

v   The right to vote was given earlier under certain conditions. Details not provided.

w   Twenty seats reserved for women.

x   Data refer to nominations.

y   According to Article 69 of the Constitution (1971), "each Emirate shall be left to determine the method of selection of the citizens who shall represent it on the Federal National Council".

z   Data refer to the former Yemen Arab Republic. For the former Democratic Yemen, the corresponding figure is 9.9 per cent.

aa   Data refer to the former Yemen Arab Republic. For the former Democratic Yemen, the corresponding year is 1967.

3
Education and training

In much of the world, women have progressed towards equal educational enrolment rates with men at all levels of schooling, but huge gaps persist between men's and women's educational achievement. Many girls and women still do not receive equal access to educational and training resources and this has critical consequences for women in both their productive and reproductive roles.

Despite broad progress towards literacy, a huge historical deficit of literacy remains among today's adult women, especially rural women. In 1985 there were 597 million illiterate women and 352 million illiterate men. This deficit will persist well into the next century in all the developing regions.

Girls are achieving universal primary education—accepted as a fundamental goal by all countries—in most countries of Asia and Latin America and the Caribbean, but not in southern Asia and sub-Saharan Africa.

For mass secondary education, there has been substantial progress for both boys and girls in Latin America and the Caribbean, little for girls in sub-Saharan Africa and southern Asia, and only moderate progress in the other regions.

In advanced training, there has been good progress in many fields traditionally dominated by men in developed regions, Latin America and the Caribbean and some of Asia—while progress has been much more limited in northern and sub-Saharan Africa and southern Asia.

Advancing literacy for women

The extensive primary education of the past few decades has boosted literacy rates—particularly among young people. But there still are more illiterate women than men in every region of the world. Moreover, illiteracy rates have fallen faster for men, so the literacy gap between men and women is still growing (chart 3.2).

In most countries in the developed regions and in some countries in developing regions, decades of universal primary education have led to near-universal literacy for young people, and large-scale censuses and surveys no longer measure it. But in most of the developing world, generations of educational neglect have left very high illiteracy rates among older women. In sub-Saharan Africa, southern Asia and western Asia illiteracy rates are highest—more than 70 per cent of women aged 25 and over are illiterate (chart 3.1). In eastern and south-eastern Asia more than 40 per cent of women aged 25 and over are still illiterate and in Latin America and the Caribbean over 20 per cent. [29]

Growing populations in some developing regions are outpacing educational efforts, so that while illiteracy rates have dropped, the actual number of illiterate girls and women has increased. According to United Nations estimates, the number of illiterate women was 597 million in 1985, up from 543 million in 1970. The number of illiterate men increased much less—to 352 million from 348 million—showing that women are still disproportionately disadvantaged.[1]

Contributing to national illiteracy rates is the continuing high illiteracy in rural areas. The urban-rural contrast is sharpest in Latin America—where the rural illiteracy rate among women aged 15–24 is 25 per cent, compared with 5 per cent in urban areas. In Asia and the Pacific, rural rates are double urban rates (43 per cent compared with 22 per cent), and in Africa three-quarters of rural women aged 15–24 are illiterate, compared with less than half in urban areas (chart 3.3). [21]

Illiteracy

An illiterate person cannot, with understanding, both read and write a short, simple statement on their everyday life. A person who can only write figures, his or her name or a memorized ritual phrase is not considered literate.

Literacy (or illiteracy) is a good measure of educational achievement in developing regions. For young people, literacy is a better measure of education than enrolment since it usually reflects a minimal level of successfully completed schooling.

For many countries or areas, estimates of illiteracy are not available from UNESCO for one or more of the following reasons: (a) illiteracy has been reduced to minimal levels through several decades of universal primary education, (b) it has not been possible to establish revised estimates following recent mass literacy campaigns, (c) not even a minimal database is available for making rough estimates, or (d) countries have preferred that no estimate be published.

3.1

Three-quarters of women aged 25 and over in much of Africa and Asia are still illiterate

Illiterate women 25 and over, 1990 (%)

Latin America and Caribbean

Northern Africa and western Asia[a]

Sub-Saharan Africa[b]

Eastern and south-eastern Asia

Southern Asia

Note: Based on total population of women aged 25 years and over in each region.

Source: Prepared by the Statistical Office of the United Nations Secretariat from UNESCO and Statistical Office databases.

a   Includes Somalia and Mauritania; excludes Cyprus, Israel and Turkey.
b   Includes Sudan; excludes South Africa.

Primary and secondary school enrolments

It will take several generations to reach parity in male and female literacy rates, due to the historical deficit in women's education. But it will take far less time to achieve equality in school enrolments among young children where educational resources keep pace with the population of children.

Girls' enrolments have caught up with boys' in most countries in the developed regions and in Latin America and the Caribbean. But they still lag far behind in sub-Saharan Africa and in southern Asia, where they have been increasing faster than boys' but from a lower base (chart 3.4). [30,31] One reason for this is early child-bearing, clearly incompatible with schooling.

University and college enrolments [31]

Women increasingly are enrolling in colleges and universities, but enormous disparities remain among countries. In the developed regions, western Asia, some countries of southern Africa, and Latin America and the Caribbean, the numbers of women and men in higher education have become nearly equal due to rapid increases in female enrolment. In 33 countries women actually outnumber men in higher education (list 3.5).

By contrast, the sub-Saharan African and southern Asian countries enrol fewer than 30 women per 100 men in higher education. In northern Africa the ratio of women to men rose substantially from 1970 to 1990. But the region's average

3.2

Illiteracy rates are falling for young women but are still much higher for young women than men

Over 40 per cent of young women are still illiterate in Africa and southern and western Asia

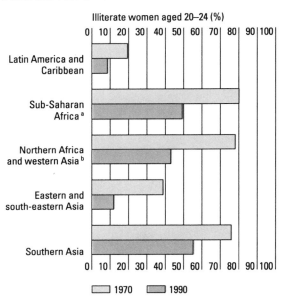

The widest gaps between women and men are in Africa and southern and western Asia

Women   Men

A   Latin America and Caribbean
B   Sub-Saharan Africa[a]
C   Northern Africa and western Asia[b]
D   Eastern and south-eastern Asia
E   Southern Asia

Note: Based on total population of women and men aged 20-24 years in each region.

Source: United Nations Educational, Scientific and Cultural Organization, *Compendium of Statistics on Illiteracy–1990 edition*, No. 31 (Paris, 1990).

a   Includes Sudan; excludes South Africa.
b   Includes Somalia and Mauritania; excludes Cyprus, Israel and Turkey.

3.3
Illiteracy rates among young women are much higher in rural areas of developing regions

Illiterate women aged 15–24, 1980 (%)

☐ Urban   ▨ Rural

A   Africa
B   Latin America and Caribbean
C   Asia and Pacific

Note: Averages based on a limited number of countries in each region for census years around 1980.

Sources: Prepared by the Statistical Office of the United Nations Secretariat from UNESCO and Statistical Office databases.

is still only 51 women per 100 men. The ratio is much higher in eastern and south-eastern Asia, averaging 73 women per 100 men. But some of the largest countries in the Asia and Pacific region still average fewer than 50 women per 100 men in higher education—with 42 per 100 in China and 48 per 100 in Indonesia.

Fields of advanced study and training [2]

As more women enrolled in college programmes in the 1970s and 1980s, more enrolled in fields once dominated by men. In Latin America and the Caribbean and in the developed regions, more women entered male-dominated fields of study between 1970 and 1985. But in Africa, there are fewer women than men in all fields, including those where women's enrolments surpassed men's in the other regions (liberal arts, social sciences and education).

Women can make a substantial contribution to economic development if they are trained in agriculture, forestry and fishing, particularly in developing countries, where such activities predominate. But they are still denied access to this training, and men continue to dominate the field. In 1970 the average ratio of women to men in advanced studies in these fields was 1 to 10 in all developing regions. Women's representation improved significantly by 1984 in developed regions and in Latin America and the Caribbean, reaching about 1 to 2, but it lagged far behind in Africa and in Asia and the Pacific, where the ratio was still about 1 to 5 in 1984.

Women everywhere (except Africa) made rapid gains relative to men in advanced training for law and business. They have nearly caught up with men in the developed regions and in Latin America and the Caribbean. Women represent on average 26 per cent of those enrolled in advanced training for law and business in Africa, and 38 per cent in Asia and the Pacific. Although women are far from

3.4
Girls' secondary enrolment still lags behind boys' in much of Africa and Asia

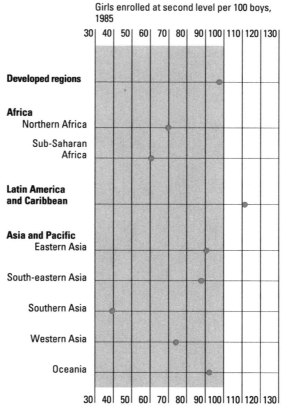

Girls enrolled at second level per 100 boys, 1985

Source: Prepared by the Statistical Office of the United Nations Secretariat from UNESCO, *Statistical Yearbook* (Paris, various years).

Educational enrolments

Enrolment data are provided by schools or other educational authorities to national educational ministries. They offer an easy way of comparing numbers of boys and girls registered in schools each year but do not reflect differences between boys and girls in rates of absenteeism, repetition and dropping out.

UNESCO defines education at the primary level as usually beginning between the ages of 5 and 7 and lasting for about five years. Education at the second level is defined as beginning at about age 10–12 and lasting for about three years at the first stage and as beginning at about age 13–15 and lasting for about four years at the second stage. Education at the third level, including universities and colleges, is defined as beginning at about age 17–19 and lasting for at least three or four years.

3.5
In higher education more women are enrolled than men in many countries and areas
Women per 100 men

Developed regions
Bulgaria (124)
Canada (113)
Germany:
former German Dem. Rep. (114)
Hungary (115)
Iceland (113)
Norway (113)
Poland (127)
Portugal (113)
United States (110)

Africa
Lesotho (172)

**Latin America
and Caribbean**
Argentina (113)
Cuba (123)
Dominica (200)
Grenada (123)
Jamaica (132)
Nicaragua (122)
Panama (136)
Puerto Rico (153)
St. Vincent/Grenadines (224)
St. Kitts and Nevis (101)
Suriname (116)
Trinidad and Tobago (101)
Uruguay (130)
US Virgin Islands (259)

Asia and Pacific
Bahrain (147)
Brunei Darussalam (101)
Kuwait (117)
Mongolia (149)
Oman (102)
Philippines (119)
Qatar (202)
Tonga (129)
United Arab Emirates (139)

Source: UNESCO.

reaching equality in these fields, the gains over the past 20 years have been substantial in many countries.

Advanced study in science and engineering prepares women to take an active role in technological development in their countries. Women made significant gains in these fields in all regions, increasing their representation by half. In all regions except Africa, women now represent at least 30 per cent of the people training in these fields.

Women in teaching

Teaching has always been one of the first professions open to women, making the number of women teachers a revealing indicator of employment opportunities. In addition, women teachers are important role models for young girls, particularly where their education is not encouraged or supported or in societies where male teaching of females is forbidden.

The proportion of women primary school teachers increased everywhere over the past two decades—but with continuing wide regional disparities (chart 3.6). Women have long been employed as primary school teachers in developed regions and in Latin America and the Caribbean, where they respectively constitute two thirds and three fourths of all primary school teachers. In Asia and the Pacific, nearly half the primary school teachers are now women, compared with 38 per cent 20 years ago. Although men still have a lock on educational and employment opportunities in Africa, the proportion of women teachers increased from 28 per cent in 1970 to 39 per cent in 1984.

The higher the level of education, the fewer the women teaching. Men outnumber women as secondary-school teachers in every region except Latin America and the Caribbean, where they are equal. In Africa there is only one woman teaching secondary school for every three men.

3.6
More women are becoming teachers but mainly at the lower levels

Half or more of first level teachers are now women except in Africa

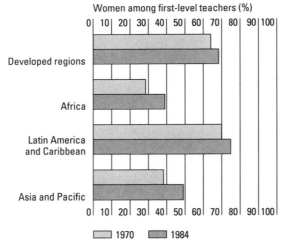

Women among first-level teachers (%)

Developed regions

Africa

Latin America and Caribbean

Asia and Pacific

☐ 1970   ☐ 1984

The percentage of teachers who are women is much lower at the second level

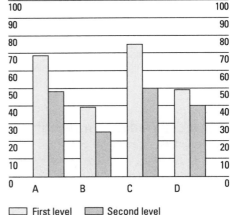

Teachers who are women, 1984 (%)

A   B   C   D

☐ First level   ☐ Second level

A   Developed regions
B   Africa
C   Latin America and Caribbean
D   Asia and Pacific

Source: Prepared by the Statistical Office of the United Nations Secretariat from UNESCO, *Statistical Yearbook 1984* and *1986* (Paris, 1984 and 1986).

Indicators

Indicators in table 4 measure illiteracy among women and men in the population 15–24 years of age and aged 25 years and over, and the ratio of females to males in enrolments at the first (primary), second (secondary) and third (post-secondary) levels of regular education.

The definitions recommended by the United Nations Educational, Scientific and Cultural Organization (UNESCO) for illiteracy and educational enrolment levels are described on pages 45 and 47. The UNESCO definition of illiteracy is widely used in national population censuses and surveys but its interpretation and application may vary to some extent among countries, depending on national, social and cultural circumstances. Furthermore, this concept of illiteracy does not include persons who, though familiar with the basics of reading and writing, might still be considered functionally illiterate. Thus, a measure of functional illiteracy would also be useful, but such statistics are collected in only a few countries at present.

These indicators on illiteracy have been compiled from statistics prepared by UNESCO and the Statistical Office of the United Nations Secretariat on the basis of data from national population censuses and surveys.

Indicators on enrolment have been compiled mainly from statistics published by UNESCO in its *Statistical Yearbook.* [31] UNESCO prepares enrolment statistics from data provided by Governments in response to UNESCO questionnaires.

Notes
1   Calculated by the Statistical Office of the United Nations Secretariat from [15] and [29].
2   Indicators in this section have been calculated by the Statistical Office of the United Nations Secretariat from [31].

Table 4
Indicators on education and training

Country or area	Illiterates (%)								Ratio of female to male enrolment (x100)				
	Age group 15-24 years				Age group 25 years and above				First level		Second level		Third level
	1970/74		Latest year		1970/74		Latest year		1970	1985/87	1970	1985/87	1985/87
	f	m	f	m	f	m	f	m					
Developed regions													
Albania	..	..	..	..	..	..	..	..	90	90	..	83	91[a]
Australia	..	..	..	..	..	..	..	..	94	95	..	99	91
Austria	..	..	..	..	..	..	..	..	95	94	98	98	80
Belgium	..	..	..	..	..	..	..	..	94	96	94	96	89
Bulgaria	..	..	..	..	..	..	..	..	94	94	..	96	124[a]
Canada	..	..	..	..	..	..	..	..	95	93	..	95	113
Czechoslovakia	..	..	..	..	..	..	..	..	96	97	154	170	73
Denmark	..	..	..	..	..	..	..	..	97	96	..	95	97
Finland	..	..	..	..	..	..	..	..	90	95	104	112	99
France	..	..	..	..	..	..	..	..	95	94	105	102	97[b]
Germany[c]													
Federal Rep. of Germany	..	..	..	..	..	..	..	..	96	96	94	100	72
former German Dem. Rep.	..	..	..	..	..	..	..	..	..	94	..	92	114[a]
Greece	2.2	1.7	1.1	0.9	28.5	8.0	17.6	4.7	92	94[b]	75	92[b]	94
Hungary	0.8	0.6	0.6	0.6	2.8	1.8	1.7	0.7	93	95	74	95	115[a]
Iceland	..	..	..	..	..	..	..	..	95	95	78	90	113
Ireland	..	..	..	..	..	..	..	..	95	95[b]	104	105[b]	76
Italy	1.0	1.2	0.4	0.3	8.8	5.6	5.5	3.4	94	95[b]	80	92[b]	88
Japan	..	..	..	..	..	..	..	..	97	95	98	97	56[d]
Luxembourg	..	..	..	..	..	..	..	..	97	94	90	94	52
Malta	..	..	..	..	..	..	..	..	93	90	..	92	53
Netherlands	..	..	..	..	..	..	..	..	96	97	81	93	70
New Zealand	..	..	..	..	..	..	..	..	94	95	..	98	89
Norway	..	..	..	..	..	..	..	..	105	96	94	100	113
Poland	0.1	0.2	0.2	0.2	4.3	1.8	2.2	0.9	93	95	104	103	127[a]
Portugal	3.7	3.3	1.8	2.3	43.1	28.1	31.7	19.1	95	91[b]	83	116[b]	113
Romania	..	..	..	..	..	..	..	..	97	95	72	86	81[a]
Spain	2.2	1.8	1.0	0.9	17.0	6.9	12.3	5.0	99	93	72	101	96
Sweden	..	..	..	..	..	..	..	..	96	97[b]	93	107[b]	89
Switzerland	..	..	..	..	..	..	..	..	98	97	91	104	47
USSR	..	..	..	..	..	..	..	..	..	..	..	..	..
United Kingdom	..	..	..	..	..	..	..	..	95	95	94	99	81
United States	..	..	0.6	0.7	..	..	3.1	3.4	..	94	..	97	110
Yugoslavia	7.0[e]	1.8[e]	2.0	0.8	36.7[f]	13.5[f]	19.8	5.6	91	93	82	90	88
Africa													
Algeria	69.7	35.4	40.5	15.5	95.9	70.8	85.7	61.3	60	79	39	71	46
Angola	..	..	..	..	..	..	..	..	55	..	72	..	..
Benin	..	..	81.7	54.3	..	..	94.3	82.8	45	50	42	41[b]	20[b]
Botswana	36.0	45.9	..	..	65.0	70.0	..	..	113	108	83	109	71[b]
Burkina Faso	..	..	93.2	77.5	..	..	98.2	89.0	57	59	39	51	29[b]
Burundi	..	..	..	..	..	..	..	..	49	75	25	56	32
Cameroon	..	..	40.9	20.4	..	..	84.2	56.5	74	84[b]	40	61[b]	..
Cape Verde	..	..	..	..	..	..	..	..	..	97	100	84	..
Central African Rep.	..	..	82.0[e]	46.0[e]	..	..	98.5[f]	87.5[f]	49	62	23	41	12
Chad	..	..	..	..	..	..	..	..	34	38	8	18[b]	9
Comoros	..	..	45.1	30.6	..	..	66.8	50.0	46	78	34	66	..
Congo	..	..	..	..	..	..	..	..	78	94	43	77	15[b]
Côte d'Ivoire	..	..	..	..	..	..	..	..	57	70[b]	27	43[b]	..
Djibouti	..	..	..	..	..	..	..	..	43	70	37	63	..
Egypt	..	..	61.9	37.0	..	..	84.7	51.0	61	76	47	65	50[g]
Equatorial Guinea	..	..	..	..	..	..	..	..	78	..	35	..	11[b]
Ethiopia	99.6	88.4	..	..	99.9	92.9	..	..	46	64	33	..	22

Table 4. Indicators on education and training [*cont.*]

Country or area	Illiterates (%)								Ratio of female to male enrolment (x100)				
	Age group 15-24 years				Age group 25 years and above				First level		Second level		Third level
	1970/74		Latest year		1970/74		Latest year		1970	1985/87	1970	1985/87	1985/87
	f	m	f	m	f	m	f	m					
Gabon	..	..	..	..	..	..	..	..	91	98 [b]	40	71 [b]	40
Gambia	..	..	..	..	..	..	..	..	44	63	32	44	..
Ghana	60.4	31.4	..	..	91.4	68.8	..	..	75	78 [b]	38	60 [b]	21 [b]
Guinea	..	..	..	..	..	..	..	..	46	44	26	34	16
Guinea-Bissau	..	..	82.2	40.3	..	..	95.7	77.8	43	52 [b]	57	27 [b]	..
Kenya	..	..	..	..	..	..	..	..	71	93	42	68 [b]	36
Lesotho	10.9 [h]	46.6 [h]	..	..	41.1 [h]	60.3 [h]	..	..	150	125	118	148 [b]	172
Liberia	80.6	48.3	..	..	94.4	80.5	..	..	49	61 [b]	30	39 [b]	38 [i]
Libyan Arab Jamahiriya	62.5	8.8	..	..	95.2	51.9	..	..	59	90 [b]	22	71 [b]	34 [b]
Madagascar	..	..	..	..	..	..	..	..	86	93 [b]	66	..	62
Malawi	75.3 [h]	49.0 [h]	..	..	93.4 [h]	74.2 [h]	..	..	59	77	37	46	40
Mali	..	..	86.5	73.3	..	..	97.9	92.4	55	59	28	40 [b]	15 [b]
Mauritania	..	..	..	..	..	..	..	..	39	63	..	40	..
Mauritius	..	..	..	..	..	..	..	..	94	98	..	90	50
Morocco	77.3	46.8	..	..	95.7	75.3	..	..	51	62	39	65	50
Mozambique	..	..	74.7	36.0	..	..	93.8	65.8	..	78	..	49	30
Namibia	..	..	..	..	..	..	..	..	..	..	..	..	..
Niger	..	..	..	..	..	..	..	..	53	56	37	..	23
Nigeria	..	..	..	..	..	..	..	..	59	79 [b]	47	..	..
Reunion	..	..	2.5	6.2	..	..	28.2	33.2	..	93	..	115	..
Rwanda	..	..	55.3	40.3	..	..	84.6	55.6	79	97	49	52	16
Sao Tome and Principe	..	..	25.9	9.2	..	..	74.4	36.9	79	..	71	..	..
Senegal	..	..	..	..	..	..	..	..	63	68	40	49	26
Seychelles	17.7	28.0	..	..	48.1	51.4	..	..	101	98	124	82	..
Sierra Leone	..	..	..	..	..	..	..	..	67	69 [b]	39	..	..
Somalia	..	..	..	..	..	..	..	..	33	52	26	53	25
South Africa	..	..	..	..	..	..	..	..	..	..	..	..	..
Sudan	92.4 [h]	69.6 [h]	..	..	98.2 [h]	77.3 [h]	..	..	61	68	39	73	68
Swaziland	..	..	25.0	23.9	..	..	58.6	52.2	94	98	77	97	62 [b]
Togo	83.1	51.5	64.1 [e]	26.8 [e]	96.4	81.4	90.4 [f]	67.9 [f]	45	62	29	31	18
Tunisia	..	..	36.8	9.7	..	..	84.5	54.9	64	80	38	70	58
Uganda	..	..	..	..	..	..	..	..	65	74 [b]	..	49 [b]	30
United Rep. Tanzania	..	..	45.9	19.3	..	..	80.0	46.2	65	100	40	62	16
Western Sahara	..	..	..	..	..	..	..	..	..	..	..	..	..
Zaire	..	..	..	..	..	..	..	..	58	75 [b]	27	40 [b]	..
Zambia	39.7	17.5	..	..	78.2	47.8	..	..	80	89	48	54 [b]	21
Zimbabwe	..	..	..	..	..	..	..	..	79	97	65	..	50

Latin America and Caribbean

Country or area	f	m	f	m	f	m	f	m	1970	1985/87	1970	1985/87	1985/87
Antigua and Barbuda	..	..	..	..	..	..	..	..	93	86 [b]	..	..	..
Argentina	3.9	4.4	2.7	3.6	9.6	7.3	7.5	6.4	98	97	110	112	113
Bahamas	..	..	..	..	..	..	..	..	..	97	..	..	..
Barbados	0.2	0.3	..	..	0.9	1.0	..	..	96	94 [b]	..	101 [b]	96
Belize	3.1	3.2	..	..	11.4	11.7	..	..	96	93	..	118	..
Bolivia	..	..	24.2	8.5	..	..	60.6	32.3	69	88	..	86	..
Brazil	25.1	25.7	14.8	17.5	43.1	33.1	33.6	26.9	98	95 [b]	102	..	100 [b]
Chile	4.5	4.6	2.8	3.8	15.0	12.7	12.1	10.9	98	95	113	106	75
Colombia	11.6 [e]	12.6 [e]	..	..	28.6 [f]	23.1 [f]	..	..	101	100	95	100	95
Costa Rica	4.6	5.2	2.4	3.3	16.1	15.0	10.1	9.6	96	94	104	104	..
Cuba	..	..	1.2	1.9	..	..	7.2 [j]	5.8 [j]	96	89	..	102	123
Dominica	0.8	0.9	..	..	8.0	8.8	..	..	91	94	144 [k]	116	200
Dominican Republic	20.8	22.2	..	..	43.2	36.5	..	..	99	100	..	..	..
Ecuador	15.6	12.4	7.3	5.2	37.3	27.0	25.9	17.0	93	..	83	98 [b]	64
El Salvador	30.2	26.7	29.5 [l]	27.1 [l]	54.9	45.8	56.1 [f]	44.5 [f]	92	99 [b]	88	112 [b]	72

Table 4. Indicators on education and training [cont.]

	Illiterates (%)								Ratio of female to male enrolment (x100)				
	Age group 15-24 years				Age group 25 years and above				First level		Second level		Third level
	1970/74		Latest year		1970/74		Latest year		1970	1985/87	1970	1985/87	1985/87
Country or area	f	m	f	m	f	m	f	m					
French Guiana	7.9[m]	7.7[m]	10.8	6.9	12.5	15.6	20.5	20.4	99	..	118	110[b]	..
Grenada	0.9	1.2	..	..	3.1	2.4	..	..	98	92[b]	84	..	123[b]
Guadeloupe	1.4[n]	2.0[n]	1.1	1.9	19.2	18.8	13.3	14.8	95	91[b]	..	113	..
Guatemala	52.4	38.1	..	..	66.8	51.1	..	..	79	82	70	83[b]	92
Guyana	2.0	1.7	..	..	16.1	8.1	..	..	96	96[b]	102	..	92
Haiti	72.0	63.9	49.0	48.7	88.3	78.5	76.0	69.4	..	86[b]	..	..	46
Honduras	27.8	29.5	..	..	55.4	48.0	..	..	99	99	88	116[b]	61[b]
Jamaica	1.1	1.7	..	..	4.5	5.6	..	..	100	97[b]	..	105[b]	132
Martinique	..	..	0.8	1.4	..	..	9.0	11.6	96	91	..	120[b]	..
Mexico	18.1	14.5	9.2	6.9	35.9	25.7	26.4	17.7	92	95	63	95	66
Netherlands Antilles	3.2	4.7	1.7	2.8	9.2	8.5	8.5	7.2	..	97[b]	..	111[b]	..
Nicaragua	33.6	37.2	..	..	48.2	44.9	..	..	101	107	90	208	122
Panama	13.2	12.1	6.6	5.1	27.1	25.5	19.5	17.8	92	92	108	109	136
Paraguay	11.3	8.3	6.4	5.3	31.5	18.4	19.9	12.1	89	92	99	..	53[b]
Peru	19.8	7.1	10.2	3.5	47.5	21.8	34.6	13.2	85	93	75	83[b]	53[b]
Puerto Rico	3.4	4.6	5.4	6.6	17.8	13.4	13.8	11.8	..	..	..	..	153[b]
St. Kitts and Nevis	1.4	1.5	..	..	2.7	2.9	..	..	93[k]	98	..	93[b]	101
St. Lucia	4.0	6.5	..	..	23.7	25.8	..	..	106	94	88	156	84
St. Vincent/Grenadines	2.0	2.1	..	..	5.7	5.6	..	..	98	94	98	140[b]	224
Suriname	..	..	..	..	..	..	..	..	92	93[b]	119	..	116
Trinidad and Tobago	1.3	1.1	0.8	0.8	15.1	7.5	9.7	4.9	97	99	107	101[b]	101
Uruguay	..	..	1.1	2.3	..	..	7.0	7.8	91	95	113	112[b]	130[b]
US Virgin Islands	..	..	..	..	..	..	..	..	..	..	..	..	259[b]
Venezuela	12.9	12.7	6.3	7.8	34.8	24.7	22.9	16.8	99	96	103	119	..

Asia and Pacific

	Illiterates (%)								Ratio of female to male enrolment (x100)				
	Age group 15-24 years				Age group 25 years and above				First level		Second level		Third level
	1970/74		Latest year		1970/74		Latest year		1970	1985/87	1970	1985/87	1985/87
Country or area	f	m	f	m	f	m	f	m					
Afghanistan	..	..	88.9	54.2	..	..	97.6	77.3	16	52	15	..	16
Bahrain	45.4	22.8	17.9	10.3	84.6	63.3	56.2	28.9	73	98	69	93	147
Bangladesh	77.7	53.3	72.8	55.4	90.6	66.7	86.7	62.3	47	66	..	39	24
Bhutan	..	..	..	..	..	..	..	..	5	54	3	21[b]	6[b]
Brunei Darussalam	17.8	9.0	6.8	5.9	70.9	33.5	45.4	19.8	92	93	81	105[b]	101
Cambodia	..	..	..	..	..	..	..	..	..	..	..	..	..
China	..	..	17.9	4.8	..	..	62.3	27.6	..	82	..	69	42
Cyprus	..	..	..	..	..	..	..	..	94	93	86	99	89
East Timor	..	..	..	..	..	..	..	..	..	..	..	..	..
Fiji	..	..	9.2	5.6	..	..	34.7	19.7	93	95	73	99	53
French Polynesia	..	..	..	..	..	..	..	..	94	93[b]	125	122	94[b]
Guam	..	..	4.1	4.6	..	..	3.3	3.1	..	92[b]	..	93[b]	..
Hong Kong	4.8	2.8	..	..	49.3	12.9	..	..	90	91[b]	72	100[b]	53
India	66.7	37.8	59.7	33.7	86.3	58.0	80.6	50.2	60	65[b]	39	..	35[i]
Indonesia	25.8	13.3	18.3	10.4	67.8	37.4	54.2	28.2	84	93	52	74[b]	48
Iran (Islamic Rep. of)	..	..	57.7	29.1	..	..	85.4	63.2	55	78	49	65	39
Iraq	..	..	..	..	..	..	..	..	41	81	41	57	48[b]
Israel	5.8[e]	2.7[e]	0.4	0.4	23.9[f]	10.8[f]	14.3	6.4	92	97	105	105	84
Jordan	..	..	23.5[m]	5.2[m]	..	..	..	..	78	91	52	92	82
Kiribati	..	..	..	..	..	..	..	..	..	97	63	96	..
Korea, D. People's R.	..	..	..	..	..	..	..	..	..	..	..	..	..
Korea, Republic of	1.2	0.7	..	..	26.6	7.8	..	..	92	94	61	88	43
Kuwait	39.9	28.5	23.9	18.7	62.7	36.3	49.7	30.4	73	95	74	90	117
Lao People's Dem. Rep.	..	..	..	..	..	..	..	..	59	81	36	69	55
Lebanon	28.6[m]	11.0[m]	..	..	58.6	32.1	..	..	83	88[b]	..	..	64
Macau	13.5	8.7	..	..	33.6	19.8	..	..	89	..	81	..	..
Malaysia	..	..	16.8[e]	10.2[e]	..	..	62.2[f]	30.2[f]	88	98	69	96	80
Maldives	..	..	12.9	15.8	..	..	20.8	18.4	..	..	..	..	..
Mongolia	..	..	..	..	..	..	..	..	..	100	..	..	149

Table 4. Indicators on education and training [*cont.*]

Country or area	Illiterates (%) Age group 15-24 years 1970/74 f	m	Latest year f	m	Age group 25 years and above 1970/74 f	m	Latest year f	m	Ratio of female to male enrolment (x100) First level 1970	1985/87	Second level 1970	1985/87	Third level 1985/87
Myanmar	26.1	12.3	18.6	11.4	48.9	17.6	33.3	15.6	89	..	64	..	..
Nepal	94.4	66.7	85.1	54.9	98.6	82.1	93.4	74.0	18	41 [b]	..	30 [b]	25 [b]
New Caledonia	..	..	2.1	3.0	..	..	13.1	9.8	98	96	84	109	79
Oman	..	..	..	..	..	..	..	..	16	82	..	54	102
Pacific Islands	..	..	..	..	..	..	..	..	90	..	..	..	45 [b]
Pakistan	81.9	58.8	75.1	54.6	92.4	74.4	89.2	68.3	36	50	25	37	17
Papua New Guinea	..	..	..	..	..	..	..	..	57	75 [b]	36	..	32
Philippines	7.7	8.0	7.6	8.9	25.2	19.5	22.7	19.9	..	94	..	99	119
Qatar	..	..	..	..	..	..	..	..	81	90	47	111	202
Samoa	0.0	0.0	..	..	3.4	3.6	..	..	94	94	108	96 [b]	89 [b o]
Saudi Arabia	..	..	..	..	..	..	..	..	46	80	24	64	65
Singapore	15.5	8.1	3.8	3.6	62.4	22.0	36.8	10.9	88	89 [b]	91	98 [b]	72
Solomon Islands	..	..	..	..	..	..	..	..	57	77	34	..	..
Sri Lanka	15.9	10.4	10.3	8.9	39.9	15.8	22.9	9.4	89	93	..	..	68
Syrian Arab Republic	64.6	21.9	..	..	87.5	49.8	..	..	57	86	35	67	53
Thailand	8.0	4.5	3.8	2.4	40.7	17.1	22.9	9.7	88	93 [b]	72	..	..
Tonga	..	..	0.2	0.2	..	..	0.7	0.4	92	91	92	98	129
Turkey	44.2	13.2	24.7	6.4	76.2	39.6	62.3	25.0	73	89	40	55	50
United Arab Emirates	..	..	43.7	34.4	..	..	70.2	44.4	61	94	..	95	139
Vanuatu	..	..	32.3	24.2	..	..	64.4	52.9	78	84 [b]	73	60 [b]	..
Viet Nam	..	..	6.0	3.9	..	..	32.3	12.8	97 [k]	91	95 [b]	..	31 [b d]
Yemen	..	..	..	..	..	..	..	..	19	24 [b]	5 [p]	22 [b]	40 [b]

Sources:
United Nations Educational, Scientific and Cultural Organization: education statistics database, *Statistics of Educational Attainment and Illiteracy, 1970–1980*, CSR-E-44 (Paris, 1983), *Statistical Yearbook* (Paris, various years up to 1988) and *Compendium of Statistics on Illiteracy*, No. 31 (Paris, 1990); *Demographic Yearbook 1983* (United Nations publication, Sales No. E/F. 84.XIII.1); and national publications of Central African Republic and Comoros.

a   Including evening and correspondence courses.
b   1980/84.
c   Through the accession of the German Democratic Republic to the Federal Republic of Germany with effect from 3 October 1990, the two German States have united to form one sovereign State. As from the date of unification, the Federal Republic of Germany acts in the United Nations under the designation "Germany". All data shown for Germany pertain to end-June 1990 or earlier and are indicated separately for the Federal Republic of Germany and the former German Democratic Republic.

d   Including correspondence courses.
e   Age group 15–29.
f   Age group 30+.
g   Excluding Al Azhar University.
h   1966.
i   1979.
j   Age group 25–49.
k   1975/76.
l   Age group 10–29.
m   Age group 20–24.
n   Age group 10–24.
o   Data exclude the School of Agriculture.
p   Data refer to the former Yemen Arab Republic only.

4
Health and child-bearing

Almost everywhere, women live longer than men and die of different causes—though the trends in some causes of death, such as heart disease and cancer, are converging.

Throughout life, women's concerns about their health differ from men's, and they face different threats. Child-bearing exposes women to a particular array of health risks and in many developing countries the complications from pregnancy and childbirth are a major (and avoidable) cause of death for women.

Good health and family planning services are very important for the well-being of women and their children—giving them opportunities to choose whether they will have children, when and how many. And reduced infant mortality means that women can reach their desired family size with fewer pregnancies.

With the growing availability of family planning and greater freedom in its use, child-bearing rates have fallen considerably in recent decades, except in Africa. The increased availability is far from universal, however, and global trends mask high rates of child-bearing and maternal deaths for some regions and countries.

Life expectancy

Life expectancy at birth increased for both men and women in every region of the world between 1970 and 1990. And women's life expectancy increased faster than men's in every region (charts 4.1 and 4.2). The increase for women was eight to nine years on average in developing regions and about four years in the developed regions. These increases among women were about one year more than the increases among men. [23]

Women tend to outlive men everywhere except Bangladesh, Bhutan, Maldives and Nepal (table 5). In the developed regions, women's life expectancy is 6.5 years longer than men's. In the developing regions, the average difference is 5 years in Latin America and the Caribbean, 3.5 years in Africa and 3 years in Asia and the Pacific. As a result, women are more likely than men to be widowed in their later years and become dependent on the state, their children, or savings.

Because of differences in women's and men's life expectancy in all regions except southern Asia and differences in the average age of marriage, women can expect to outlive their husbands by 8 to 10 years. In southern Asia, the difference in the age of marriage is high—5 years—but average life expectancy is the same for women and men.

Women's life expectancy varies greatly among regions. In the developed regions, it is now 75 years or more in almost every country, and in many developing countries it is more than 70 years—including 15 countries in Latin America and the Caribbean, 11 in Asia and the Pacific and 1 in Africa.

Despite progress in some countries, the average life expectancy at birth for African women is only 54 years. In Asia and the Pacific, where the average is 64 years, many countries still have female life expectancies below 50 years. Globally, the lowest life expectancies for women are in Afghanistan, East Timor, Ethiopia and Sierra Leone—only 42 or 43 years. In Latin America and the Caribbean, only Bolivia and Haiti still have life expectancies under 60 years.

Life expectancy

Data here refer to life expectancy at birth, which is an overall estimate of the expected average number of years to be lived by a female or male born alive. Life expectancy calculations are based on national statistics of mortality by age in a given period and assume that age-specifc mortality levels will remain unchanged for the lifetime of the cohort. To the extent that mortality rates change over time, the actual average life expectancy of persons born in a given year will differ from the estimate.

Causes of death

The definition and classification of causes of death are
recommended by the World
Health Organization in the
International Classification
of Diseases, Injuries and
Causes of Death. Causes of
death are commonly
grouped as infectious and
parasitic diseases, neo-
plasms (cancers), circulatory
diseases, respiratory diseases and so on. However,
the only reliable source of
statistics on causes of death
is civil registration of deaths
with certification of cause
of death by trained health
personnel. These data are
generally not available, or
are available only for a small
percentage of the popula-
tion, for most developing
regions.

4.1

Women's life expectancy is increasing everywhere

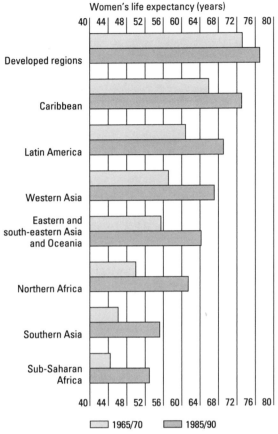

Source: Averages for each region calculated by the Statistical Office of the United Nations Secretariat from *World Population Prospects 1988* (United Nations publication, Sales No. E.89.XIII.7).

Causes of death

Widespread reductions in infectious and parasitic diseases were a major factor in lengthening
life expectancy in developing regions over the past
two decades. Due mainly to better nutrition, safer
water and sanitation, improved preventive health
and broader education and primary health care services, these reductions have played a large part in
reducing infant and child mortality and increasing
overall life expectancy.

But evidence from the developed regions indicates that women's deaths from chronic diseases,
accidents and violence have increased from levels
well below men's to levels closer to men's—the
dark side of equality. Women traditionally have
suffered less than men from threats linked to personal behavior such as alcohol consumption, smoking, motor vehicle accidents and other violence,
and their death rates in these categories remain
lower than men's. But with women adopting life

styles more like men's, they have become increasingly susceptible to some of the same major causes
of death. For example, their deaths from motor
vehicle accidents increased 20 per cent in the developed regions while men's were the same in the
late 1980s as the early 1950s. And the prevalence
of lung cancer among women has risen much more
rapidly than among men (chart 4.3). [41]

Maternal mortality remains a significant cause
of death for women in the developing regions, [37]
and in many countries women still suffer from
other causes of death specifically related to the
their gender, such as infanticide, bride burning,
dowry deaths and domestic homicide (see page 19).

4.2

Women live longer than men almost everywhere

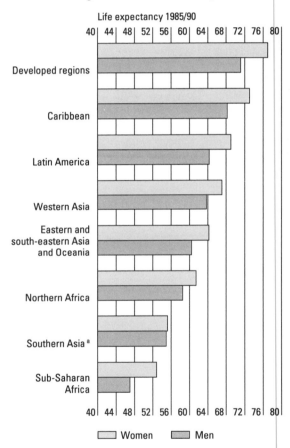

Source: Averages for each region calculated by the Statistical Office of the United Nations Secretariat from *World Population Prospects 1988* (United Nations publication, Sales No. E.89.XIII.7).

a   Estimated life expectancy at birth is lower for women than men in Bangladesh, Bhutan, Maldives and Nepal.

4.3

Differences between women's and men's death rates are diminishing for some causes in developed regions

Change in age-standardized death rate from 1950/54 to 1986 (%)

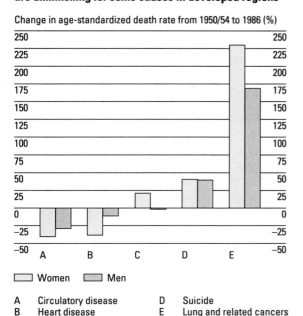

☐ Women   ▨ Men

A Circulatory disease   D Suicide
B Heart disease   E Lung and related cancers
C Motor vehicle accidents

Source: *World Health Statistics Annual 1988* (World Health Organization, Geneva, 1988).

Women's health

If women are inadequately nourished—as are about half the women in most of Asia and Africa—it limits their physical development, compromises their health and threatens their ability to bear healthy children. Malnourished women are sick more, have smaller babies and die earlier. And where infant and child mortality is high, birth rates are also high—increasing the stress on women's bodies and trapping them and their children in a cycle of poor health and nutrition.

Better nutrition, broader access to appropriate health care, improved education and good family planning are keys to improving women's health and reducing their reproductive burden. Such services allow women to have more control over their child-bearing and their lives. But the benefits are quickly lost if these essential services are withdrawn or cut back because of social and economic pressures.

Maternal mortality

Rates of maternal mortality show a greater disparity between the developed and developing regions than any other health indicator (chart 4.4). [37] Almost all countries in the developed regions have reduced maternal deaths to very low levels—in some cases close to zero. Many developing countries have also made dramatic reductions—often with very limited resources, such as Zambia (to 151 deaths per 100,000 live births)—but many others still have very high rates, such as Bhutan (at 1700 per 100,000).

Women who become pregnant in developing regions face a risk of death due to pregnancy that is 80 to 600 times higher than women in developed regions. The reasons are that births are not attended by trained personnel, there are few backup services for high-risk pregnancies and malnutrition is endemic among pregnant women. The southern Asian countries have the highest maternal mortality rates—650 maternal deaths per 100,000 births—and the largest numbers of births without trained attendants (chart 4.4). Women in these regions also bear two to three times as many children as do their counterparts in the developed regions.

Abortion is a major cause of maternal mortality in developing regions but not in the developed regions (except Czechoslovakia and Romania). Each year, at least half a million women worldwide die from pregnancy-related causes, of whom roughly 200,000 die from illegal abortions, most performed by unskilled attendants under unsanitary conditions or self-inflicted. More than half the abortion-related deaths occur in southern and south-eastern Asia, followed by sub-Saharan Africa and then Latin America and the Caribbean.[1] Fewer women die from legal abortions than from illegal abortions. In some developed countries, there are only 0.6 deaths from legal abortion per 100,000 procedures. But in such places as India, where abortion is legal, mortality is still high because of inadequate health care.

Family planning is not a substitute for general health services. Maternal deaths are also linked to lack of health service facilities and personnel, especially for women in rural areas. Poor transport networks in developing countries do not allow easy access to medical care, which often is centred in cities. Other detrimental health care factors include lack of treatment for complications in rural areas, improper treatment and shortages of staff and supplies.

Maternal mortality rate

Maternal mortality is calculated on the basis of maternal deaths and live births for a given year, using national civil registration and demographic survey statistics on births and deaths. Rates of less than 5 are found in a few countries in the developed regions, while rates of more than 1,000 maternal deaths per 100,000 live births have been estimated in some developing areas.

Source: World Health Organization estimates.

Anaemia and women's nutrition

A majority of women in developing countries are malnourished, as measured by the incidence of anaemia. Anaemia increases women's susceptibility to illness, pregnancy complications and maternal death—and contributes to higher overall death rates. Women in their reproductive years require three times as much iron a day as do adult men. Because anaemia starves the body of oxygen, it makes women tired and listless. It also increases the danger of haemorrhaging and other complications in childbirth. [38]

Nearly two thirds of the pregnant women in Africa and in southern and western Asia are clinically anaemic, compared with half the women who are not pregnant. Among women aged 15–49 in eastern Asia and in Latin America and the Caribbean, 17–18 per cent are anaemic. In Latin America and the Caribbean, however, anaemia among pregnant women is disproportionately high at 30 per cent, compared with 20 per cent in eastern Asia. For the developed regions, the World Health Organization estimates the rate of anaemia as 11 per cent among all women aged 15–49 and 14 per cent among pregnant women (chart 4.6).

Iron deficiency is widespread among women in the developing regions and most common in southern Asia and parts of Africa. In India and Mexico, where the preference for sons is strong, girls are often given less protein-rich and iron-rich food than boys of the same age. In Ethiopia, the Sudan and Nigeria, cultural taboos discourage pregnant women from eating fruits, vegetables, milk, rice and other high-calorie foods, endangering the mother and unborn child. And in many societies it is still the custom for adult women and young children to eat after the men have had their fill, leaving them less of the more nutritious foods. This tendency for girls and women to eat less food (or food with less nutritional value) is part of what diminishes the usually longer life expectancy of infant girls at birth compared with boys.[2]

The correlation with maternal mortality is clear. A woman stunted from poor eating and weakened by anaemia starts pregnancy in poor condition. Resulting high rates of complications of pregnancy threaten her chances of surviving and she is more likely to have low-weight babies susceptible to permanent damage from anaemia, iodine deficiency and other nutritional problems.

4.4

Maternal mortality is much higher in developing regions, especially where women give birth with no trained attendant

Maternal mortality rates in Africa and southern Asia are over 30 times those in developed regions

In Africa and southern and south-eastern Asia more than half of births are without trained attendants

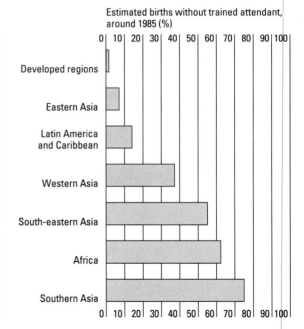

Note: Rates are based on estimated totals in each region, not country averages.

Sources: World Health Organization: "Maternal mortality rates: a tabulation of available information (second edition)" (Geneva, WHO/FHE/86.3), and "Coverage of maternity care: a tabulation of available information (second edition)" (Geneva, WHO/FHE/89.2).

Breast-feeding

The link between infant nutrition and breast-feeding is also clear. Breast-feeding confers immunities and provides more sterile and digestible food for babies. UNICEF estimates that well over a million deaths a year could be avoided if all children were breast-fed optimally (four to six months of a baby's consuming only breast milk), and many more would avoid debilitating illnesses. [27] Breast-feeding is practiced most in Africa, where the percentage of mothers breast-feeding at six months is 90 per cent. It is practiced least in Europe, where 25 per cent of the mothers breast-feed.

Breast-feeding can have a contraceptive influence but is taxing. It depletes a woman's nutritional reserves—which may already be dangerously low. A woman needs more food while she is breast-feeding, but she is unlikely to get it if she is poor or suffering from social prejudices that deny her adequate rest and nutrition.

4.6

Inadequate nutrition is widespread among women in developing regions, especially Africa and much of Asia

Women aged 15–49 with anaemia, around 1980 (%)

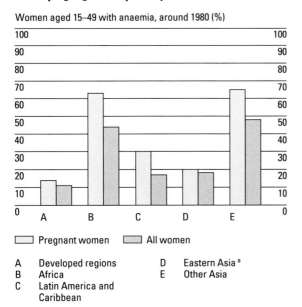

☐ Pregnant women   ▨ All women

A   Developed regions   D   Eastern Asia [a]
B   Africa   E   Other Asia
C   Latin America and
     Caribbean

Note: Anaemia is defined according to WHO reference values for age, sex and pregnancy status. Rates are estimated from various studies and refer to totals in each region, not country averages.

Source: WHO, *World Health Statistics Quarterly*, 38 (Geneva, 1985).

a   Excluding China.

The health of girls

Several United Nations agencies paid special attention in 1990 to the girl child—to focus attention on the health, nutritional, socio-economic and educational discrimination that girls suffer in many developing regions. This discrimination denies girls the stepping stones to a better life, leaving them with little knowledge and training and little chance to improve their condition.

Historical patterns of discrimination against girls are evident in long-term statistics comparing women's mortality with men's. Although current indicators clearly show considerable convergence almost everywhere in female and male mortality at the youngest ages, there still is strong evidence of higher mortality among girls than boys aged 2–5 in some countries (table 4.7). Higher mortality for girls aged 1–5 has also been reported in northeast Brazil, Burundi, Guatemala, Indonesia and Togo.[3] For infants, reliable mortality data by sex are hard to come by in developing countries, especially in rural areas. The data that are available—mainly for developing countries where infant mortality rates are already lower in general—show no differences by sex.

Although girls contribute much to the family—in Africa and Asia they often work seven or more hours a day—many societies consider them a burden. They are discriminated against as children and married off early. In addition, some societies expect women to start having children at a very young age.

Adolescent pregnancy—sometimes the cause of early marriage, and sometimes the result— is very common in some regions. Pregnancy adds an undue burden to an adolescent girl's maturing body. And teenage mothers have a higher risk for maternal and infant mortality—twice that of mothers aged 20 to 24. Besides posing a threat to health, pregnancy can limit a young girl's chances for education and a paying job, continuing the cycle of disadvantaged mothers passing on their vulnerability to their daughters, and their daughters to theirs. The figures are even more striking for individual countries—especially for younger girls. In Mauritania, 39 per cent of girls are married by age 15 and 15 per cent have given birth. In Bangladesh, 73 per cent of girls are married by age 15, and 21 per cent have had at least one child. [13]

Adolescent child-bearing rates are much lower in the developed regions, except in Bulgaria, Czechoslovakia, Romania and the United States of America, where they were over 50 per 1000 in the late 1980s. [26]

Anaemia

Anaemia is a condition in which the haemoglobin content of the blood is lower than normal as a result of a deficiency of one or more essential nutrients. While anaemia can be caused by various illnesses, the most common cause is malnutrition. The prevalence of anaemia is therefore a good indicator of inadequate nutrition.

Total fertility rate

The total fertility rate is an estimate of the average number of children that would be born to each woman if the fertility patterns of a given period were to stay unchanged. This measure gives the approximate total number of children an average woman will bear in her lifetime, assuming no mortality among women of child-bearing age.

4.7

Higher mortality rates among girls aged 2–5 years have been found in demographic and health surveys in a significant number of countries

	Deaths per year per 1,000 population aged 2–5 years	
	Girls	Boys
Pakistan	54.4	36.9
Haiti	61.2	47.8
Bangladesh	68.6	57.7
Thailand	26.8	17.3
Syria	14.6	9.3
Colombia	24.8	20.5
Costa Rica	8.1	4.8
Nepal	60.7	57.7
Dominican Republic	20.2	17.2
Philippines	21.9	19.1
Sri Lanka	18.7	16.3
Peru	30.8	28.8
Mexico	16.7	14.7
Panama	8.7	7.6
Turkey	19.5	18.4
Republic of Korea	12.7	11.8
Venezuela	8.4	7.6

Source: Compiled by UNICEF from national survey reports of the World Fertility Survey programme.

Child-bearing

Across the world, women are having fewer children now than 20 years ago. Child-bearing rates dropped from an average of 2.6 to 1.8 births per woman in the developed regions and from a range of 5–7 to a range of 3–6 in developing regions from 1970 to 1990. However, these averages hide marked differences among countries (table 5). [23]

In the developed regions, the total fertility rate of 1.8 births per woman is slightly below what it takes for a population to maintain itself. This rate reflects the long-term decline in child-bearing that was interrupted in the 1950s in some countries by the baby boom.

The developing regions experienced much steeper average declines during the 1970s. For many of the least developed countries, however, fertility rates have only recently begun to decline, if at all (chart 4.8). Sub-Saharan Africa shows only a small drop over the past twenty years after decades of very high child-bearing rates, and at 6.2 births per woman, fertility rates there remain much higher than in any other region.

Every country in Latin America and the Caribbean experienced a decline in child-bearing, with the average total fertility rate dropping from 5.5 in 1965/70 to 3.6 in 1985/90. The Caribbean countries had the lowest rates—as low as 1.7 in Cuba. Central American countries still have the highest rates in the region but they also experienced steep declines.

Average child-bearing decreased from 6.1 births per woman in 1970/75 to 4.6 in 1985/90 in Asia and the Pacific—with broad variation. Eastern Asia, led by China, had far greater declines in child-bearing (to 2.4 births per woman, excluding Mongolia), compared with southern Asia (5.4 births) or western Asia (5.3 births). The decline in south-eastern Asia (to 3.9 births per woman) was moderate.

4.8

Fertility rates have declined significantly in all regions except sub-Saharan Africa

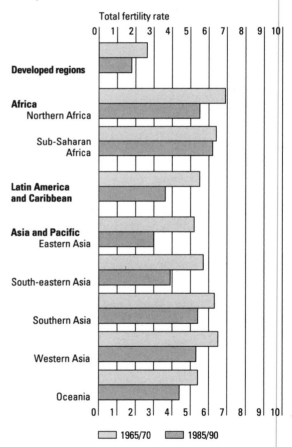

Source: Averages for each region calculated by the Statistical Office of the United Nations Secretariat from *World Population Prospects 1988* (United Nations publication, Sales No. E.89.XIII.7).

Urbanization and child-bearing

Regional averages mask the disparities between urban and rural child-bearing rates. In the developing regions, mothers tend to have fewer children in urban areas than in rural areas. The gap is clearest in Latin America and the Caribbean, where rural rates are much higher than in cities and towns. Although the gaps are smaller, the same pattern of rural-urban variation has developed over the past 20 years in Asia and the Pacific, and to some extent in Africa. [10]

It is difficult to say how urbanization by itself affects child-bearing, but urban life's greater employment and educational opportunities may be more conducive to smaller families, as might the urban life style. Children may also cost more in urban environments. With higher costs of education, health and housing, the costs of rearing children go up and the children's contribution to the family economy goes down.

Family planning

Modern family planning methods make it far easier to limit fertility, and their use is increasing almost everywhere. [16] Over half the couples in the developed regions, Latin America and the Caribbean and eastern Asia now use some modern method of family planning. This represents increases in some cases of five times or more from the 1960s to the 1980s (chart 4.9). The acceptance and availability of family planning methods are nevertheless uneven. There are marked differences between these high-use regions (averaging 70 per cent) and Africa and Asia and the Pacific outside of eastern Asia (list 4.10).

Family planning and contraceptive use were widespread in the developed regions from the early 1960s to the 1980s. In developing regions, use rose sharply from under 15 per cent in all regions in 1960/65 to over 33 per cent in the early 1980s except in Africa.

Recent data show ranges of contraceptive use from 2 per cent to 75 per cent in sub-Saharan Africa, from 7 per cent to 70 per cent in Latin America and the Caribbean, and from 1 per cent to 70 per cent in Asia and northern Africa (table 5). The World Fertility Survey in the 1970s and 1980s revealed this: a majority of women in many developing countries say they do not want more children but are not using any form of family planning because of cost, inaccessibility or cultural barriers. In Brazil, it has been reported that nearly a third of the married women resort to illegal and expensive sterilization operations because they have no easy and accessible alternatives.[4]

Inadequate access to health and family planning services exposes poor women to serious health risks from inappropriate contraceptive methods. Teenage girls and unmarried women are also at a great disadvantage, because family planning programmes often overlook them.

Determinants of child-bearing

The circumstances of individual women determine their child-bearing. Some of these circumstances are directly linked to child-bearing, such as when they marry and whether they practice family planning and breast-feed. Others are indirectly linked, such as decisions about timing and spacing of child-bearing, government policies and the socio-economic environment (list 4.11).[5]

Couples in developing regions seldom use contraception before the birth of their first child. And a woman's age at marriage is an important determinant of her age when her first child is born. The younger she is when she marries, the more likely she is to bear more children.

4.9

Contraceptive use has increased in every region but is still far from common in much of Africa and Asia

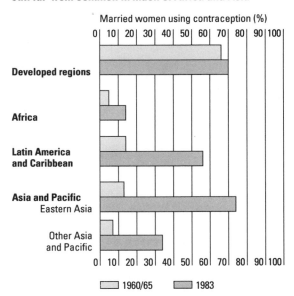

Note: Rates are based on estimated totals in each region, not country averages.

Source: *Levels and Trends of Contraceptive Use as Assessed in 1988*, Population Studies No. 110 (United Nations publication, Sales No. E.89.XIII.4).

4.10

In at least 26 countries and areas, mainly in Africa and Asia, less than 30 per cent of currently-married women practice contraception

Percentage currently-married women who use contraception, 1980/87

Africa
Benin (9)
Burundi (9)
Cameroon (2)[a]
Côte d'Ivoire (3)
Ghana (13)
Kenya (27)
Lesotho (5)[a]
Liberia (6)
Malawi (7)[b]
Mali (5)
Mauritania (1)
Nigeria (6)[c]
Rwanda (10)
Senegal (11)
Sudan (5)[a][d]
Uganda (5)

Latin America and Caribbean
Bolivia (26)
Guatemala (23)
Haiti (7)
Nicaragua (27)

Asia and Pacific
Bangladesh (25)
Jordan (27)[e]
Nepal (14)
Pakistan (8)
Syrian Arab Republic (20)[a]
Yemen (1)[a][f]

Source: Population Division of the United Nations Secretariat.

a   Data from 1975/79.
b   Including unmarried women.
c   Ondo state only.
d   North Sudan.
e   Excluding abstinence, douche and folk methods.
f   Data refer to former Yemen Arab Republic only.

Exclusive breast-feeding—when a child is fed only breastmilk—provides women with 98 per cent protection from pregnancy during the first four to six months after birth if menses have not returned. And only in conjunction with family planning does it help substantially thereafter.

Good-quality family planning allows couples to choose the timing and spacing of their children. In countries where fertility rates have begun to decline and large families are desired less, access to modern family planning methods speeds the decline.

What, then, of the indirect determinants? In some countries, despite skyrocketing populations and the accompanying social and economic stresses, children are still an asset to families. Starting at a young age, they provide needed labour and contribute to the family's survival. And parents, especially mothers, depend on children to take care of them in their old age—particularly where there are no social safety nets for the elderly.

Besides the economic imperative, women in some countries have many children because they are the only route to status in the family and community. When a woman's status is no longer strictly associated with her bearing and rearing children, and as living conditions improve, child-bearing decisions change. With greater development, education, social security and economic opportunities, couples are more likely to substitute quality for quantity in their family decisions. Rather than rely on their children as extra economic resources for the family, they invest in their children's education and future. And they have smaller families.

Reductions in infant mortality rates have been followed by reductions in total fertility rates in the developed regions, Latin America and the Caribbean and parts of Asia. Opinions differ on whether the least developed countries will experience lower fertility rates as infant mortality falls. (And it is unclear how the high prevalence of AIDS among young women in Africa will affect mortality and child-bearing rates there.) But efforts to reduce infant mortality can be expected to lay the groundwork for subsequent efforts to reduce child-bearing. This will be difficult, however, where political and cultural barriers block family planning efforts.

Education improves the likelihood that a woman will know about and use modern family planning. Higher levels of education among women are also associated with delays in marriage and child-bearing and with a desire for smaller families.

Government programmes to spread education and health services, or to reduce discrepancies in living standards among social classes, are also conducive to smaller families. But whether couples' desired family size translates to reduced child-bearing depends on social and cultural factors.

AIDS and other threats to women's health
AIDS [39]

Until recently, the social, economic and demographic impacts of acquired immunodeficiency syndrome (AIDS) on women were largely neglected, but that is changing because of the steady increases of AIDS reported among heterosexuals.

A third of all those infected with AIDS in the world are women—an estimated 2 million of the 6 million or more people infected (table 4.12). Although AIDS has primarily affected men in the developed regions and in Latin America and the Caribbean, it is also spreading among women and infants in those regions—and at alarming rates among African women. In many African countries nearly as many women as men are infected, and in some sub-Saharan cities up to 40 per cent of the women aged 30 to 39 are estimated to be infected. Although AIDS appeared more recently in Asia, it is spreading rapidly there among intravenous drug users and people with multiple sex partners. There has also been a sharp rise in the number of American women found to be infected. In cities the picture is particularly grim. According to the World Health Organization, AIDS is now the leading cause of death for women aged 20–40 in some major cities of western Europe, sub-Saharan Africa and the Americas including New York.

Sexually transmitted diseases [6]

Sexually transmitted diseases (STDs) render millions of women subfertile or infertile and give them recurrent infections. Often much harder to detect in women than in men, many STDs reach more advanced stages in women, so the mortality and morbidity rates associated with these diseases are higher in women. Despite the prevalence of STDs, they are not high on the list of health priorities—because the biomedical payoff is felt to be too low given the perceived cost and technical difficulty of interventions.

STDs primarily affect women between the ages of 15 and 44 years—their child-bearing and most economically productive years. STDs account for 0.5 to 1.0 per cent of the maternal deaths in sub-Saharan Africa and for 20 per cent in the United States of America, where overall maternal mortality rates are much lower.

Sexually transmitted diseases may be a factor in the rapid spread of AIDS among women in Africa and in some urban areas of Latin America and the United States where reproductive tract infections are associated with an increased risk of transmission of the AIDS virus.

Sexual assault and rape

Women are victimized not only in their families but also in public places and at work. Sexual assaults against children and women who are unable to understand or control them include defilement, indecent exposure, unlawful carnal knowledge and rape. For example: [7]

- In Canada women are about seven times more likely to be sexually assaulted than men.
- In Trinidad and Tobago from 1970 to 1980, while the population increased 28 per cent, the number of men charged with rape rose 134 per cent.
- In the United Kingdom there were 1,334 rapes recorded in 1983, 1,433 in 1984 and 1,842 in 1985. Much of the increase apparently was due

to the greater willingness of victims to report violations because of the more sympathetic and understanding treatment by police.

Disability [12]

It is impossible to compare rates of disability for countries and regions because statistics collected do not use a universal definition for the term. Overall, however, it is known that men are more likely than women to be disabled in their 20s, 30s and 40s due to war and violence. Because women generally live longer than men, their disability rates increase rapidly in their 50s, 60s and older.

Rates of profound disability among the general population—including deafness and loss of limbs—are small (0.5 per cent). Rates of disabling disease and mental retardation are about 1 to 2 per cent. Between 5 and 10 per cent of the population suffers from less profound disability. These rates, though small, can have a big impact well beyond women who are themselves disabled because the care of disabled persons falls disproportionately on women.

Disability

Disability is defined by the World Health Organization from a health perspective as any restriction or lack of ability to perform an activity in the manner or within the range considered normal for a human being. The main emphasis is on the restriction of abilities manifested in the form of deficits in activities and behaviours, including limitations in bodily functions.

4.12

Over two million females were estimated to be infected with the AIDS virus in 1989

A. Estimated numbers of infected persons

	Total	Ratio of f to m	Infected females	Pattern of infection
Northern America, western Europe, Australia and New Zealand; some Latin America and Caribbean	under 3 million	1 to 9	0.3 million	Low among females but steadily increasing
Sub-Saharan Africa; some Latin America and Caribbean	over 3 million	approx. 1 to 1	over 1.5 million	Spreading rapidly among both sexes from sexual intercourse, contaminated medical equipment and blood, and from mothers to infants
Eastern Europe; northern Africa and eastern Mediterranean; Asia and Pacific	0.1 million	1 to 2	33 thousand	Low among both sexes but increasingly found among persons of both sexes with risk behavior
Total	6 million +	1 to 3	2 million +	

B. Symptomatic cases, both sexes (cumulative)

	Total
Cases reported to World Health Organization to August 1990	275,000
Estimated actual cases to August 1990	800,000
Projected cases to mid/late 1990s	3 million +
Projected cases to 2000	5–6 million

Source: World Health Organization, Global Programme on AIDS, Surveillance, Forcasting and Impact Assessment Unit, 1989 and 1990.

Cigarette smoking

A quarter or more of adult women smoke in most developed and developing regions except Africa (chart 4.13). As more women smoke, more can be expected to die of smoking-related diseases. Since 1985, approximately 126,000 women have died each year from smoking-related diseases, and the prevalence of lung cancer among women increased 400 per cent in the past 30 years.[8] In Canada, men were more likely than women to be regular smokers, but for people under age 25, a higher proportion of women than men smoked regularly.[9]

Just as many countries in the developed regions are waging antismoking campaigns, a counter-campaign by the international tobacco industry is opening new markets for tobacco in developing countries. Africa has the lowest proportion of women smokers (14 per cent) and Latin America and the Caribbean the highest (30 per cent). [40]

Indicators

Statistics and indicators on women's health and child-bearing in table 5 concern (a) mortality, including life expectancy and infant and child mortality; (b) selected indicators of maternal health and health services; (c) selected indicators of fertility and contraceptive use; and (d) prevalence of smoking, which has a significant long-term negative impact on health.

Life expectancy at birth is an overall estimate of the expected average number of years to be lived by a female or male born alive. This indicator is taken from the estimates and projections prepared by the Population Division of the United Nations Secretariat. [23] Many developing countries lack complete and reliable statistics of births and deaths based on civil registration, so various estimation techniques are used to calculate life expectancy using other sources of data, mainly population censuses and demographic surveys. Life expectancy at

4.13

Fewer women than men smoke but they are catching up in many countries and world-wide consumption is still increasing in most regions, especially Asia and the Pacific

Smoking among women is highest in Latin America and the Caribbean

Per capita consumption of cigarettes is highest in the developed regions

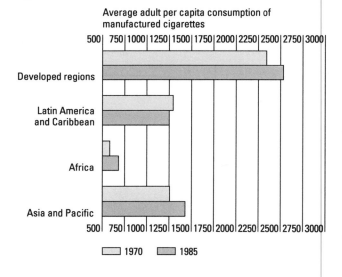

Average percentage of adults who smoke, 1980s

☐ Women   ☐ Men

A   Developed regions   C   Africa
B   Latin America   D   Asia and Pacific
      and Caribbean

Average adult per capita consumption of manufactured cigarettes

☐ 1970   ☐ 1985

Source: Prepared by the Statistical Office of the United Nations Secretariat from World Health Organization, "Tendances et effets du tabagisme dans le monde" by R. Masironi and K. Rothwell, *World Health Statistics Quarterly*, 41 (Geneva, 1988).

birth by sex gives a statistical summary of current differences in male and female mortality across all ages and the second column of table 5 shows the difference in years between female and male life expectancy. However, trends and differentials in infant and child mortality rates are the predominant influence on trends and differentials in life expectancy at birth in most developing countries. Thus, life expectancy at birth is of limited usefulness in these countries in assessing levels and differentials in male and female mortality at other ages.

Child mortality rates refer to the number of deaths each year per 1,000 boys or girls between the ages of one and five. These series have been compiled by the Statistical Office of the United Nations Secretariat for the *Demographic Yearbook* [10], by the Pan American Health Organization (unpublished) and by UNICEF and are subject to the limitations of national reporting in this field described in those sources.

The infant mortality rate is the number per 1,000 children born alive who die within one year of birth. This series is also taken from the estimates and projections of the Population Division of the United Nations Secretariat, based on a review of all available national sources. In most developing countries where civil registration data are deficient, the most reliable sources are demographic surveys of households. Where these are not available, other sources and general estimates are made which are necessarily of limited reliability. Where countries lack comprehensive and accurate systems of civil registration, infant mortality statistics by sex are difficult to collect or to estimate with any degree of reliability because of reporting biases, and thus are not shown here.

Table 5 includes four different indicators of maternal health and health services. Data on maternal mortality are compiled in the *Demographic Yearbook* [10] and by the World Health Organization (WHO) in a comprehensive review of available information up to 1986. [37] The maternal mortality rate is calculated on the basis of maternal deaths and live births for a given year and expressed per 100,000 live births. These statistics are based on national civil registration and demographic survey statistics on births and deaths computed by national statistical services. When official statistics are not available, other sources such as results of community surveys, evaluation studies and reports of consultants were utilized as deemed appropriate by WHO. Maternal deaths are defined as those caused by deliveries and complications of pregnancy, child-birth and the puerperium. However, the exact definition varies from case to case and is not always clear in the original source, particularly as regards the inclusion of abortion-related deaths. Furthermore, WHO observes that most maternal deaths go unregistered in areas where maternal mortality rates are highest.

The estimated total fertility rate is calculated as the average number of children that would be born to each women if the fertility patterns of a given period did not change. This measure gives the approximate total number of children an average women will bear in her lifetime, assuming no mortality. Estimates and projections of fertility are prepared every two years by the Population Division of the United Nations Secretariat. [23]

Data in table 5 on contraceptive use among currently married women aged 15–44 years have been compiled by the Population Division of the United Nations Secretariat from the results of national surveys associated with the World Fertility Survey and other surveys. Detailed information on the concepts and methods used in the collection of these statistics and the results are contained in a publication prepared by the Population Division. [16]

The percentage of births attended by trained personnel has been widely found to be a sensitive indicator in developing countries of access to maternal health services which are essential to the survival and health of mothers and infants. These data are compiled by WHO from a variety of national sources in connection with monitoring the global strategies for achieving health for all by the year 2000. [35]

Statistics on prevalence of smoking among adults have also been compiled by WHO, based on available national surveys. [40]

Notes

1   Stanley Henshaw, "Induced abortion: a world review, 1990", *Family Planning Perspectives,* March/April 1990; and Health Statistics Database of the World Health Organization. See also Jodi L. Jacobson, "The global politics of abortion", Worldwatch Paper 97 (Washington, D.C., Worldwatch Institute, 1990).

2   Judith S. McGuire and Barry M. Popkin, "Helping women improve nutrition in the developing world: beating the zero sum game", Technical Paper, No. 114 (Washington, D.C., World Bank, 1990); and *Special Challenges in Third World Women's Health—Presentations at the 117th Annual Meeting of the American Public Health Association, Chicago, Illinois, October 1989* (New York, International Women's Health Coalition, 1990).

3   Unpublished statistics compiled by United Nations Children's Fund from national reports of the Demographic and Health Surveys programme (DHS). See also Demographic and Health Surveys *Newsletter* (Columbia, Maryland).

4   Henshaw, loc. cit.

5   Nafis Sadik, *Investing in Women: The Focus of the '90s* (New York, United Nations Population Fund).

6   Based on Mead Over and Peter Piot, "HIV infection and other sexually transmitted diseases", in *Evolving Health Sector Priorities in Developing Countries,* Dean T. Jamison and W. Henry Mosley, eds. (Washington, D.C., World Bank, 1990).

7   Information compiled from national reports by the Division for the Advancement of Women, Centre for Social Development and Humanitarian Affairs, United Nations Secretariat (United Nations Office at Vienna).

8   United States Centers for Disease Control, "Reducing the health consequences of smoking: 25 years of progress: A report of the Surgeon General" (Atlanta, 1989).

9   Craig McKie, "Lifestyle risks: smoking and drinking in Canada", *Canadian Social Trends* (Ottawa, Statistics Canada), Spring 1987.

Table 5
Indicators on health and child-bearing

Country or area	Life expectancy (years) 1985/90 f	f minus m	F change, 1970 to 1990	Maternal (per 100t births)	Child (per 1000 aged 1–4) f	m	Infant (per 1000 births)	Total fertility rate (births per woman) 1970	1990	% women using con-traception	% trained attendant at birth	% of adults who smoke f	m
Developed regions													
Albania	74.2	5.0	6.8	..	..	..	39	5.1	3.0	..	..	..	..
Australia	79.5	6.6	5.2	5	0.5	0.6	8	2.9	1.9	..	99	30	37
Austria	77.8	7.2	4.4	7	0.5	0.6	11	2.5	1.5	71	..	22	33
Belgium	78.1	6.6	3.8	9	0.6	0.6	10	2.3	1.6	81	100	21	35
Bulgaria	75.0	5.8	1.9	25	..	..	16	2.2	1.9	76[a]	100	..	..
Canada	80.3	7.0	5.0	4	0.4	0.5	7	2.5	1.7	73	99	28	31
Czechoslovakia	75.0	7.5	1.6	8	0.4	0.5	15	2.1	2.0	95[a b]	100	14	57
Denmark	78.3	5.7	3.0	4	0.4	0.4	7	2.2	1.5	63[a]	100[a]	38	49
Finland	78.8	7.8	5.3	7	0.2	0.3	6	2.1	1.7	80[a]	100[a]	17	35
France	79.8	8.1	4.4	12	0.4	0.5	8	2.6	1.9	64[c]	..	26	49
Germany[d]													
Federal Rep. of Germany	78.2	6.6	4.8	8	0.4	0.5	9	2.3	1.4	78	100[a]	29	44
former German Dem. Rep.	76.2	5.8	2.2	17	0.5	0.7	9	2.3	1.7	..	99[a]	..	..
Greece	77.9	4.4	5.1	7	..	..	17	2.4	1.7	..	97[a]	13	54
Hungary	74.0	7.5	1.7	15	0.5	0.5	20	2.0	1.8	73	99	25	50
Iceland	80.4	5.6	4.1	..	0.1	0.2	5	3.2	2.1	..	100	..	..
Ireland	76.9	5.4	3.5	6[e]	0.4[e]	0.5[e]	9	3.9	2.5	..	..	32	39
Italy	79.1	6.7	5.2	9	0.6	0.6	11	2.5	1.5	78[a]	100[a]	18	46
Japan	81.1	5.7	7.2	14[f]	0.4[f]	0.6[f]	5	2.0	1.7	64	100	14	66
Luxembourg	77.7	6.7	4.5	..	0.4	1.2	10	2.2	1.5	..	99	..	..
Malta	74.6	3.6	3.2	36	..	..	10	2.2	1.9	..	98	..	..
Netherlands	80.2	6.7	3.8	8	0.4	0.5	8	2.7	1.5	72[c]	100[a]	33	41
New Zealand	77.9	6.1	3.5	14	0.6	0.5	11	3.2	1.9	70[a]	99	29	35
Norway	80.2	6.7	3.5	4	0.4	0.5	7	2.7	1.7	71[a]	100	32	42
Poland	75.5	8.0	2.5	13	0.5	0.7	18	2.3	2.2	75[a g]	100	29	63
Portugal	76.8	6.8	7.5	9	0.9	1.0	15	2.9	1.8	66	87[a]	10	37
Romania	73.0	5.5	2.8	149	..	..	22	3.1	2.2	58[a g]	99	13	48
Spain	79.7	6.1	5.4	11	..	..	10	2.9	1.7	59	96	27	58
Sweden	80.1	5.9	3.6	3	0.3	0.3	6	2.1	1.7	78	100	30	26
Switzerland	80.4	6.6	5.3	4	0.5	0.5	7	2.3	1.6	71	99[a]	29	46
USSR	74.2	9.2	0.7	48	..	..	24	2.4	2.4	..	100	11	48
United Kingdom	78.1	5.7	3.5	7[h]	0.4	0.4	9	2.5	1.8	83	98	32	36
United States	79.0	7.1	4.9	8	0.4	0.6	10	2.6	1.8	68	100	24	30
Yugoslavia	75.0	5.9	6.1	16	1.1	1.1	25	2.5	2.0	55[a g]	86[a]	10	57
Africa													
Algeria	64.1	3.1	11.6	140[i]	12.8[j]	12.5[j]	74	7.5	6.1	36	15	..	..
Angola	46.1	3.2	8.6	..	..	..	137	6.4	6.4	..	15	..	..
Benin	48.1	3.2	8.5	..	..	..	110	6.9	7.0	9	45	..	..
Botswana	61.5	6.0	11.0	200-300	..	..	67	6.9	6.3	33	77	..	..
Burkina Faso	48.9	3.3	8.1	810	..	..	138	6.7	6.5	..	30	..	..
Burundi	50.7	3.3	5.0	..	..	..	112	5.8	6.3	9	12[a]	..	..
Cameroon	53.0	4.0	8.0	300[i]	..	..	94	5.8	5.8	2[a]	10	..	..
Cape Verde	62.8	3.5	11.2	107	..	..	66	6.0	5.2	..	10	..	..
Central African Rep.	47.1	3.2	5.5	600	..	..	132	5.7	5.9	..	66	..	..
Chad	47.1	3.2	8.5	860[k]	..	..	132	6.1	5.9	..	24	..	..
Comoros	53.8	3.5	7.2	..	..	..	80	6.3	6.2	..	24	..	..
Congo	50.2	3.3	8.1	1000[k]	..	..	73	5.9	6.0	..	..	..	..
Côte d'Ivoire	54.2	3.4	9.6	..	..	..	96	7.4	7.4	3	20	1	24
Djibouti	48.7	3.3	8.1	..	..	..	122	6.6	6.6	..	73	..	..
Egypt	62.0	2.7	11.0	318	19.1[l]	15.6[l]	85	6.6	4.8	38	47	2	33
Equatorial Guinea	48.1	3.2	8.5	..	..	..	127	5.7	5.7	..	58	..	..
Ethiopia	42.6	3.2	2.1	..	..	..	154	6.7	6.2	..	10	3[a]	28[a]

Table 5. Indicators on health and child-bearing [*cont.*]

Country or area	Life expectancy (years) 1985/90 f	f minus m	F change, 1970 to 1990	Maternal (per 100t births)	Child (per 1000 aged 1–4) f	m	Infant (per 1000 births)	Total fertility rate (births per woman) 1970	1990	% women using contraception	% trained attendant at birth	% of adults who smoke f	m
Gabon	53.2	3.3	8.6	..	..	..	103	4.2	5.0	..	80	..	..
Gambia	44.6	3.2	8.1	..	..	..	143	6.5	6.4	..	85	..	..
Ghana	55.8	3.6	6.1	1000	..	..	90	6.8	6.4	13	40	1 [a]	50 [a]
Guinea	43.8	3.2	7.1	..	..	..	147	6.4	6.2	..	25	..	..
Guinea-Bissau	46.6	3.2	7.0	..	..	..	132	5.2	5.4	..	31 [a]	..	..
Kenya	60.5	4.0	10.0	170 [i]	..	..	72	8.1	8.1	27	28	..	..
Lesotho	60.5	9.0	10.5	..	..	..	100	5.7	5.8	5 [a]	40	..	..
Liberia	56.0	3.0	9.5	..	..	..	87	6.4	6.5	6	87	..	..
Libyan Arab Jamahiriya	62.5	3.4	..	80 [i]	..	..	82	..	6.9	..	76 [a]	..	..
Madagascar	55.0	3.0	9.8	240	..	..	120	6.6	6.6	..	62	..	..
Malawi	47.7	1.4	7.5	100 [m]	87.2 [i]	97.7 [i]	150	6.9	7.0	7 [c]	45	..	..
Mali	45.6	3.2	7.0	..	41.9 [l]	44.8 [l]	169	6.6	6.7	5	16	..	..
Mauritania	47.6	3.2	8.0	..	..	..	127	6.5	6.5	1	20	..	..
Mauritius	71.7	5.3	8.2	126	1.3	1.2	23	4.3	1.9	75	85	7	58
Morocco	62.5	3.4	10.7	300 [n]	..	..	82	7.1	4.8	36	29	..	..
Mozambique	48.1	3.2	5.5	..	..	..	141	6.5	6.4	..	28	..	..
Namibia	57.5	2.5	10.0	..	..	..	106	6.1	6.1	..	..	..	..
Niger	46.1	3.2	7.0	420	..	..	135	7.1	7.1	..	47	..	..
Nigeria	52.2	3.4	8.1	800	..	..	105	7.1	7.0	6 [o]	40	3	53
Reunion	75.5	8.5	11.4	..	..	..	14	4.8	2.4	..	..	..	..
Rwanda	50.2	3.3	4.5	210 [p]	..	..	122	8.0	8.3	10	22	..	..
Sao Tome and Principe	..	..	..	..	..	..	..	..	..	..	88	..	..
Senegal	47.4	3.2	7.1	600	..	..	128	6.7	6.4	11	50 [a]	35	43
Seychelles	74.1 [q]	8.8 [q]	6.1	..	..	..	..	6.1	3.3	..	99	..	..
Sierra Leone	42.6	3.2	7.6	450	..	..	154	6.4	6.5	..	25	..	..
Somalia	46.6	3.2	6.0	1100	..	..	132	6.6	6.6	..	2	..	..
South Africa	63.5	6.0	9.0	83 [r]	..	..	72	5.9	4.5	48	..	..	..
Sudan	51.0	2.4	8.9	660	..	..	108	6.7	6.4	5 [a s]	60	..	..
Swaziland	57.3	3.6	10.8	..	..	..	118	6.5	6.5	..	50	72	80
Togo	54.8	3.5	10.2	..	..	..	94	6.2	6.1	34	..	..	..
Tunisia	66.1	1.5	13.5	310 [k]	..	..	59	6.8	4.1	50	68	6	60
Uganda	52.7	3.3	5.1	300	..	..	103	6.9	6.9	5	20-30 [a]	..	33
United Rep. Tanzania	54.7	3.4	9.0	340 [t]	..	..	106	6.9	7.1	..	60	..	..
Western Sahara	..	..	..	..	..	..	..	..	..	..	..	..	..
Zaire	54.2	3.4	8.6	..	..	..	98	6.0	6.1	..	..	..	..
Zambia	54.5	2.1	7.6	151	..	..	80	6.7	7.2	..	..	7	39
Zimbabwe	60.1	3.6	9.4	480 [n]	..	..	72	7.5	5.8	43	69	..	..

Latin America and Caribbean

Antigua and Barbuda	..	..	..	..	1.3 [n]	2.1 [n]	..	..	..	39	83	..	..
Argentina	74.0	6.7	4.7	60	1.3	1.6	32	3.1	3.0	..	87 [a]	18	58
Bahamas	..	..	..	18	..	..	..	3.5	2.5	..	99	..	..
Barbados	77.0	6.0	6.9	71	0.5	0.9	11	3.5	2.0	47	98	..	10
Belize	..	..	..	..	2.2	2.3	..	6.3	..	..	73 [a]	..	..
Bolivia	55.4	4.5	8.1	480	7.8 [l]	8.7 [l]	110	6.6	6.1	26	47 [a]	61	84
Brazil	67.6	5.3	7.7	120	..	..	63	5.3	3.5	66	83	53	59
Chile	75.1	7.0	11.3	50	..	..	20	4.4	2.7	..	98	18	52
Colombia	67.2	4.6	6.5	110	4.5	4.8	46	6.0	3.6	65	51	31	57
Costa Rica	77.0	4.6	9.5	24	0.7	0.8	18	5.8	3.3	70	93	..	..
Cuba	75.8	3.6	5.5	47	0.7	0.8	15	4.3	1.7	..	99	..	..
Dominica	..	..	..	..	0.3	0.5	..	..	..	49	96	..	..
Dominican Republic	68.1	4.2	9.4	74	2.9	3.2	65	6.7	3.8	50	98	..	..
Ecuador	67.6	4.2	9.4	160 [u]	3.3 [u]	3.5 [u]	63	6.7	4.7	44	27	..	..
El Salvador	66.5	8.5	8.7	70	2.7	2.9	59	6.6	4.9	47	35	..	..

Table 5. Indicators on health and child-bearing [*cont.*]

Country or area	Life expectancy (years) 1985/90 f	f minus m	F change, 1970 to 1990	Maternal (per 100t births)	Child (per 1000 aged 1–4) f	m	Infant (per 1000 births)	Total fertility rate (births per woman) 1970	1990	% women using contraception	% trained attendant at birth	% of adults who smoke f	m
French Guiana	..	..	..	..	0.5	1.4	..	3.8	..	..	..	..	..
Grenada	..	..	..	..	1.6	1.4	..	..	..	31	81	..	..
Guadeloupe	76.7	6.6	8.2	..	..	..	12	5.2	2.2	44 [a]	..	..	..
Guatemala	64.4	4.7	13.1	76	..	..	59	6.6	5.8	23	34	10	36
Guyana	72.3	5.0	7.6	..	1.7	2.1	30	5.3	2.8	31 [a]	93	4	48
Haiti	56.4	3.3	8.8	230	..	..	117	6.2	4.7	7	40	..	..
Honduras	66.1	4.2	13.4	50	2.9	2.8	69	7.4	5.6	35	50	..	..
Jamaica	76.7	5.4	8.6	110	1.5	1.4	18	5.4	2.9	51 [v]	89	..	..
Martinique	76.5	4.5	7.9	..	0.5	0.3	13	5.0	2.1	51 [a]	..	..	..
Mexico	72.3	6.6	10.1	91	2.3	2.3	47	6.7	3.6	53	94	44	47
Netherlands Antilles	..	..	..	..	..	..	..	3.1	..	..	..	..	..
Nicaragua	64.6	2.6	11.8	47	3.3 [n]	3.4 [n]	62	7.1	5.5	27	..	..	..
Panama	74.1	4.0	8.6	57	1.5	1.6	23	5.6	3.1	58 [v]	89	..	..
Paraguay	69.1	4.3	2.1	365	3.2	3.3	42	6.4	4.6	45	22	..	..
Peru	63.4	3.9	10.4	89 [w]	5.7 [w]	5.6 [w]	88	6.6	4.5	46	44	7 [a]	34 [a]
Puerto Rico	78.4	6.9	4.9	13	0.4	0.7	15	3.4	2.4	70	..	..	..
St. Kitts and Nevis	..	..	..	..	2.1	0.5	..	..	..	41	97	..	..
St. Lucia	74.8 [q]	6.8 [q]	..	..	1.6	1.6	..	..	3.8	43	98	..	..
St. Vincent/Grenadines	..	..	..	..	0.7	1.3	..	..	..	42	73	..	..
Suriname	72.1	5.0	6.4	82	2.2	2.0	31	5.9	3.0	..	80	..	..
Trinidad and Tobago	72.8	5.1	5.1	54	1.1	1.1	20	3.9	2.7	53	98	5	35
Uruguay	74.4	6.6	2.5	43	0.7	0.9	27	2.8	2.6	..	96 [a]	45	45
US Virgin Islands	..	..	..	..	0.6	0.8	..	5.3	..	..	..	..	..
Venezuela	72.8	6.1	6.7	59 [w]	..	..	36	5.9	3.8	49 [a]	82	67	69

Asia and Pacific

Country or area	1985/90 f	f minus m	F change, 1970 to 1990	Maternal (per 100t births)	Child f	m	Infant (per 1000 births)	1970	1990	% women using contraception	% trained attendant at birth	f	m
Afghanistan	42.0	1.0	6.0	690 [n]	25.8 [x]	28.9 [x]	172	7.1	6.9	..	8	..	..
Bahrain	72.9	4.3	10.9	19	..	..	26	7.0	4.1	..	98	..	..
Bangladesh	50.4	-0.7	7.9	600	25.3 [y]	22.4 [y]	119	6.9	5.5	25	5	20	70
Bhutan	47.1	-1.5	7.2	1710	..	..	128	5.9	5.5	..	7	..	..
Brunei Darussalam	72.7 [q]	2.6 [q]	10.6	..	..	..	..	6.0	3.5	..	100	..	..
Cambodia	49.9	2.9	3.0	..	..	..	130	6.2	4.7	..	100	..	..
China	70.9	2.9	10.5	44	..	..	32	6.0	2.4	74	..	8	62
Cyprus	78.2	4.9	6.2	..	..	..	12	2.8	2.3	..	100	..	..
East Timor	43.4	1.8	5.3	..	..	..	166	6.2	5.4	..	..	..	..
Fiji	72.7	4.5	8.5	41	1.2	1.8	27	4.6	3.2	..	98	44 [z]	76 [z]
French Polynesia	..	..	..	..	..	..	..	..	..	..	100	46 [aa]	50 [aa]
Guam	..	..	..	31	..	..	..	4.8	..	..	100	..	..
Hong Kong	79.1	5.7	5.6	3 [bb]	0.4 [bb]	0.5 [bb]	8	4.0	1.7	81	92	4	33
India	57.9	0.1	10.6	340	..	..	99	5.7	4.3	34	33	3	52
Indonesia	57.4	2.8	11.3	450	..	..	84	5.6	3.3	48	31	5	75
Iran (Islamic Rep. of)	65.5	0.5	12.6	..	..	..	63	7.0	5.6	..	..	..	..
Iraq	64.8	1.8	10.9	..	1.9 [i]	2.2 [i]	69	7.2	6.4	..	60	6	45
Israel	77.2	3.6	4.8	8 [cc]	0.6 [cc]	0.5 [cc]	12	3.8	2.9	..	99	25	38
Jordan	67.8	3.6	14.6	..	2.0 [dd]	2.4 [dd]	44	8.0	7.2	27 [v]	75	..	..
Kiribati	..	..	..	..	..	..	..	..	..	..	..	70	85
Korea, D. People's R.	72.7	6.5	13.3	41	..	..	24	5.7	3.6	..	100	..	..
Korea, Republic of	72.5	6.3	13.1	14	1.9	2.0	25	4.5	2.0	70	70	7	69
Kuwait	75.0	4.3	8.6	4	0.7	1.0	19	7.5	4.8	..	99	12	52
Lao People's Dem. Rep.	50.0	3.0	8.2	2	..	..	110	6.2	5.7	..	15 [a]	..	..
Lebanon	69.0	3.9	4.2	..	..	..	40	6.1	3.4	..	45 [a]	..	..
Macau	..	..	..	40	..	..	..	2.0	..	..	..	..	..
Malaysia	71.6	4.1	10.6	59	1.4	1.5	24	5.9	3.5	51	82	4	41
Maldives	49 [q]	-3.9 [q]	..	..	..	..	..	..	..	..	61	..	..
Mongolia	65.6	4.1	5.8	100	..	..	45	5.9	5.4	..	100	..	..

Table 5. Indicators on health and child-bearing [*cont.*]

Country or area	Life expectancy (years) 1985/90 f	f minus m	F change, 1970 to 1990	Mortality rates, 1980/90 Maternal (per 100t births)	Child (per 1000 aged 1–4) f	m	Infant (per 1000 births)	Fertility, attended births Total fertility rate (births per woman) 1970	1990	% women using con- traception	% trained attendant at birth	Smoking % of adults who smoke f	m
Myanmar	61.8	3.5	10.8	135	..	..	70	5.7	4.0	..	25	..	..
Nepal	50.3	-1.2	9.8	830	..	..	128	6.2	5.9	14	6	58	79
New Caledonia	..	..	..	160	..	..	..	..	..	..	..	22ᵃ	58ᵃ
Oman	56.8	2.7	11.9	..	..	..	100	7.2	7.2	..	60	..	..
Pacific Islands	..	..	..	..	..	..	..	5.7	..	..	..	..	..
Pakistan	56.5	0.0	11.0	400-600	15.8ˡ	12.5ˡ	109	7.0	6.5	8	24ᵃ	6	44
Papua New Guinea	54.8	1.6	9.9	900	..	..	59	6.2	5.7	..	34	80	85
Philippines	65.4	3.8	7.6	93	6.1	7.0	45	6.0	4.3	45	57	..	78
Qatar	71.8	4.9	11.0	..	..	..	31	7.0	5.6	..	90	..	..
Samoa	..	..	..	40	..	..	..	5.8	..	..	95	..	..
Saudi Arabia	65.2	3.5	13.9	..	..	..	71	7.3	7.2	..	74	..	..
Singapore	75.7	5.5	5.7	13	0.4	0.5	9	3.5	1.7	74	100	3	35
Solomon Islands	..	..	..	10	..	..	..	..	..	..	80	..	..
Sri Lanka	72.5	4.2	7.5	60	..	..	33	4.7	2.7	62ᵉᵉ	87	2	48
Syrian Arab Republic	66.9	3.7	11.4	280	2.9ᶠᶠ	2.8ᶠᶠ	48	7.8	6.8	20ᵃ	37ᵃ	..	..
Thailand	67.1	4.1	8.2	81	..	..	39	6.1	2.6	68	33	13	59
Tonga	..	..	..	..	..	..	..	..	..	..	60	38	62
Turkey	65.8	3.3	9.3	210	..	..	76	5.6	3.6	51	70	50	50
United Arab Emirates	72.9	4.3	12.1	..	..	..	26	6.8	4.8	..	96	..	..
Vanuatu	..	..	..	107	..	..	..	..	..	..	86	..	..
Viet Nam	63.6	4.4	13.4	140	..	..	64	5.9	4.1	..	100	2	38
Yemen	52.4	2.9	10.6	..	..	..	117	7.0	6.9	1ᵃ ᵍᵍ	12	..	..

Sources:
Demographic Yearbook (United Nations publication, various years); *Levels and Trends of Contraceptive Use as Assessed in 1988,* Population Studies No. 110 (United Nations publication, Sales No. E.89.XIII.4); *World Population Prospects 1988,* Population Studies No. 106 (United Nations publication, Sales No. E.88.XIII.7);United Nations Children's Fund, *The State of the World's Children 1990* (New York, 1990);World Health Organization,"Maternal mortality rates: a tabulation of available information (second edition)" (Geneva, FHE/86.3) and "Coverage of maternity care: a tabulation of available information (second edition)" (Geneva, WHO/FHE/89.2); R. Masironi and K. Rothwell "Tendances et effets du tabagisme dans le monde", *World Health Statistics Quarterly,* 41 (Geneva,1988);and unpublished data from Pan American Health Organization.

a   Data refer to 1970s.
b   Past or current use (percentage naming a method "normally" or most often" used).
c   Including unmarried women.
d   Through the accession of the German Democratic Republic to the Federal Republic of Germany with effect from 3 October 1990, the two German States have united to form one sovereign State. As from the date of unifi- cation, the Federal Republic of Germany acts in the United Nations under the designation "Germany". All data shown for Germany pertain to end- June 1990 or earlier and are indicated separately for the Federal Republic of Germany and the former German Democratic Republic.
e   Deaths registered within one year of occurrence.
f   For Japanese nationals in Japan only.
g   Excluding sterilization.
h   England and Wales only.
i   1977/78.

j   For Algerian population only.
k   1970/72.
l   1976.
m   All health institutions.
n   1974/75.
o   Ondo state only.
p   All hospitals.
q   1981/86.
r   From 267 hospitals.
s   North Sudan.
t   From 48 hospitals.
u   Excluding nomadic Indian tribes.
v   Excluding abstinence, douche and folk methods.
w   Excluding Indian jungle population.
x   1979.
y   Based on life tables calculated by the United Nations Population Division ("Age structure of mortality in developing countries", ST/ESA/SER.R /66).
z   Melanesian population only.
aa   Maori population only.
bb   Excluding Vietnamese refugees.
cc   Including data for East Jerusalem and Israeli residents in certain other territories under occupation by Israeli military forces since June 1967.
dd   1979. Excluding data for Jordanian territory under occupation since June 1967 by Israeli military forces.
ee   Excluding several northern and eastern areas containing roughly 15 per cent of the population.
ff   Excluding deaths for which cause is unknown.
gg   Data refer to the former Yemen Arab Republic only.

5
Housing, human settlements and the environment

Women in developing regions face extra hardships and burdens unknown to women in developed regions, who can take for granted their access to safe water, sanitation and electricity.

In most developing regions, women in rural areas live in serious deprivation. Urban women have better (though still very limited) access to housing, schools, transport, safe water, sanitation, fuel and electricity.

All countries in the developing regions are experiencing rapid urban growth, but women in Latin America and the Caribbean have much better opportunities from urbanization than their counterparts in Africa and Asia.

Environmental degradation, a product of economic forces directed mainly by men, creates new problems for women. Especially in rural areas, pollution threatens their health and the health of their children, clean water is difficult to find, and fuel for cooking and heating is scarce.

Human settlements

During the past two decades the number and proportion of people in cities and towns has increased greatly all over the world, but the proportion urban and rates of change have varied considerably from one region to another (chart 5.2).

Women, like men, are attracted to towns and cities because of the perceived opportunities. In developed regions, women outnumber men in urban areas by 107 to 100, but the number of rural women is about equal to the number of rural men. In Latin America and the Caribbean, women outnumber men in urban areas by 108 to 100, but are outnumbered by men in rural areas 94 to 100. In Africa, there are many fewer women than men in urban areas (95:100) and more women than men in rural areas (105:100). In Asia and the Pacific, too, there are fewer women than men in urban areas (91:100), but women are also outnumbered in rural areas (95:100). [6]

Urban women and rural women

Over the past 20 years the population of urban women worldwide increased 71 per cent and rural women only 23 per cent. Overall, rural populations are growing only in Africa and Asia and the Pacific (list 5.1 and chart 5.3).

The largest increases in the proportions of women urban were in Oceania (from 18 to 47 per cent), western Asia (from 42 to 60 per cent), northern Africa (from 37 to 52 per cent) and Latin America and the Caribbean (from 59 to 73 per cent) (chart 5.2).

In 1990 urban women outnumbered rural women by about three to one in the developed regions and in Latin America and the Caribbean. In northern Africa, western Asia and Oceania, the ratio was about even. But in sub-Saharan Africa and eastern, south-eastern and southern Asia, there were more than twice as many rural women as urban women (chart 5.2). By far the largest numbers of rural women today are in Africa and Asia and the Pacific—these two regions account for about 85 per cent of the world's rural women.

Urban and rural areas and urbanization

The definition of urban areas in population censuses and surveys is usually based on size of locality (that is, number of inhabitants of the city, town or village). Definitions vary considerably among countries but commonly consider localities larger than, say, 1,000–2,000 inhabitants as urban areas. Rural areas consist of all other areas. Urbanization does not refer simply to the growth of population in urban areas, but more broadly to the increase in the proportion (or percentage) of a country's population living in urban areas.

5.1
Where rural population is still growing more than 2 per cent per year
Percentage increase in rural population per year, 1985–1990

Africa
Northern Africa
Algeria (2.4)
Sudan (2.6)
Sub-Saharan Africa
Botswana (2.4)
Burkina Faso (2.4)
Burundi (2.5)
Comoros (2.5)
Côte d'Ivoire (2.5)
Gambia (2.2)
Ghana (2.7)
Kenya (3.3)
Lesotho (2.0)
Madagascar (2.3)
Malawi (2.7)
Mali (2.7)
Niger (2.2)
Nigeria (2.2)
Rwanda (3.1)
Senegal (2.0)
Somalia (2.2)
Togo (2.2)
Uganda (3.3)
Zaire (2.3)
Zimbabwe (2.4)

Latin America and Caribbean
Guatemala (2.2)

Asia and Pacific
Southern Asia
Bangladesh (2.3)
Bhutan (2.0)
Iran (Islamic Rep. of) (2.2)
Nepal (2.1)
Pakistan (2.9)
Western Asia
Bahrain (2.3)
Oman (3.0)
Syrian Arab Republic (2.6)
United Arab Emirates (3.3)
Eastern and south-eastern Asia and Oceania
Cambodia (2.3)
Mongolia (2.9)
Papua New Guinea (2.3)

Source: Population Division of the United Nations Secretariat.

Problems of growth and housing

Latin America and the Caribbean have the largest proportion of urban dwellers in the developing world—73 per cent of the people there live in towns and cities. And more of them are women than men. The growth of mega-cities in this region poses acute problems for city planners and managers as services are outstripped and slums and squatter settlements proliferate. In Asia and the Pacific, where the number of urban women doubled from 1970 to 1990, the challenge of housing an increasing number of poor people, many of them women, is equally daunting. Seven of the world's ten largest cities are in the developing regions and are growing at the rate of nearly 3 per cent per year. [19]

5.2
The pace of urbanization everywhere is rapid

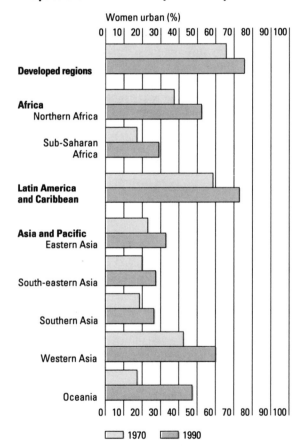

Note: Based on total populations of women and women in urban areas in each region.

Source: *Age and Sex Structure of Urban and Rural Populations, 1970–2000: The 1980 Assessment* (United Nations publication, ESA/P/WP.81).

5.3
Rural populations are still growing in Africa and Asia

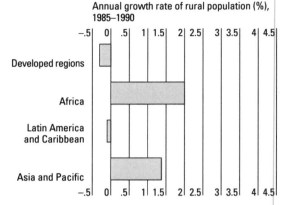

Note: Based on growth of total population of women in rural areas in each region.

Source: *Prospects of World Urbanization 1988*, Population Studies No. 112 (United Nations publication, Sales No. E.88.XIII.8).

One major problem for urban women is housing. Laws in such countries as Kenya and Tanzania prevent women from owning a home. They are often denied access to loans and other forms of credit and are last on the list for housing schemes. That forces them into substandard housing and unhealthy living environments for raising their children.[1]

Urban growth and rural women

Urban growth also places stress on women left in rural areas. The migration of men leaves them with total responsibility for themselves and their dependents. And it leaves them with fewer resources to meet those responsibilities—especially when the land has been depleted. In Kenya more than two fifths of rural households are now headed by women, and the size of the average family plot has halved since 1969. Around 60,000 men leave drought-ridden Burkina Faso each year to find work in neighbouring Côte d'Ivoire, and two thirds do not return.[2] As a result, rural women's burdens continue to increase. Male and female migration to the cities leaves many elderly people behind, most of them women and most of them with very few resources.

Migration

Rural-to-urban migration

Over the past two decades, women have increasingly moved to new homes in rural areas, urban areas and different countries, temporarily or permanently. Migrant women are vulnerable because they leave family and social networks and bring along few skills and resources. They also face physical hardships and dangers—as well as serious adjustment problems—because of their religion, language and nationality.

Women migrants have greater economic opportunities in cities, but remain poor and are denied decent living conditions. In developing regions, over 70 per cent of the migrants to urban areas are under the age of 25 and 40 per cent are under 15. Girls under 15 make up a majority of female migrants in many Latin American countries, in some African countries, for example Ghana and Morocco, and Asian countries, for example Bangladesh, the Islamic Republic of Iran and Syria. [24] In India only 4 per cent of the women migrate for employment reasons, 47 per cent because of marriage.[3]

Women who remain in rural areas but whose husbands migrate to urban areas find themselves with even more family and economic responsibilities. A few receive remittances, but most do not, making them widows in all but name. In Lesotho, where 45 per cent of rural households were headed by women in 1980, one survey found that fewer than half those women received any money at all from their absent men.[4] Research in Pakistan and India showed that migrant men sent remittances to their fathers—to pay debts or buy land—rather than to their wives.[5]

Rural-to-urban migration has been predominantly male in Africa and in Asia and the Pacific and predominantly female in the developed regions and in Latin America and the Caribbean (chart 5.4). In Uruguay and the United States in the 1970s, for example, at least three times as many women moved to towns and cities as men. [24]

International migration

International migration by women has not received much attention and little is known about its extent or character. The incompleteness of the information fosters the view that the typical migrant is a young, economically motivated man.

According to data from population censuses taken since 1970, 48 per cent of the 77 million foreign-born persons counted were women, so the overall sex disparity is relatively small. Women were more numerous than men among foreign-born migrants in more than a quarter of the 157 countries or areas considered, including the United States of America, which hosts the largest number of international migrants. In three-quarters of the countries considered, women accounted for at least 44 per cent of all foreign-born persons. [22]

In most countries of Africa and Asia and the Pacific, male migrants have tended to outnumber female migrants. In the Americas, however, the situation was more balanced, with half the countries having at least as many female migrants as male. Only in Europe did women predominate over men among migrants in most countries.

Women's participation in flows of short-term migrant workers is increasing. During the 1980s, growing numbers of women from southern and south-eastern Asia migrated—mainly to Japan, Hong Kong, Singapore and western Asia—to work in household and entertainment services.[6]

Migration

Long-term migrants are generally defined as persons who move their place of residence with the intention of staying at least one year. Very limited data are available directly on age and sex of international or internal migrants (such as migrants from rural to urban areas). Some limited conclusions on the relative magnitudes of female and male migration can be inferred from differential female-to-male sex ratios in urban and rural areas and foreign-born populations.

5.4

Many more women than men migrate to urban areas in the developed regions and Latin America and the Caribbean

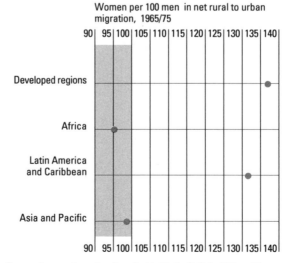

Women per 100 men in net rural to urban migration, 1965/75

Source: Averages for each region calculated by the Statistical Office of the United Nations Secretariat from *World Population Trends and Policies, 1987 Monitoring Report*, Population Studies No. 103 (United Nations publication, Sales no. E.88.XIII.3).

Access to safe water, sanitation facilities and electricity

Access to safe drinking water as defined by the World Health Organization refers to safe drinking water available in the home or within 15 minutes walking distance. Safe water supply includes treated surface waters and untreated but uncontaminated water from protected sources.

Access to adequate sanitation facilities refers to facilities for hygienic waste disposal in the home or immediate vicinity. Facilities are considered adequate if they effectively prevent contact with and access to excreta by humans, animals and insects. WHO uses a variety of national sources and methods of estimation for these series, including population and housing censuses, household surveys and special surveys.

Access to electricity is based on percentage of housing units with electric lighting, as enumerated in national population and housing censuses.

Refugee women

Women and children make up an estimated 70 to 80 per cent of the world's 14 million refugees—of the 6.8 million in Asia, 55,000 in Oceania, 4.6 million in Africa, 1.2 million in Latin America and the Caribbean, 1.4 million in northern America and 745,000 in Europe. Most of the refugees come from developing areas—including Afghanistan, Bangladesh, the Islamic Republic of Iran and Sri Lanka in southern Asia; Cambodia, China, Lao People's Democratic Republic and Viet Nam in eastern and south-eastern Asia; Iraq and Yemen in western Asia; the Sudan and Western Sahara in northern Africa; Angola, Burundi, Ethiopia, Liberia, Mozambique, Rwanda, Somalia and Zaire in sub-Saharan Africa; and El Salvador, Guatemala and Nicaragua in Latin America.[7]

Refugee women are particularly vulnerable during their flight. If they flee because of sex discrimination, they often have trouble establishing refugee status. They usually are not participants in the administration of camps and other refugee assistance programmes. A high proportion of refugee households are headed by women who have no secure source of income.

Water, sanitation and electricity [7, 36]

By the late 1960s urban and rural people in the developed regions had universal access to safe water and sanitation facilities. But even today, developing regions still have a long way to go to catch up with the developed regions in the quality of basic services and infrastructure (chart 5.5). During the early 1980s, 70 per cent of Africa's rural population still lacked access to safe water, and more than 90 per cent in at least seven countries. In Latin America and the Caribbean, nearly 60 per cent of rural populations lacked access to safe water, and in Asia and the Pacific, 50 per cent.

Safe water was more widely available in urban areas, except in Africa where 33 per cent of the population still lacks adequate access.

Sanitation is even worse. During the early 1980s in Africa, close to 80 per cent of the people in rural areas and 50 per cent in urban areas lacked adequate sanitation facilities—and in Latin America and the Caribbean and Asia and the Pacific, 60 per cent in rural areas and nearly 30 per cent in urban.

Electricity was available to nearly all urban and rural households in the developed regions by

5.5

In developing regions, access to safe water, adequate sanitation and electricity is very limited in rural areas

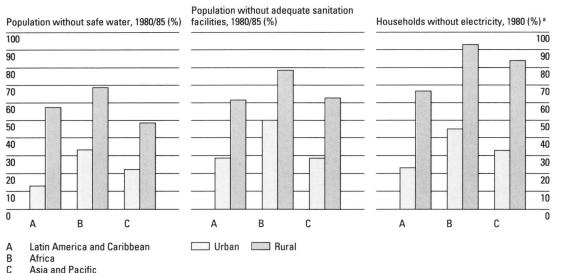

A Latin America and Caribbean
B Africa
C Asia and Pacific

Source: Compiled by the Statistical Office of the United Nations Secretariat from Statistical Office and WHO databases.

a   Averages based on a small number of countries or areas in each region.

the 1970s. But by the early 1980s, a quarter of the urban households in Latin America and the Caribbean, a third in Asia and the Pacific and a half in Africa had no access to electricity. Only about a third of the rural households had such access in Latin America and the Caribbean, a sixth in Asia and the Pacific and less than a tenth in Africa.

The environment[8]

Women are direct consumers of basic natural resources in most developing countries, because they are the primary providers of household water, food and fuel for cooking and heating. Indoor water, sanitation, electricity and heating are taken for granted in most countries in the developed regions. By contrast in developing regions women spend a considerable amount of time providing fuel, water, and basic amenities for their families. How much time? Small-scale studies in Asia and Africa indicate that women and girls spend on average 5 to 17 hours per week collecting and carrying water (table 5.6). And fragmentary data from small surveys show that women spend 7.5 hours a week collecting fuel in India, 2.5 hours a week in Nepal and Bangladesh, and about an hour a week in Guatemala, Indonesia and Burkina Faso.[9]

In most regions (both developed and developing), women constitute 40–90 per cent of unpaid labour in family enterprises, mostly agricultural (table 9). And in developing regions, women and girls have a greater role in subsistence agriculture than men—in fact some studies show that they produce most of the food consumed in rural areas.

But women rarely have any say in major decisions and practices that directly affect their environment and their resource needs. Many development projects exploit raw materials for export or produce cash crops, also for export. These activities ignore long-term effects on natural resources and the people who depend on those resources. Women and their families have been deeply affected by projects that have depleted the resource bases on which many of their productive activities depend (subsistence agriculture, food processing and so forth).[10]

5.6

Women in many developing regions must spend hours each week drawing and carrying water

	Hours per week
Africa	
Botswana, rural areas	5.5
Burkina Faso, Zimtenga region	4.4
Côte d'Ivoire, rural farmers	4.4
Ghana, northern farms	4.5
Kenya, villages	
dry season	4.2
wet season	2.2
Mozambique, villages	
dry season	15.3
wet season	2.9
Senegal, farming village	17.5
Asia	
India, Baroda region	7.0
Nepal, villages	
aged 5–9 years	1.5
aged 10–14 years	4.9
aged 15+ years	4.7
Pakistan, village survey	3.5

Source: Compiled by the Statistical Office of the United Nations Secretariat from local survey studies and reports.

Programmes aimed at protecting the environment have also ignored women's interests—and their exposure to pollution. Because of their childbearing role, women are even more physiologically sensitive to environmental pollutants than men. Because of their daily responsibilities, women are exposed to other health threats. Smoke emitted from burning fuelwood, charcoal, crop residues or dung causes serious eye and respiratory diseases. One study in India estimated that while women were cooking they were inhaling as much of the carcinogen, benzopyrene, as if they smoked 20 packs of cigarettes a day.[11]

Women in developed and developing regions have been active grass-roots participants in environmental movements. And planners are finally recognizing women's intuitive knowledge of the environment, and have begun addressing their concern for environmental protection. Investment in water supplies is a good way to give women the means to contribute more productively to development. For example, rural Mexican women participating in a UNIFEM project decided to use a loan fund to purchase a community water pump. The pump revolutionized their lives so greatly that they embarked on a project to manufacture and distribute the pumps at a factory their association built on land donated by the government.[12]

Indicators

Table 6 presents selected statistics on urban and rural population and basic household facilities available to them.

Data on urban and rural population are compiled by the Statistical Office of the United Nations Secretariat for the *Demographic Yearbook* from reports of national statistical services. Data are generally obtained from nation-wide population censuses or are estimates based on the results of sample surveys. International estimates of urban and rural population are prepared by the Population Division of the United Nations Secretariat.

Urban-rural classification of population follows the national census definition and varies from one country or area to another. National definitions are usually based on criteria that may include any of the following: size of population in a locality, population density, distance between built-up areas, predominant type of economic activity, legal or administrative boundaries and urban characteristics such as specific services and facilities.

The main source of data for percentage of women living in urban areas and females per 100 males in rural and in urban areas is the *Demographic Yearbook,* [10] supplemented by estimates of urban and rural population by sex made by the Population Division of the United Nations Secretariat. [6] The computation of annual growth rate is described in the notes for table 1.

Rural to urban migration is a key population movement that is of major interest to urban planners and national administrators and policy makers. Net rural-urban migration is commonly estimated indirectly through an application of the census survival ratio technique. Employing this technique, the Population Division of the United Nations Secretariat has estimated net rural-urban migration, for males and females separately, for countries which have had at least two censuses between 1960 and 1982. [24]

Statistics on population without access to safe water and adequate sanitation facilities are compiled by the World Health Organization in connection with the International Drinking Water Supply and Sanitation Decade and implementation of the Global Strategy for Health for All by the Year 2000 and issued in [36]. WHO uses a variety of national sources for these series, including population and housing censuses, household surveys and special surveys and estimates.

The series on percentage of housing units without electricity is based on national housing census results compiled by the Statistical Office of the United Nations Secretariat and issued in [6]. In the United Nations housing census recommendations, a housing unit is defined as a separate and independent place of abode basically intended for habitation by one household. Housing units without electricity refer to housing units with no electric lighting.

Notes

1. *Engendering Adjustment for the 1980s: Report of the Commonwealth Expert Group on Women and Structural Adjustment* (London, Commonwealth Secretariat Publications, 1989).

2. Nafis Sadik, *Investing in Women: The Focus of the '90s* (New York, United Nations Population Fund).

3. *State of India's Urbanisation* (New Delhi, National Institute of Urban Affairs, 1988).

4. *Investing in Women....*

5. Ibid.

6. Population Division of the United Nations Secretariat, "Measuring the extent of female international migration", paper presented at the United Nations Expert Group Meeting on International Migration Policies and the Status of Female Migrants", San Miniato, Italy, 27–30 March 1990 (IESA/P/AC.31/2); "World Migrant Populations: The Foreign-born" (wall chart) (United Nations publication, Sales No. E.89.XIII.7A); and unpublished data.

7. Information compiled by the Division for the Advancement of Women, Centre for Social Development and Humanitarian Affairs, United Nations Secretariat (United Nations Office at Vienna), based on reports of the United Nations High Commissioner for Refugees.

8. This section was prepared with the assistance of the Interregional Project for the Promotion of Women in Water and Environmental Sanitation Services (PROWWESS) of the United Nations Development Programme.

9. Information compiled by the Statistical Office of the United Nations Secretariat from national reports. See "Sources of statistics on time use", following table 8.

10. *Adjustment with a Human Face,* vol. I, *Protecting the Vulnerable and Promoting Growth: A Study by UNICEF,* G.A. Cornia, Richard Jolly and Frances Stewart, eds. (Oxford and New York, Oxford University Press, 1987).

11. "Biomass fuel combustion and health" (Geneva, World Health Organization, 1984).

12. *Strength in Adversity: Women in the Developing World; Report on the United Nations Development Fund for Women 1988–1989* (New York, United Nations Development Fund for Women).

Table 6
Indicators on housing, human settlements and environment

| Country or area | Urban and rural population | | | | | | | Safe water, sanitary facilities and electricity, 1980/85 | | | | | |
| | % of women living in urban areas | | Annual change in population, 1985-1990 (%) | | Females per 100 males, latest year | | F/100 M, rural-urb migration | Population without safe water (%) | | Population without adequate sanitation (%) | | Households without electricity (%) | |
	1970	latest	Urban	Rural	Urban	Rural	1965/75	Urban	Rural	Urban	Rural	Urban	Rural
Developed regions													
Albania	..	35	2.6	1.4	96	93	..	..	..	..	..	..	..
Australia	87	87	1.2	1.2	103	89	90	..	..	..	..	..	..
Austria	53	56	0.5	-0.8	117	105	117	..	..	..	..	..	..
Belgium	..	95 [a]	0.2	-3.7	105 [a]	99 [a]	..	..	..	..	..	..	..
Bulgaria	..	65	1.2	-2.3	101	102	107	..	..	..	..	..	..
Canada	77	77	1.0	0.4	106	94	..	..	..	..	..	..	..
Czechoslovakia	56	66	1.1	-1.7	107	103	..	..	..	..	..	..	..
Denmark	47	85	0.3	-1.8	106	88	..	..	..	..	..	..	..
Finland	66	61	1.5	-2.0	111	100	102	..	..	..	..	..	..
France	..	74	0.5	-0.1	107	100	110	..	..	..	..	..	..
Germany [b]													
Federal Rep. of Germany	..	..	0.0	-1.3	..	..	..	..	..	..	..	..	..
former German Dem. Rep.	74	77	0.3	-0.9	112	107	110	..	..	..	..	..	..
Greece	53	59	1.1	-1.1	106	100	105	..	..	..	..	..	..
Hungary	46	59	1.0	-1.8	109	104	175	..	..	..	..	..	..
Iceland	..	90	1.2	-1.2	100	86	..	..	..	..	..	..	..
Ireland	55	58	1.6	0.0	106	91	116	..	..	..	..	..	..
Italy	..	..	0.4	-0.7	..	..	..	..	..	..	..	..	..
Japan	72	77	0.5	0.2	103	105	117	..	..	..	..	..	..
Luxembourg	68	..	0.6	-2.9	..	..	101	..	..	..	..	..	..
Malta	94	84	0.9	-1.9	110	104	..	..	..	..	..	..	..
Netherlands	..	89	0.4	0.2	103	97	..	..	..	..	..	..	..
New Zealand	70	85	0.9	0.2	104	89	251	..	..	..	..	..	..
Norway	..	61	0.7	-1.0	111	100	..	..	..	..	..	..	..
Poland	..	61	1.3	-0.5	108	100	..	..	..	..	..	..	..
Portugal	27	30	1.6	-0.4	113	105	..	..	..	..	..	..	..
Romania	40	49	1.0	-0.1	102	103	..	..	..	..	..	..	..
Spain	..	92	1.1	-1.9	104	98	..	..	..	..	..	..	..
Sweden	83	84	0.1	-0.7	105	89	176	..	..	..	..	..	..
Switzerland	59	62	0.6	-0.5	109	100	..	..	..	..	..	..	..
USSR	..	66	1.4	-0.4	113	114	..	..	..	..	..	..	..
United Kingdom	79	89	0.3	-1.8	109	99	..	..	..	..	..	..	..
United States	74	74	0.9	0.7	108	100	..	..	..	..	..	..	..
Yugoslavia	39	47	2.3	-0.9	105	100	..	..	..	..	..	..	..
Africa													
Algeria	45	61	4.2	2.4	102	100	..	0	30	5	30	..	..
Angola	..	..	5.7	1.7	..	..	..	10	88	71	85	..	..
Benin	..	31	6.9	1.0	98	111	..	55	91	55	96	..	..
Botswana	9	20	7.9	2.4	95	115	..	2	28	21	88	..	..
Burkina Faso	..	..	5.5	2.4	..	..	..	50	74	62	95	..	..
Burundi	2	4	8.7	2.5	79	108	..	67	78	10	75	..	..
Cameroon	..	27	5.8	0.0	93	104	..	54	70	..	..	81	99
Cape Verde	..	..	5.8	-1.0	..	..	..	1	79	64	91	..	..
Central African Rep.	..	35 [a]	4.4	1.0	109 [a]	108 [a]	..	76	95	64	91	..	..
Chad	..	..	6.9	0.7	..	..	..	73	70	..	..	..	..
Comoros	..	23	5.1	2.5	101	100	..	1	48	..	..	..	..
Congo	..	35	4.2	1.8	92	110	..	58	93	83	..	..	..
Côte d'Ivoire	..	..	6.4	2.5	..	..	..	70	90	87	80	..	..
Djibouti	..	..	3.8	0.1	..	..	..	47	80	57	81	..	..
Egypt	..	44	3.6	1.7	95	96	..	7	39	5	51	23	81
Equatorial Guinea	..	..	4.0	-0.2	..	..	..	53	..	72	..	..	..
Ethiopia	..	11	4.4	1.7	115	98	..	7	58	..	95	..	..

Table 6. Indicators on housing, human settlements and environment [*cont.*]

	Urban and rural population							Safe water, sanitary facilities and electricity, 1980/85					
	% of women living in urban areas		Annual change in population, 1985-1990 (%)		Females per 100 males, latest year		F/100 M, rural-urb migration	Population without safe water (%)		Population without adequate sanitation (%)		Households without electricity (%)	
Country or area	1970	latest	Urban	Rural	Urban	Rural	1965/75	Urban	Rural	Urban	Rural	Urban	Rural
Gabon	..	33	5.8	1.8	90	112	..	25	66	..	..	..	..
Gambia	..	..	5.2	2.2	..	..	..	0	67	..	..	..	..
Ghana	..	..	4.1	2.7	..	..	100	28	61	53	83	..	..
Guinea	..	18	5.5	1.6	95	104	..	9	98	46	99	..	..
Guinea-Bissau	..	..	4.7	1.1	..	..	..	79	63	79	87	..	..
Kenya	8	14	8.2	3.3	82	105	78	39	79	25	61	..	..
Lesotho	..	5	6.9	2.0	118	100	..	63	86	78	89	..	..
Liberia	24	31	5.5	1.7	..	..	..	50	76	76	80	..	..
Libyan Arab Jamahiriya	..	..	5.5	0.2	..	..	..	0	23	..	..	..	..
Madagascar	..	17 [a]	6.2	2.3	103 [a]	99 [a]	..	27	91	92	..	..	..
Malawi	..	8	7.7	2.7	86	110	..	18	46	..	..	..	..
Mali	..	17 [a]	4.3	2.7	103 [a]	105 [a]	..	42	80	10	95	..	..
Mauritania	..	21	6.8	0.3	85	104	..	20	84	93	..	..	..
Mauritius	45	41	1.3	1.2	100	99	..	0	2	0	5	..	..
Morocco	..	43	4.2	1.2	99	100	125	..	..	..	..	..	..
Mozambique	..	12	9.5	0.7	88	108	..	18	98	..	..	..	..
Namibia	..	43	5.4	0.7	90	112	..	..	..	..	..	..	..
Niger	..	..	7.0	2.2	..	..	..	52	66	64	97	..	..
Nigeria	..	19	6.1	2.2	93	105	..	40	70	70	..	..	..
Reunion	..	..	3.1	-0.4	..	..	..	..	..	..	..	..	..
Rwanda	3	4	7.9	3.1	82	107	..	45	40	40	40	..	..
Sao Tome and Principe	..	..	..	..	..	..	..	..	..	..	..	..	..
Senegal	..	34 [a]	3.9	2.0	103 [a]	102 [a]	..	37	73	13	98	..	..
Seychelles	27	38	..	..	102	97	..	..	..	..	..	..	..
Sierra Leone	..	..	5.2	1.4	..	..	..	42	92	57	90	..	..
Somalia	..	..	5.7	2.2	..	..	..	40	80	40	95	..	..
South Africa	45	55	3.3	0.8	99	107	..	..	..	..	..	..	..
Sudan	..	19	4.3	2.6	88	99	..	..	..	80	99	..	..
Swaziland	7	..	8.3	1.5	..	..	..	..	..	38	90	..	..
Togo	13	17	6.3	2.2	..	..	..	32	74	66	92	..	..
Tunisia	..	53	2.9	1.8	97	96	113	2	21	34	71	32	94
Uganda	7	11	5.7	3.3	86	104	..	55	88	60	90	..	..
United Rep. Tanzania	5	13	10.1	1.3	93	106	91	15	53	9	24	..	..
Western Sahara	..	..	..	..	..	..	..	..	..	..	..	..	..
Zaire	..	17	4.8	2.3	97	105	..	57	95	92	90	..	..
Zambia	..	39	6.3	1.2	97	109	..	30	68	44	59	..	..
Zimbabwe	14	22	5.6	2.4	88	110	..	0	90	0	95	..	..

Latin America and Caribbean

Antigua and Barbuda	34	..	..	..	..	..	..	..	..	..	..	..	..
Argentina	..	85	1.7	-0.9	105	86	..	28	81	7	63	..	..
Bahamas	59	76	..	..	107	102	..	41	..	36	..	..	..
Barbados	..	..	1.8	-0.3	..	..	..	0	80	0	..	..	..
Belize	..	..	..	..	..	..	..	..	..	..	..	..	..
Bolivia	..	50	4.3	1.3	105	100	..	22	88	59	91	24	94
Brazil	..	72 [c]	3.2	-1.3	103 [c]	93 [c]	105	..	48	67	99	..	..
Chile	78	85	2.2	-1.0	107	84	111	0	82	0	90	..	..
Colombia	..	70	2.9	0.2	110	88	197	0	24	4	86	..	..
Costa Rica	43	46	4.2	1.1	109	93	120	7	14	0	60	..	..
Cuba	..	73	1.6	-1.6	103	89	106	..	..	..	..	1	54
Dominica	..	..	..	..	..	..	..	..	..	..	..	..	..
Dominican Republic	..	..	3.9	0.0	..	..	115	15	67	59	90	..	..
Ecuador	43	53 [d]	4.6	0.7	103 [d]	94 [d]	101	2	79	36	74	..	..
El Salvador	40	41	2.8	1.3	110	99	146	29	57	48	66	..	..

Table 6. Indicators on housing, human settlements and environment [*cont.*]

| Country or area | Urban and rural population | | | | | | | Safe water, sanitary facilities and electricity, 1980/85 | | | | | |
| | % of women living in urban areas | | Annual change in population, 1985-1990 (%) | | Females per 100 males, latest year | | F/100 M, rural-urb migration | Population without safe water (%) | | Population without adequate sanitation (%) | | Households without electricity (%) | |
	1970	latest	Urban	Rural	Urban	Rural	1965/75	Urban	Rural	Urban	Rural	Urban	Rural
French Guiana	71	..	..	..	..	..	..	..	..	..	..	..	..
Grenada	..	..	..	..	..	..	..	..	..	..	..	..	..
Guadeloupe	..	..	1.5	-0.7	..	..	..	..	..	..	..	..	..
Guatemala	..	38	3.9	2.2	105	93	132	10	74	47	72	..	..
Guyana	..	23	3.2	1.0	108	98	105	0	39	46	19	..	..
Haiti	..	28	4.1	1.0	125	101	..	27	75	46	88	..	..
Honduras	..	41	5.2	1.9	107	95	122	9	45	56	60	..	..
Jamaica	..	43	2.7	0.3	114	98	..	1	7	8	10	..	..
Martinique	..	..	1.2	-2.5	..	..	..	..	..	..	..	..	..
Mexico	60	67	3.1	0.2	105	97	107	10	60	7	88	..	..
Netherlands Antilles	..	..	..	..	..	..	..	..	..	..	..	..	..
Nicaragua	50	56	4.6	1.9	116	92	..	2	91	27	84	..	..
Panama	49	54	3.0	1.1	105	88	..	3	74	39	29	9	67
Paraguay	..	44	4.3	1.8	107	94	..	54	90	8	5	..	..
Peru	..	68 c	3.4	0.7	100 c	96 c	..	27	82	43	98	83	96
Puerto Rico	59	68	2.4	-0.9	109	99	..	..	..	..	..	..	..
St. Kitts and Nevis	35	36	..	..	110	106	..	..	..	..	..	..	..
St. Lucia	..	..	..	..	..	..	..	..	..	..	..	..	..
St. Vincent/Grenadines	..	..	..	..	..	..	..	..	..	..	..	..	..
Suriname	..	..	2.3	0.8	..	..	..	7	13	0	4	..	..
Trinidad and Tobago	13	48	3.2	-1.5	103	98	..	3	23	0	2	8	24
Uruguay	..	86 a	1.0	-0.4	110 a	76 a	290	5	73	41	41	11	66
US Virgin Islands	25	40	..	..	113	106	..	..	..	..	..	..	..
Venezuela	79	84 c	3.3	-2.7	100 c	87 c	119	12	35	43	94	..	..

Asia and Pacific

Afghanistan	..	17 e	6.0	1.8	94 e	94 e	..	70	90	..	..	..	..
Bahrain	77	80	4.0	2.3	70	76	..	0	0	0	0	..	..
Bangladesh	8	14	5.6	2.3	79	97	75	71	57	79	98	..	..
Bhutan	..	..	5.6	2.0	..	..	..	60	86	..	..	..	..
Brunei Darussalam	..	59	..	..	88	87	..	..	..	..	..	..	..
Cambodia	..	14	4.0	2.3	97	101	..	..	..	..	..	..	..
China	..	20 f	2.2	1.2	91 f	96 f	..	..	..	..	..	..	..
Cyprus	..	46	2.4	-0.3	98	103	..	0	0	0	0	..	..
East Timor	..	..	4.6	1.9	..	..	..	..	..	..	..	..	..
Fiji	33	39	3.0	0.6	100	95	131	..	..	..	..	..	..
French Polynesia	38	..	..	..	..	..	..	..	..	..	..	7	49
Guam	25	..	..	..	..	..	..	..	..	..	..	..	..
Hong Kong	..	93	1.5	-0.7	95	90	..	..	..	..	..	..	..
India	19	25 g	4.0	1.4	89 g	96 g	86	20	53	70	99	..	..
Indonesia	17	26	4.3	0.7	101	101	104	60	68	70	70	53	94
Iran (Islamic Rep. of)	..	46 a	4.7	2.2	91 a	97 a	79	10	48	5	65	..	..
Iraq	57	67	4.6	0.9	92	99	89	0	54	0	85	..	..
Israel	86	89 h	1.9	-1.4	101 h	94 h	..	..	..	..	..	..	..
Jordan	..	59	5.2	1.7	93	94	..	0	10	0	5	..	..
Kiribati	23	..	..	..	..	..	..	..	..	..	..	..	..
Korea, D. People's R.	..	..	3.5	0.3	..	..	..	0	0	0	0	..	..
Korea, Republic of	41	66	3.2	-3.1	101	98	108	..	..	..	..	..	..
Kuwait	..	..	4.5	-3.1	..	..	..	0	0	0	0	..	..
Lao People's Dem. Rep.	15	..	5.9	1.8	..	..	..	..	..	..	..	..	..
Lebanon	..	76	3.0	-1.6	104	103	..	2	2	6	82	..	..
Macau	97	..	..	..	..	..	..	..	..	..	..	..	..
Malaysia	27	35	4.4	0.9	99	100	..	..	..	..	..	..	..
Maldives	12	23	..	..	78	99	..	47	92	31	99	..	..
Mongolia	44	52	3.3	2.9	101	98	..	0	0	..	..	..	..

Table 6. Indicators on housing, human settlements and environment [*cont.*]

	Urban and rural population							Safe water, sanitary facilities and electricity, 1980/85					
	% of women living in urban areas		Annual change in population, 1985-1990 (%)		Females per 100 males, latest year		F/100 M, rural-urb migration	Population without safe water (%)		Population without adequate sanitation (%)		Households without electricity (%)	
Country or area	1970	latest	Urban	Rural	Urban	Rural	1965/75	Urban	Rural	Urban	Rural	Urban	Rural
Myanmar	..	24	2.7	1.9	101	102	..	64	79	66	85	..	..
Nepal	4	6	7.1	2.1	87	96	..	29	89	84	99	..	..
New Caledonia	..	42	..	..	99	93	..	..	..	..	..	..	..
Oman	..	..	7.3	3.0	..	..	..	30	90	40	..	..	..
Pacific Islands	32	30	..	..	96	95	..	..	..	..	..	..	..
Pakistan	26	28[i]	5.0	2.9	87[i]	92[i]	..	16	72	44	95	29	85
Papua New Guinea	9	12	4.8	2.3	73	94	..	46	90	49	97	..	..
Philippines	..	38	3.9	1.6	105	96	..	..	..	..	..	..	..
Qatar	..	..	4.6	1.6	..	..	..	2	50	30	..	..	..
Samoa	22	22	..	..	96	92	..	..	..	..	..	..	..
Saudi Arabia	..	..	5.2	0.5	..	..	..	0	32	0	67	..	..
Singapore	..	75	1.1	..	98	91	..	..	..	..	..	..	..
Solomon Islands	5	7[a]	..	..	64[a]	95[a]	..	9	..	14	..	..	..
Sri Lanka	22	21	1.6	1.3	91	98	..	24	74	..	..	53	92
Syrian Arab Republic	..	49[i]	4.6	2.6	94[i]	98[i]	91	23	35	30	..	..	..
Thailand	13	17	4.3	0.8	104	100	111	30	30	50	56	8	88
Tonga	..	..	..	..	..	..	..	..	..	..	..	42	88
Turkey	..	43	3.1	1.1	91	102	86	..	..	..	..	..	..
United Arab Emirates	..	84	3.3	3.3	47	36	..	0	0	7	78	..	..
Vanuatu	10	17	..	..	84	89	..	..	..	..	..	..	..
Viet Nam	..	18	3.8	1.9	94	109	..	10	70	..	..	..	..
Yemen	31[k]	35[k]	6.6	1.8	90[k]	111[k]	..	10	76	27	67[k]	..	..

Sources:
Demographic Yearbook, 1974, 1977, 1983 and *1987* (United Nations publications); *Prospects of World Urbanization 1988,* Population Studies No. 112 (United Nations publication, Sales no. E.88.XIII.8); *World Population Trends and Policies, 1987 Monitoring Report,* Population Studies No. 103 (United Nations publication, Sales. No. E.88.XIII.3); *Age and Sex Structure of Urban and Rural Populations, 1970-2000: The 1980 Assessment* (United Nations, ESA/P/WP.81); World Health Organization, "Evaluation of the Strategy for Health for all 1985-1986: Detailed Analysis of Global Indicators" (Geneva, WHO/HST/87.2/1987); *Compendium of Human Settlements Statistics 1983* (United Nations publication, Sales No. E/F.84.XVII.5).

a   1975/76.
b   Through the accession of the German Democratic Republic to the Federal Republic of Germany with effect from 3 October 1990, the two German States have united to form one sovereign State. As from the date of unification, the Federal Republic of Germany acts in the United Nations under the designation "Germany". All data shown for Germany pertain to end-June 1990 or earlier and are indicated separately for the Federal Republic of Germany and the former German Democratic Republic.
c   Excluding Indian jungle population.

d   Exluding nomadic Indian tribes.
e   Excluding nomads.
f   Covering only the civilian population of 29 provinces, municipalities and autonomous regions
g   Including Indian-held part of Jammu and Kashmir, the final status of which has not yet been determined.
h   Including East Jerusalem and Israeli residents in certain other territories under occupation by Israeli military forces since June 1967.
i   Excluding Jammu and Kashmir, the final status of which has not yet been fully determined, Junagardh, Manavadar, Gilgit and Baltistan.
j   Including Palestinian refugees.
k   Data refer to the former Democratic Yemen only.

6
Women's work and the economy

Both women and men work, but many aspects of their work are different: total hours, the kind of work, rates of pay, age of participation and domestic responsibilities, which women generally have considerably more of than men.

Since 1970 women's share in the labour force has been rising. And almost everywhere, women are working more outside the household.

Job segregation and wage discrimination persist almost everywhere, with a big gap between what women produce and what they earn. They also have less access to training and capital.

What women do is often unrecorded, undervalued or not valued at all, but statistical concepts and methods are being revised in order to better incorporate these omissions.

Women's concerns have largely been ignored in national and international programmes to deal with economic crises and promote investment in developing regions.

Women's working world [1]

The household is a major centre of work for women. Women's work in the home can include many different kinds of economic activity, for example, subsistence agriculture, production of goods for trade and keeping accounts for their husbands' business. It also includes unpaid housework. That so much work takes place in the home and is caught up with the daily routine in housework makes it difficult to measure women's work accurately. Enumerators and women themselves often do not understand that they should be counted as economically active and traditional measures do not cover unpaid housework. To understand more fully the burden of work in women's lives and how it compares to men's, this chapter begins with the time spent working.

Time-budget statistics measure how people spend their time throughout the course of each day and provide an essential starting point for understanding women's work. They cover productive activities in and out of the household, and unlike traditional statistics they capture unstructured work patterns more characteristic of housework and informal sector work. They thus overcome the common perception affecting other methods of measuring work that women engage primarily in housework and that all other tasks are of marginal importance. (See also the section below on women and the United Nations System of National Accounts.)

Women's longer working day

Time-use statistics considering all work (paid and unpaid economic activity and unpaid housework) reveal that women spend more of their time working than men in all developed and developing regions except northern America and Australia, where the hours are almost equal (chart 6.1).

Women are spending more time working in the labour force in western Europe and less time in housework everywhere in the developed regions (table 6.2). Men, by contrast, are spending less time working in the labour force than before in all the developed regions and slightly more in housework in northern America, Australia and western Europe.

These rates reflect substantial changes in the 1970s and 1980s. Before 1975 men and women in the developed regions worked very similar hours everywhere, except eastern Europe and the USSR. But since then, women have been working two hours more a week than men in Japan and five to six more hours a week than men in western Europe. The gap between women and men in eastern Europe and the Soviet Union has narrowed from nine hours more a week to just over seven—still a considerable difference.

In the developed regions, women and men are working less today than before 1975, and women are spending less time doing housework. Part of the reason for this is women's lower fertility, but other possible factors are time-saving home appliances, smaller homes, smaller households, lower standards and the use of housekeepers or domestic services.

Despite the limited data for developing regions, there are clear indications that women there are also working longer hours than men (chart 6.1). Studies in Latin America and the Caribbean up to 1975 showed that women there worked almost three hours a week less than men, but recent studies show that they are now working 5.6 more hours a week than men. The widest gaps are in Africa and in Asia and the Pacific, where studies have found that women average 12 to 13 hours more work a week than men. A 1976 study in the Philippines found that when housework and child care were taken into account, the average hours worked per week by mothers was 70, compared to 57 for men.

In many developing countries hit by the economic ravages of the 1980s, women—especially very poor women—are now working 60–90 hours a week just to try to maintain their meagre living standards of a decade ago.[2]

A simple distinction between paid and unpaid work does not capture the unique features of wo-

men's work, particularly in developing countries. Unpaid work may include work in a family enterprise or in subsistence activities. In rural Côte d'Ivoire and Nepal, men's and women's hours spent at economic activity are almost identical. But women's non-market economic activity takes more than eight additional hours a week than men's (table 6.3).

6.1

Women in most regions spend as much or more time working than men when unpaid housework is taken into account

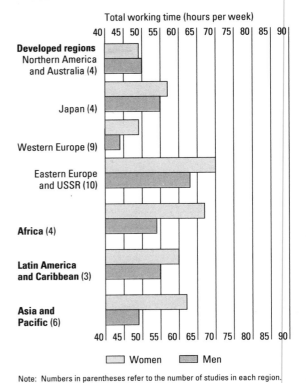

Note: Numbers in parentheses refer to the number of studies in each region.

Source: Data are averages from a small number of studies in each region, 1976/88, compiled by the Statistical Office of the United Nations Secretariat.

6.2

Since 1975, both women and men have spent less time in total work in most of the developed regions

Time spent in work (hours per week)

| | 1975 or earlier | | | | | | 1976 or later | | | | | |
| | Economic activity | | Unpaid housework | | Total working time | | Economic activity | | Unpaid housework | | Total working time | |
	f	m	f	m	f	m	f	m	f	m	f	m
Northern America and Australia	18	44	36	10	54	54	19	35	30	15	49	50
Japan	28	56	31	3	59	59	27	52	29	3	57	55
Western Europe	15	41	35	8	50	49	18	34	31	11	49	44
Eastern Europe and USSR	36	52	39	15	75	66	37	48	33	15	70	63

Source: Data are averages from a small number of studies in each region, compiled by the Statistical Office of the United Nations Secretariat.

Unpaid housework

Women everywhere retain the primary responsibility for household work—even when they have economic responsibility inside and outside the home. Far more is known about unpaid housework in the developed regions than in the developing regions, where the data are generally based not on national studies but on small scattered surveys. It is nevertheless possible to make two generalizations. First, women everywhere have nearly total responsibility for housework. Second, men in developing regions generally do even fewer household chores than men in the developed regions.

Data from the developed regions show that household chores and caring for children are mostly done by women (table 7). Everywhere, cooking and dishwashing are the least shared household chores with no more than one fourth of this work done by men. Shopping is more evenly shared. In northern America, Australia, western Europe and the USSR men do nearly 40 per cent of the family's shopping. There are other chores such as taking out garbage, outdoor work and household repairs which men tend to do but these tasks are a relatively small part of household responsibilities. In the United States of America and certain countries of western

6.3

Women's time in economic activity is comparable to men's in developing regions when non-market economic activity is taken into account

Time spent in work (hours per week)

| | Economic activity | | | | | |
| | Market work | | Non-market economic activity* | Total | Unpaid housework | Total work |
	Wage-salary	Own-account and family				
Côte d'Ivoire (rural)						
Women	..	11.9	10.3	22.1	25.4	47.6
Men	..	20.3	3.0	23.3	4.2	27.5
Nepal						
Women	3.2	29.1	15.1	47.5	28.2	75.7
Men	8.7	23.1	6.4	47.1	5.5	52.6

*Includes unpaid work in family enterprises and subsistence agriculture and other unremunerated economic activity in households such as water carrying, fuel gathering and own construction.

Source: Data from national studies compiled by the Statistical Office of the United Nations Secretariat.

Europe, housework is more evenly shared than it once was. But there is also evidence that the increase in men's share is not due to a more equal division of routine cooking, cleaning and laundry. Rather women's hours in housework have decreased sharply and men have increased the time they spend in tasks such as shopping.[3]

Women in the labour force

Of the 828 million women officially estimated to be economically active in 1990, more than half (56 per cent) live in Asia, 29 per cent in the developed regions, 9 per cent in Africa and 5 per cent in Latin America and the Caribbean (chart 6.4). [1]

Women's share in the labour force increased between 1970 and 1990, but not in all regions (chart 6.5). It rose to 39 per cent from 35 in the developed regions, to 29 per cent from 24 in Latin America and the Caribbean, and to 17 per cent from 12 in northern Africa and western Asia. In the rest of Asia, there was little change. It stayed at high levels in eastern and south-eastern Asia (40 and 35 per cent, respectively), and in southern Asia at lower levels (about 20 per cent). In Oceania, women's share rose from 26 to 29 per cent of the labour force. In sub-Saharan Africa it showed a decline—39 per cent in 1970, 37 per cent in 1990.

In all developing regions, and recently in some of the developed, the growth in the female labour force has been undercut by economic recession. Women generally continue to be the last to benefit from job expansion and the first to suffer from job contraction—particularly in the stagnant or declining economies of Africa and Latin America and the Caribbean.[4] In Africa, due to especially severe economic conditions, the growth in the female labour force has fallen well behind population growth.

6.4

More than half the world's women in the labour force live in Asia

Percentage distribution of the world's female labour force, 1990

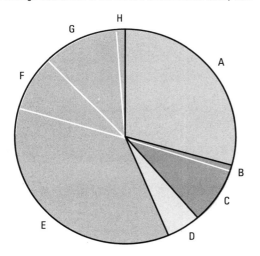

Developed regions		**Asia and Pacific**	
A	All developed regions (29.3)	E	Eastern Asia (35.8)
Africa		F	South-eastern Asia (8.2)
B	Northern Africa (0.7)	G	Southern Asia (10.9)
C	Sub-Saharan Africa (8.6)	H	Western Asia (1.4)
Latin America and Caribbean			Oceania (0.1)
D	All Latin America and Caribbean (5.0)		

Source: International Labour Office, *Economically Active Population—Estimates, 1950–1980, Projections, 1985–2025,* six volumes (Geneva, 1986).

6.5

Women's share in the labour force increased between 1970 and 1990 in almost every region

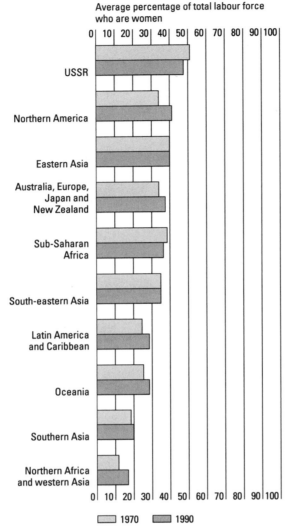

Source: Prepared by the Statistical Office of the United Nations Secretariat from International Labour Office, *Economically Active Population—Estimates, 1950–1980, Projections, 1985-2025,* six volumes (Geneva, 1986).

Economic participation rates [1]

According to international estimates, the proportion of women who are economically active rose between 1970 and 1990 in the developed regions (except the USSR), northern Africa and western Asia, eastern Asia and Latin America and the Caribbean. But it declined slightly in the other regions, except for a sharp decline in sub-Saharan Africa (chart 6.6). (As explained in the section "Counting economically active women", women's economic participation and economic activities may be substantially undercounted in some regions, especially in rural areas, and do not in any case include unpaid housework).

The highest rates of economic activity for women are in eastern Asia (59 per cent) and the USSR (60 per cent). The other developed regions, sub-Saharan Africa and south-eastern Asia show high average rates ranging from 45 to 50 per cent. Northern Africa has the lowest rate of any region (16 per cent) followed by western and southern Asia (21 and 24 per cent) and Latin America and the Caribbean (32 per cent).

6.6

Women's economic activity rates rose in most developed and developing regions from 1970 to 1990

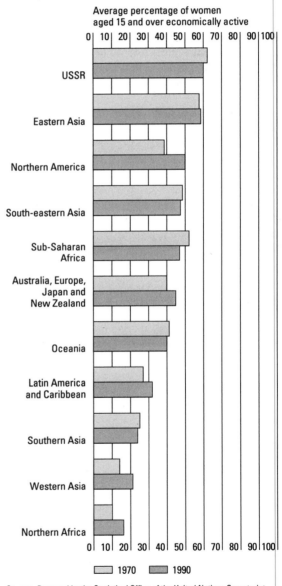

Source: Prepared by the Statistical Office of the United Nations Secretariat from International Labour Office, *Economically Active Population—Estimates, 1950–1980, Projections, 1985–2025,* six volumes (Geneva, 1986).

Counting economically active women

It is not easy in a population census or household survey to decide whether a person is working or not and what people are working at, particularly women in developing regions. Statistical definitions, the language used, the order of questions and the time-reference period all affect responses to inquiries concerning economic activity.

Terms such as *employment, job, work* and *main activity* mean different things to different people. Unless respondents are given clear examples of work that encompasses what women do as well as men, women may define themselves as not economically active when in fact they are. In Chile, for example, an interviewer found that many women defined planting and harvesting as homemaking rather than agricultural work.*

Interviewers also contribute to bias when they assume that women or children are not economically active.

Defining economic activity

Many ambiguities arise in applying the concept of economic activity, especially where it relates to activities on the borderline between subsistence production and housework. Where does non-economic housework end and economic activity begin? Although household food and other subsistence production and processing (but not unpaid housework) and work in the informal sector are included in the international definition in principle, many countries omit such activities as gathering fuel or water, processing crops, raising a few animals, keeping a kitchen garden or managing small household-based industries and trading.

The 1982 definition of unpaid family workers reduces the work-time criterion from one-third of "normal working time" to the same minimum time used to define other workers (commonly one hour per week) but added a new stipulation: counting persons who produce solely for household consumption as economically active only if such production is an "important contribution" to the total consumption of the household. Such a contribution must be carefully defined so that interviewers do not assume—once again—that women's work is not important.

Asking questions about work

Many census and survey questionnaires begin by asking "What is your main activity?" or "What is your primary occupation?" This approach is inadequate for most women. Men usually state their economic occupation. Women are likely to say they are housewives, even

if they also produce for the market or produce food for their household. They may think their domestic housework takes more time or is more significant. If the interviewer does not include questions beyond housework, women's economic activity may never be counted.

Persons who work for a wage or salary are usually enumerated as economically active regardless of how the questions are phrased. The complications arise as one moves from wage and salary employment to self-employment—especially in the informal sector—and to unpaid labour in a family farm or business: that is, from more male-dominated to more female-dominated forms of economic activity.

For example, a methodological survey in India designed to test the effect of including different types of activities in the labour force definition found that 13 per cent of adult women were wage or salary earners.[†] When market-oriented production was included—for example, family business, self-employment, crafts and agricultural activities—the figure rose to 32 per cent. When the new ILO standard was fully applied, 88 per cent of women were found to be economically active.

Seasons are very pertinent for rural analyses and also affect many activities in the informal sector and in non-agricultural wage work. Where women's economic activity is less regular than men's, the short reference period will exclude them from being counted in the labour force.

The need for careful interpretation and better measurement

Discrepancies in statistics on economically active women could be cited from a variety of sources for many countries, especially those in which large proportions of the population live in rural areas or are engaged in unpaid family labour or small-scale self-employment. Properly applying improved statistical definitions on women's work is a slow process, however. The present chapter of *The World's Women 1970–1990* relies on available statistics on women's economic activity but looks carefully and critically at national and regional results and at related statistics on time use, where available. Careful review, country-by-country, is necessary for these data to be effectively used and further improved.

*P.M. Garret, "Some structural constraints on the agricultural activities of women: the Chilean hacienda", University of Wisconsin, Research Paper No. 70 (Madison, Wisconsin, 1976).
[†]R. Anker, M.E. Khan and R.B. Gupta, "Biases in measuring the labour force: results of a methods test survey in Uttar Pradesh, India", *International Labour Review* (Geneva, International Labour Office), March–April 1987.

Economic activity

For general purposes in this book, the terms "labour force", "economically active population", "economic activity" and "economic participation" all refer to the same international definition of the economically active population.

Statisticians use the term economic activity rather than work in order to be consistent with the concept of economic production in the United Nations System of National Accounts. The definition of economic activity has been broadened over the years but it still excludes such unpaid housework as shopping, cooking, cleaning and caring for children and other family members.

The ILO recommendation of 1982 includes all work for pay or in anticipation of profit. It also specifies that the production of economic goods and services includes all production and processing of agricultural products, whether for the market, for barter or for home consumption.

The time-frame is also crucial to determining whether a person is economically active. If a short reference period is used (commonly one week), a person is considered "currently" economically active if they work (or are looking for or available for work) at least one hour in the reference week. If a long reference period is used (commonly one year), a person is considered "usually" economically active if they worked at least one hour per week or per day during the majority of weeks or days in the reference period.

Occupational groups

Occupation refers to the kind of work done by a person during the reference period used in a census or survey. The 1968 revision of the International Standard Classification of Occupations (ISCO) classifies occupations in 7 major groups:

Professional, technical and related workers;

Administrative and managerial workers;

Clerical and related workers;

Sales workers;

Service workers;

Agriculture, animal husbandry and forestry workers, fishermen and hunters;

Production and related workers, transport equipment operators and labourers.

And even though the proportion of men who are economically active is down everywhere, the gaps between women's recorded participation and men's remain wide (chart 6.7). They are widest in northern Africa (16 per cent versus 80 per cent), western and southern Asia (21–24 per cent for women compared with 83–85 per cent for men), and Latin America and the Caribbean (32 per cent compared with 80 per cent).

6.7

The gap between women's and men's recorded economic participation remains wide

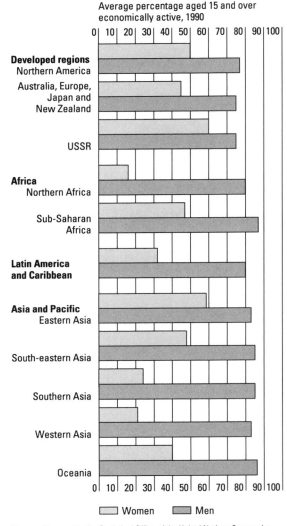

Source: Prepared by the Statistical Office of the United Nations Secretariat from International Labour Office, *Economically Active Population—Estimates, 1950–1980, Projections, 1985–2025,* six volumes (Geneva, 1986).

Economic participation at different ages [1]

The economic participation of both women and men peaks in the age group 25 to 44, during women's child-bearing years (chart 6.8). It declines in every region in the age group 45 to 59, but only slightly in sub-Saharan Africa and southern Asia. Sub-Saharan African women are generally more economically independent in their households than women in other regions. And as men migrate to cities and towns for wage labour, more and more women become the primary providers for the household. Economic activity rates remain high in sub-Saharan Africa even among women aged 60 and over.

The most important changes between 1970 and 1990 in women's economic participation at different ages were the increases in economic activity rates for women aged 25–44 in the developed regions, in Latin America and the Caribbean and in western Asia and northern Africa—and the declines for women in all age groups in sub-Saharan Africa. The large increase in the developed regions in the 25–44 age group, from 50 to 65 per cent, marked an important shift from the previous pattern of higher women's participation in the youngest age group. The declines in sub-Saharan Africa in all age groups show how the economic crises there are hurting women.

Economic participation in urban and rural areas [10]

Urban growth is providing new economic opportunities for women in Latin America and the Caribbean. The recorded economic participation rates for women in urban areas there are twice those in rural areas. In Africa and Asia, by contrast, more limited urban growth and development over the last 20 years have offered women fewer economic opportunities, at least in the wage labour market. Urban job opportunities have been primarily reserved for men, and many development policies have favoured men's production and jobs over women's. Most Asian and sub-Saharan African women remain and work in rural areas. In the developed regions, the economic activity rates of women are very similar and generally high in both urban and rural areas (chart 6.9).

6.8

Both women's and men's economic activity rates are highest for people aged 25–44 years

Average economic activity rates, 1990 (%)

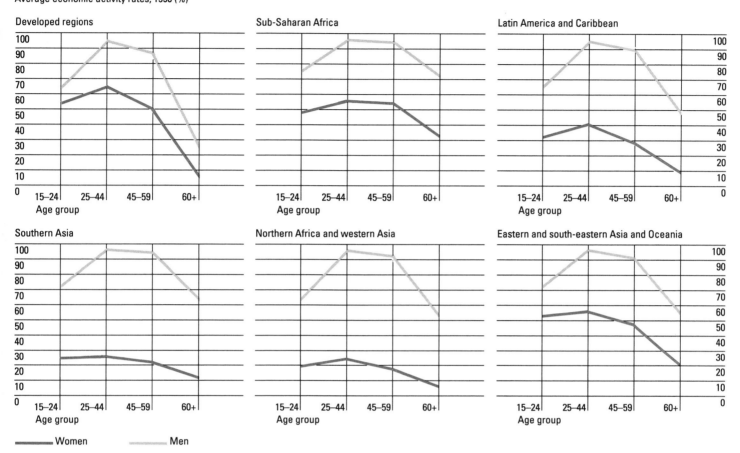

━━━ Women   ━━━ Men

Source: Prepared by the Statistical Office of the United Nations Secretariat from International Labour Office, *Economically Active Population—Estimates, 1950–1980, Projections, 1985–2025*, six volumes (Geneva, 1986).

Occupational segregation

Almost everywhere, the workplace is segregated by sex. Women fill well over half of the clerical and service jobs in the developed regions and Latin America and the Caribbean, and more than a third in Africa and in Asia and the Pacific (chart 6.10). [2]

Few women work in manufacturing and transportation—about 17 or 18 per cent of the sector's workforce. Exceptions are eastern and south-eastern Asia, where women working in industries such as textiles and electronics are 26 per cent of the manufacturing workforce.

Within an occupational group women are almost always in the less prestigious jobs. For example, there are many more women than men in lower-paid professional and technical occupations such as teaching, the largest occupation in this category. As the level, prestige and pay go up so do the numbers of men—who take an overwhelming majority of the jobs in, for example, higher education. [31]

Looking at job categories in more detail, the contrast is even starker. A study of 24 countries in the developed regions in the 1970s showed that there were many jobs—for example typists, nurses, housekeepers—where more than 90 per cent of the employees were women.[5] Much more recent data for Sweden still show the same pattern.[6]

Most occupational categories group together many different jobs. Often an occupational category appears sex neutral when in fact there is great sex segregation within the more specific job titles that comprise it. One study of firms in an area of the United States showed that most women are in jobs with completely different titles than men's. Only 10 per cent of workers studied were in jobs which included both women and men.[7]

Wages

Wages statistics compiled by the International Labour Office refer to remuneration in cash and in kind paid to employees, as a rule at regular intervals, for time worked or work done together with remuneration for time not worked, such as vacations and holidays. Data on average earnings are usually derived from payroll data supplied by a sample of establishments which often also furnish data on hours of work and on employment. The coverage, definition and methods of compiling wage statistics differ significantly from country to country. Statistics for comparisons by sex are available for only a few countries and may be based on a narrow segment of the labour force.

Wage differences

Everywhere women are paid less than men. In addition, men are more likely to have regular full-time work and receive greater seniority and benefits. However, it is difficult to measure the extent of difference and how it has changed because of limited data and the segregated nature of the labour force.

In Cyprus, Japan and the Republic of Korea women's wages are the lowest in relation to men's (about half) among those countries for which data are available (list 6.11). [2] A few countries or areas report that women have wage rates which range between 75 and 92 per cent of men's. More countries report women's wage rates below 75 per cent of men's and in some, as already noted, women's wage rates are just over half those of their male counterparts. Even in Canada—where women have made inroads into male-dominated, high status, high-paying jobs—women's earnings in these jobs are still only 71 per cent of men's.[8] For Latin America and the Caribbean there are no data available.

Wage employment [9]

Wage and salary employment is more stable and secure than self-employment but it is not always available to women—and almost never with the same wages and benefits as for men. Several factors may be responsible for the continuing exclusion of women workers from many wage and salary jobs. One is men's domination of trade unions in developing regions. Another is employ-

6.9

According to official statistics, women's economic participation rates in rural areas vary greatly among regions but are much more uniform in urban areas

Average women's economic activity rate, latest year (%)

Legend: Urban / Rural

A   Developed regions
B   Sub-Saharan Africa
C   Latin America and Caribbean
D   Asia and Pacific

Source: Regional averages calculated by the Statistical Office of the United Nations Secretariat from *Demographic Yearbook 1979* and *1984* (United Nations publications, Sales Nos. E/F.80.XIII.1 and E/F.85.XIII.1).

ers' reluctance to hire and train women. Yet a third is employers' fear that women, as potential mothers, may demand social legislation favouring maternity leave with pay. And a fourth is the perception that women, who enter and leave the labour force more often, should be confined to marginal jobs.

In the developing regions, women in Latin America and the Caribbean have benefited the most from wage and salary employment. Economically active women there were more likely than men in the 1980s to be employed as wage earners: 62 per cent of working women earned wages compared with 56 per cent of men. In Africa, women are most likely to be cut off from wage-earning opportunities, with only 30 per cent in salaried or wage-earning jobs, compared with 42 per cent of economically active men (chart 6.12). In several African countries, less than 10 per cent of economically active women have wage employment. Now, economic crises and adjustment programmes are threatening women's wage employment, for example in the public sector in Latin America and the Caribbean.[10]

Women's wage employment is highest in the developed regions. Overall, women and men are represented equally in the wage sector in developed regions (at about 77 per cent of the economically active population) and in Asia and the Pacific (at about 57 per cent).

6.10

Women make up a large part of the clerical, sales and services labour force but are largely excluded from manufacturing, transport and management

Percentage who are women, 1980s

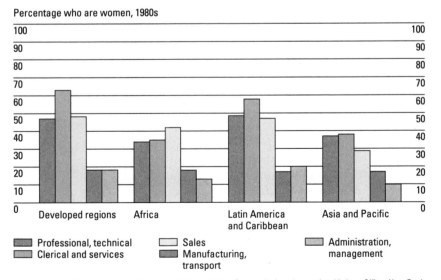

Legend:
Professional, technical
Clerical and services
Sales
Manufacturing, transport
Administration, management

Source: Prepared by the Statistical Office of the United Nations Secretariat from International Labour Office, *Year Book of Labour Statistics* (Geneva, various years).

6.12
The percentage of the economically active who are wage earners is about equal for women and men in most regions, but is lower for women in Africa

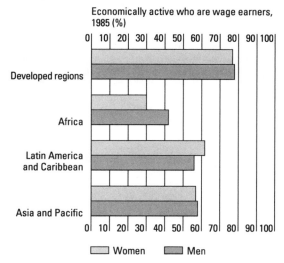

Economically active who are wage earners, 1985 (%)

☐ Women   ■ Men

Source: Prepared by the Statistical Office of the United Nations Secretariat from International Labour Office, *Year Book of Labour Statistics* (Geneva, various years).

Women in agriculture, industry and services [11]

Most women are still working in agriculture in much of Africa and Asia. Nearly 80 per cent of economically active women in sub-Saharan Africa and at least half in Asia, except western Asia, are in agriculture. Only a small minority of women work in this sector in Latin America and the Caribbean (at least according to official statistics, which may be particularly unreliable concerning women in agriculture in that region)[12] and in the developed regions (chart 6.13). In these regions services form the important sector of employment for women: they involve 71 per cent of economically active women in Latin America and the Caribbean and 62 per cent in the developed regions. In Asia and the Pacific significant numbers of women are employed in the service sector (40 per cent) but in Africa only 20 per cent of women counted as economically active work in this sector.

Fewer women world-wide are employed in industry. The range is from a high of 24 per cent of economically active women in the developed regions to 16–17 per cent in Asia and the Pacific and Latin America and the Caribbean and a low of 6 per cent in Africa.

Country examples and comparisons show even sharper contrasts. Very few women work in agriculture (5 per cent or less) in many European countries and the United States of America, in several Latin American and western Asian countries and of course in Hong Kong and Singapore. But more

than 95 per cent of economically active women work in agriculture in Burundi, Mozambique and Rwanda in Africa and Bhutan and Nepal in Asia. Services employ about 80 per cent or more of economically active women in Canada, Luxembourg, the Netherlands, Norway, Sweden and the United States in the developed regions, in Argentina, Chile and Panama in Latin America, and in six countries in western Asia, but only 2 per cent or less in Burundi, Mozambique and Rwanda.

Between 1970 and 1980 the number of women working in agriculture declined only in the developed regions. Everywhere else, agriculture continued to absorb at least some of the increasing numbers of economically active women (chart 5.2 shows where total rural populations are growing).

Chart 6.14 shows how the overall increase in the female labour force was distributed among agriculture, industry and services in each region. In sub-Saharan Africa and throughout Asia and the Pacific, agriculture absorbed more than 40 per cent of the increase.

6.13
Most women are still working in agriculture in much of Africa and Asia

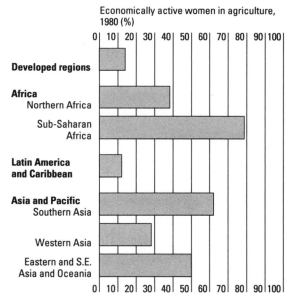

Economically active women in agriculture, 1980 (%)

Source: Prepared by the Statistical Office of the United Nations Secretariat from International Labour Office, *Economically Active Population—Estimates, 1950–1980, Projections, 1985–2025*, six volumes (Geneva, 1986).

6.11
Women are always paid less than men
Women's average wages as percentage of men's, 1983/87

Developed regions
Iceland (90)
France (89)
Australia (87)
Denmark (82)
New Zealand (79)
Netherlands (77)
Belgium (74)
Germany:
Federal Rep. of Germany (73)
United Kingdom (70)
Czechoslovakia (68)
Switzerland (67)
Luxembourg (65)
Japan (52)

Africa
United Rep. Tanzania (92)
Kenya (76)
Swaziland (73)
Egypt (64)

Asia and Pacific
Jordan (79)
Sri Lanka (75)
Hong Kong (74)
Singapore (69)
Cyprus (59)
Korea, Republic of (50)

Source: International Labour Office, *Year Book of Labour Statistics, 1986* and *1988* (Geneva, 1986 and 1988).

In economic statistics, all of
the economic units of a
country and their outputs
are commonly classified
according to each unit's
type of economic activity.
For aggregate analysis, the
nine major divisions of the
International Standard Industrial Classification of all
Economic Activities (ISIC),
1968 version, are grouped
into agriculture, industry and
services sectors. In this
grouping "agriculture" also
covers hunting, forestry and
fishing. "Industry" covers
mining and quarrying (in-
cluding oil production);
manufacturing; electricity,
gas and water; and con-
struction. "Services" covers
wholesale and retail trade
and restaurants and hotels;
transport, storage and com-
munication; financing, insur-
ance, real estate and business services; and commu-
nity, social and personal
services.

Measuring women's economic contribution in the United Nations System of National Accounts

Beginning at the global level with the World Plan of
Action for the Implementation of the Objectives of the
International Women's Year, adopted in Mexico City in
1975, women have sought better measurement of their
contribution to development and to the economies of their
countries.* There are three main problems. The first is the
national accountants' definition of an economic good or
service (the "production boundary"). The second is the
effective and unbiased application of that definition in
national accounts and labour force statistics. The third is
the separate measurement of women's and men's income
and production—to determine women's relative contribution and returns.

The current version of the United Nations System of
National Accounts (1968 SNA) recommends relatively
wide coverage of non-monetary as well as monetary
goods and services in the concept of economic activity.
For example, all kinds of agricultural production for family
consumption and own-account capital formation (such as
home construction) are included. But SNA covers other
goods and services produced in the household for its own
consumption only if those goods are also sold on the
market. It excludes child-bearing, child care, family care,
housekeeping, cooking and shopping. SNA does, however, clearly recommend that all kinds of informal, under-
ground and even illegal activities should in principle be
counted if an economic transaction is involved and some
kind of good or service is produced. Such activities are
often extensive and can cover a spectrum from, say,
smuggling to prostitution. Many countries try to cover
many of these various activities, but these efforts usually
are ad hoc, rarely comprehensive, and based on limited
statistics and speculative assumptions.

From the perspective of labour force statistics,
applying international recommendations has been even
more difficult because of problems in data collection, including sex-based stereotypes. In many developing countries, women working in subsistence activities or the
informal sector are under-counted, even though their
production may be included in the national accounts.

The major unresolved issues in measuring women's
contribution to economic output are these:

■ Many goods and services predominantly pro-
    duced by women are undercounted in national
    accounts—or are estimated with such rough
    assumptions that the resulting figures are unusable
    for policy.

■ Women's productive role is undercounted in
    labour force statistics.

■ Child-bearing and child care, family care and other
    unpaid housework are not counted at all in either
    national accounts or labour force statistics. If
    unpaid housework were valued at the cost of pur-
    chasing comparable goods and services or of
    hiring someone to do the work, the measured value
    of GDP in countries would increase by 25–30 per
    cent according to most estimates (see table 6.17).

National accounts and labour force statistics provide the fundamental picture of national economies that
governments and the public use to monitor and assess
economic development—and to prepare and implement
economic and related social policies. Failure to properly
recognize and measure women's role in production inevi-
tably leads to gross distortions and biases in economic
decision-making at both micro (individual and household)
and macro (national and international) levels. That failure
disparages and devalues women's work and perpetuates
women's segregation and exploitation in underpaid, unpaid and underfinanced sectors and occupations.

*See *Report of the World Conference of the International Women's Year,
Mexico City, 19 June–2 July 1975* (United Nations publication, Sales
No. E.76.IV.1).

In Latin America and the Caribbean the labour
force expansion accounted for by agriculture was
lowest, only 9 per cent, while services accounted
for the greatest part of the increase, 71 per cent.
Services also accounted for high percentages of net
new jobs for women in the developed regions (83
per cent) and northern Africa and western Asia
(40 per cent or more), rather less in sub-Saharan
Africa and southern Asia, and least in eastern and
south-eastern Asia and Oceania (18 per cent).

New industrial jobs accounted for a fifth or
more of all new jobs for women in the developed
regions, northern Africa (the highest of any region
at 32 per cent), Latin America and the Caribbean,
and eastern and south-eastern Asia and Oceania.
Industry contributed the least to new jobs for women in sub-Saharan Africa and southern and
western Asia (around 10 per cent).

Women in agriculture—a special case

Women's contribution to agricultural production, especially food production, continues to be
poorly estimated or ignored in many regions. Indeed, some studies show that women may have
become even more important in food production
in recent years as a result of men's increased migration to cities and towns, particularly in Africa.[13]

This comparative invisibility of women working in agriculture is due largely to the high proportion of women who work without wages on their
families' farms (about 40 per cent in every region
except Latin America and the Caribbean). Only 20
per cent of men working in agriculture are unpaid
family workers in Asia and the Pacific and the proportion is even lower in other regions. The rest
of the female agricultural labour force is divided
about equally between those who work as paid employees and those who run their own farms or are
otherwise self-employed.

A substantial proportion of women in agriculture are counted as employers or own-account workers, ranging from 24 per cent in Asia and the Pacific to 35 per cent in Africa and Latin America. However, few women are agricultural holders (2 per cent in Jordan, 6 per cent in Nepal, 13 per cent in Thailand and from 15 to 20 per cent in some developed countries). Women are most likely to control smaller holdings; the proportion of women-headed farms declines as farm size increases.[14]

Compounding the difficulty of measuring women's work in agriculture is the fact that many women work at subsistence agriculture where very little of their produce goes to the market, where unpaid labour on their own land alternates with wage or exchange labour on another's, and where home-based trade and crafts alternate with seasonal agricultural activities. The conceptual distinctions between persons who are economically active and not economically active—and between agricultural and non-agricultural occupations—can become hopelessly blurred. Yet such distinctions affect the size and composition of the labour force in fundamental ways. Regional statistics for sub-Saharan Africa, for example, show women making up 40 per cent of the agricultural labour force in 1980. But they were producing and processing (and of course cooking) most of the region's food—while men, where they had remained in agriculture at all, were concentrating on cash crops.[15]

Women's continuing invisibility in agriculture has meant that men have benefited from most of the labour-saving technology and extension services that increase productivity and profit. An FAO study in Africa found that women make up 80 per cent of the food producers in some countries but received only 2–10 per cent of the extension contacts.[16] And whether extension personnel are male or female, they tend to overlook the needs of women farmers.

Even though the number of female extension workers is rising, the thrust of agricultural training is towards export crops (involving mainly men), not household food crops and small livestock (involving mainly women). Recent recognition of women's role in agricultural production has focused more attention on female agricultural workers, and more than 100 countries have set up special units to promote the efforts of women working in agriculture. However, even given an enlightened approach to agricultural extension, women will only benefit from extension programmes if valid recommendations are available for the crops and activities of concern to them.

6.14

Much of the increase in the women's labour force has been absorbed by services in Latin America and the Caribbean and the developed regions and by agriculture in Asia and sub-Saharan Africa

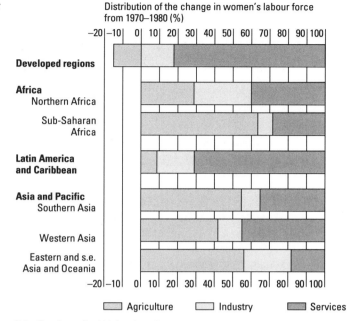

Distribution of the change in women's labour force from 1970–1980 (%)

Note: Based on regional totals, not country averages.

Source: Prepared by the Statistical Office of the United Nations Secretariat from International Labour Office, *Economically Active Population—Estimates, 1950–1980, Projections, 1985–2025,* six volumes (Geneva, 1986).

Women in industry

Between 1970 and 1980 the proportion of women in industry remained about constant (and low) in every region. In spite of this apparent stability, however, two major global trends in industrial employment illustrate the problems women face in trying to improve their employment position. First, large numbers of comparatively well-paid manual jobs held by men in the developed regions have become low-paid, exploitative jobs for women in developing regions, particularly in Asia and the Pacific. Second, a great deal of manual labour in industry in all regions has been replaced by mechanized processing. Mechanized industry is the province of administrators and technicians who are, again, overwhelmingly men.

As these trends continue, it is more important than ever to ensure that women receive training in commerce, management, science and technology to take advantage of changing employment opportunities.

Economic activity in the "formal" and "informal" sectors

The characteristics of the informal sector most often cited include simple technology, very little capital, no fixed place of business, few or no employees, quasi-legality or lack of registration, little record-keeping.

No definite distinction has been established in statistics between the formal and informal sectors and the ILO and United Nations concepts of labour force and economic production are applied without regard to "informal" sector characteristics. However, statistical recommendations do clearly distinguish economically active persons working on their own account without employees and unpaid family workers from other economically active persons. Therefore, for statistical purposes in the short term this is the definition used by INSTRAW and the Statistical Office of the United Nations Secretariat to identify women in the informal sector in Africa, Latin America and Asia. All persons working in the informal sector by this definition are also considered as economically active.

Women in services

Expanding services account for much of the increase in women's economic participation in the developed regions, in northern Africa and western Asia, and in Latin America and the Caribbean. In Latin America and the Caribbean and in the developed regions, women make up nearly half the service sector—more than would be expected from women's representation in the workforce at large. Indeed, between 60 and 70 per cent of the economically active women in these two regions are employed in services. In Asia and the Pacific and in Africa, few women work outside of agriculture, but among those who do, three times as many work in services as in industry.

The disproportionate number of women in services can be attributed to a mixture of factors. Men dominate industry, forcing women to seek work elsewhere. And service jobs—such as nursing, social, clerical and catering work—carry a more feminine label because of a real or imagined similarity with women's traditional roles. The greater availability of part-time work in service jobs may also contribute to the feminization of the sector, though it is not clear whether this is a cause or an effect.

The informal sector

In Africa and in Latin America and the Caribbean, women's opportunities for wage employment in agriculture, industry and services during the 1970s and 1980s did not improve. Due to economic crises and the impact of stabilization and adjustment policies, women's wage employment remained negligible in Africa and actually fell in Latin America.[17]

Excluded from wage employment, women have increasingly turned to work in the informal sector. In many countries the informal sector and own-account work are women's only wedges of opportunity in the face of occupational segregation, unemployment and underemployment. This is clear in Africa, where public and private wage employment are fairly well monopolized by men, and women are confined to the economic dead-end of subsistence agriculture. The informal sector is often essential for the economic survival of women—particularly poor women who work in petty trading or such home-based industries as beer brewing, soap making and tailoring. A study in Zambia shows, for example, that the importance of women's informal sector earnings to total family income increased dramatically in the 1980s.[18]

Along with discrimination in wage and salary employment, many women face cultural norms that keep them close to the home and tied to home-based production. Regular employee working hours often conflict with household responsibilities, particularly child care. And women's lack of access to education and training further handicaps them in the labour market.[19]

The informal sector is by no means a panacea for women. It is far less secure than formal sector work, and it generally pays less than the minimum wage. Low levels of investment technology, poor economies of scale, high unit prices for raw materials and limited access to large markets and marketing organizations inhibit productivity and returns.[20] And although women usually bear the costs of setting up their informal activity, they often do not control the benefits—which may be entirely taken by husbands, fathers or others.

6.15

Self-employment is an important source of livelihood for women in developing regions

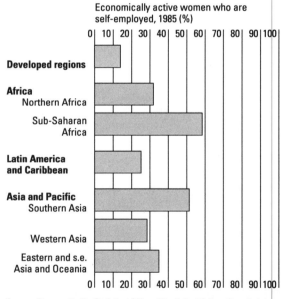

Economically active women who are self-employed, 1985 (%)

Source: Prepared by the Statistical Office of the United Nations Secretariat from International Labour Office, *Year Book of Labour Statistics* (Geneva, various years).

6.16
Economically active women are concentrated in low-productivity agricultural or services industries in developing regions. They are often forced to improvise their own economic opportunities with little resources or support in the informal sector

Despite the limitations of national accounts and labour force statistics (see pages 85 and 90), they can provide a wealth of information on women in the economy. In 1988/89, INSTRAW and the Statistical Office of the United Nations Secretariat undertook a series of case studies of women's economic activity and production in six countries in Africa, Latin America and Asia. These studies examined the role of women and the distribution of economic production by major industry groups (agriculture, mining, other industry, transport, and other services), and the contribution of women and the informal sector in manufacturing and related industries, transport and other services.

The basic statistical findings are presented in the two tables below. The first shows the percentage distribution of gross domestic product and of women and men in the labour force (in most cases according to census statis-tics), among four industry groups, which total to 100 per cent. The second shows (a) the distribution of gross domestic product and of women in the labour force in total production outside of agriculture and mining, (b) the estimated percentage of production in each industry group which is informal, and (c) the estimated percentage of informal production in each industry group which is produced by women.

The columns under "Total" refer to (a) the percentage of women in the labour force working outside of agriculture and mining activities, (b) the estimated percentage of total production outside of agriculture and mining which is informal, and (c) the estimated percentage of this informal production which is produced by women.

A. Distribution of GDP and female and male labour force by type of economic activity

		Agriculture			Mining			Industry (exc. mining), transport			Services (exc. transport)		
		% of GDP	% of labour force f	m	% of GDP	% of labour force f	m	% of GDP	% of labour force f	m	% of GDP	% of labour force f	m
Sub-Saharan Africa													
Congo	1984	7.3	72.9	35.7	45.8	0.3	2.2	21.9	3.2	28.3	25.1	23.3	33.7
Gambia	1983	33.3	85.5	63.5	–	–	–	17.9	1.1	11.5	48.1	13.4	25.0
Zambia	1986	14.0	72.7	57.4	21.0	0.2	4.1	35.5	4.3	15.2	29.5	22.8	23.5
Latin America													
Venezuela	1983	6.8	2.4	20.5	16.3	0.3	1.9	35.6	17.2	36.5	41.3	80.1	41.2
	1987	6.3	2.0	19.0	10.1	0.4	1.2	37.3	20.1	38.2	46.4	77.5	41.6
South-eastern Asia													
Indonesia	1980	24.8	53.8	57.0	25.7	0.4	0.9	22.1	12.8	16.5	27.5	33.1	25.6
	1985	23.7	53.6	55.3	16.3	0.3	0.9	26.5	12.0	18.0	33.6	34.1	25.8
Malaysia	1986	26.2	32.5	29.7	10.8	0.3	0.9	30.8	21.7	28.7	32.3	45.6	40.6

Note: The groups of economic activities shown are mutually exclusive and comprise all economic activities. Percentages of GDP, female labour force and male labour force thus each total 100 for each country across the four groups.

B. Contribution of women in the informal sector to industry and services production

		Industry (exc. mining)			Transport			Services (exc. transport)			Total [a]		
		% of fem. lab. force [a]	% of prod. informal	% of informal female	% of fem. lab. force [a]	% of prod. informal	% of informal female	% of fem. lab. force [a]	% of prod. informal	% of informal female	% of fem. lab. force [b]	% of prod. informal	% of informal female
Sub-Saharan Africa													
Congo	1984	10.3	44.0	9.9	2.0	13.4	1.3	87.9	41.9	60.4	26.8	37.9	39.3
Gambia	1983	5.6	45.0	10.9	2.0	18.0	2.2	92.2	36.4	30.6	14.5	35.8	25.0
Zambia	1986	15.0	41.3	41.4	0.9	6.8	10.8	84.1	48.4	64.7	17.3	41.7	53.3
Latin America													
Venezuela	1983	15.4	21.3	25.3	2.3	44.8	1.4	82.3	26.4	27.4	97.3	27.0	20.5
	1987	18.7	13.6	37.6	1.8	43.6	1.6	79.4	20.0	36.7	97.6	20.2	29.2
South-eastern Asia													
Indonesia	1980	27.4	44.1	45.4	0.3	44.6	0.8	71.6	59.1	46.8	45.8	52.5	43.0
Malaysia	1986	30.6	13.1	53.7	1.6	20.5	2.8	67.7	22.7	42.6	67.2	18.6	43.2

Source: "Compendium of statistics on women in the informal sector" (United Nations publication, forthcoming), INSTRAW and Statistical Office of the United Nations Secretariat.

a   Excluding agriculture and mining.
b   Female labour force in industry, transport and services as per cent of total female labour force in all branches of the economy.

Gross domestic product

Gross domestic product (GDP) is the total undup- licated output of economic goods and services pro- duced within a country as measured in monetary terms according to the United Nations System of National Accounts (SNA). GDP in- cludes subsistence products produced by households for their own use, valued at current local prices for com- parable commodities. Some countries of eastern Europe and elsewhere use net mate- rial product (NMP) as a measure of total production instead of GDP. NMP is based on the System of Mate- rial Product Balances (MPS).

GDP and NMP are measured in the local currency of each country or area. Where GDP or NMP measures are shown in terms of US dollars, the conversion has usually been done on the basis of prevailing exchange rates for international trade. These rates may differ substantially from open market rates or comparisons of actual purchasing power.

Informal sector activity is even more difficult to measure than formal. An approximation is to look at the extent of self-employment. More than half the economically active women in sub-Saharan Africa and southern Asia and a third in northern Africa and the rest of Asia are self-employed (chart 6.15). Looking only at non-agricultural production, recent United Nations estimates for six countries in Africa, Latin America and Asia show that the informal sector accounts for significant but widely varying shares of output—from 20 per cent in Malaysia and Venezuela to over 50 per cent in In- donesia (table 6.16). In services (outside transport, where women are almost completely excluded), women account for two thirds of informal sector production in African countries such as the Congo and Zambia, where their role in trade is well- known. In the developed regions by contrast, the proportion of women who are self-employed aver- ages only around 14 per cent.

Looking at women's participation rates in the informal sector in the various sectors of productive activity confirms the importance of informal eco- nomic activity for women.[20] Generally, the lower a sector's share in GDP, the higher the amount of informal activity in that sector and the greater the participation of women. In many African countries, for example, agriculture accounts for less than 25 per cent of GDP, and women make up most of the workforce. Mining, by contrast, accounts for a big part of GDP in many African countries and men make up most of the workforce. Outside agriculture and mining, the informal sector contributes much— in Indonesian industry, half—to employment and production. Except in transport generally and indus- try in Africa, the informal sector provides signifi- cant opportunities for women in the six countries studied.[21]

Economic crisis and the impact of stabilization and adjustment policies on women[22]

Women's situation in a country is also influ- enced by the level and growth of economic output. Total production and government policies deter- mine the income available and its use for consump- tion and investment and ultimately economic welfare.

The most common measure of economic pro- duction is gross domestic product (GDP). The ways in which GDP per capita may misrepresent the economic situation of countries are well- known. As an indicator of the economic welfare of populations GDP is even more deficient.[23] Table 6.17, for example, shows how much GDP fails to take account of women's unpaid housework. Women's average economic situation in most de- veloping regions is certainly worse than GDP figures show, as GDP averages do not take any ac- count of distributional considerations. (Conversely, women's economic progress in most developed regions may also be very much distorted by GDP figures.) But even according to this very crude and optimistic measure, women in most developing regions are doing very poorly indeed in economic terms.

A large majority of the world's women—62 per cent—live in countries or areas where per capita GDP per year (calculated before debt payments abroad are subtracted) is less than $US1,000. Only 14 per cent live in countries with an annual per capita GDP over $10,000. In between, 13 per cent are in countries which have just begun to make some progress out of almost universal poverty, with per capita GDPs between $1,000 and $3,000, and a mere 4 per cent are in countries which could be said to be entering a global middle class, with annual per capita GDPs of $3,000 to $10,000 (chart VI.18.).[24] (Eastern Europe and the USSR, with 8 per cent of the world's women, are excluded from these calculations as no official GDP data are avail- able for them.)

Looking at rates of growth of gross domestic product in these same groups of countries (the usual measure of economic success over time), the figures are even more pessimistic. The high-GDP countries averaged an annual increase in their GDP per year in the 1980s of over $300 per capita. The "new middle-class countries" averaged an annual increase of about $90 per person per year. By contrast the rest (with 75 per cent of the world's women), saw increases of less than $10 per person per year on average and decreases for many. (Again, eastern Europe and the USSR, as well as several small countries with very high but declin- ing oil incomes due to price fluctuations, are excluded from these calculations.)

Although some economies in Asia and the Pacific and in Latin America and the Caribbean surged in the 1970s, their GDP growth rates declined in the 1980s. In many countries throughout the developing regions GDP growth rates were actually negative (list 6.19). The countries in the developed regions maintained consistently higher growth of GDP per capita than the other regions throughout the 1970s and 1980s although their rate of growth also declined. Africa has the lowest GDPs of all the regions, and GDP per capita in the 1980s has fallen by an average of over 20 per cent.

Economic crises and stabilization and adjustment programmes have brought increased hardships to many people in much of the developing world, especially the heavily indebted countries, and these have particularly affected women. With the stabilization and adjustment processes relying heavily on cuts in government spending, women have been disproportionately squeezed out of public sector employment. Cuts in such government services as health, child care, family planning and education have hit women particularly hard, setting back women's earlier gains.[25] Women generally depend more on health services than men because of child-bearing, because of their responsibility for their family's health and because they outlive men and require more services in old age.

The burden of inflation has fallen heavily on women who are responsible for procuring staple goods for the household. Often stabilization and adjustment plans have mandated wage freezes, the resources for obtaining goods have dwindled, and women have had to increase their working hours just to ensure their families' survival. In addition, the costs of imported processed goods or time-saving technologies have become prohibitive for many people—and again the increased work burden has fallen mainly on women.[26]

Rising interest rates, another result of structural adjustment, also have an insidious effect on women. Because women lack collateral and are discriminated against by formal lending institutions, they have much less access to formal credit than men. So, they must rely more on informal lending institutions that charge very high interest rates—pushed up even higher by rising formal rates. An increasing part of women's meagre operating surplus then has to be spent on these payments, adding even more to their work burden.[27]

6.17
Estimates of addition to GDP if women's unpaid housework were included

Country	Year	Value of unpaid housework as % of GDP*	Sponsoring organization or researcher
A. For all women			
Developed regions			
Canada	1961	27	Statistics Canada
	1971	28	
Denmark	1949	50	Denmark Statistics
Finland	1979	31	Ministry of Social Affairs and Health
France	1975	24	INSEE
Norway	1972	41	A. L. Brathaug and A. B. Dahle
	1981	28	
United States	1929	25	National Bureau of Economic Research
	1960	29	M. Murphy
	1970	27	
	1975	30	J. Peskin
	1980	23	
Developing regions			
India	1970	33	M. Mukherjee
Pakistan	1975	35[a]	T. Alauddin
Philippines	1982	11	National Commission on the Role of Filipino Women
B. Housewives not economically active			
Chile	1981	15[a]	V. L. Pardo and N. P. Cruz
Japan	1955	11	Economic Council
	1970	9	
Venezuela	1982	22[a]	Central Bank

*Methods of valuation based on equivalent market wages or services were used except in the case of Japan where overall average female wage was used.

Sources: Compiled by Luisella Goldschmidt-Clermont as consultant to the United Nations Secretariat, based on the following—
Canada: H. J. Adler and O. Hawrylyshyn, "Estimates of the value of household work, Canada, 1961 and 1971", *Review of Income and Wealth* (New Haven, USA, December 1978);
Chile: V. L. Pardo and N. P. Cruz, "La dueña de casa en sus actividades de trabajo: su valoración en el mercado y dentro del hogar", Documento Serie Investigación, No. 59 (Santiago, Universidad de Chile, Departamento de Economía, 1983);
Denmark: Statistics Department, "Nationalproduktet og national-indkomsten 1946–1949", in *Statistiske Meddelelser* (Copenhagen), Series 4, Vol. 140, Fasc. 2 (1951);
Finland: Ministry of Social Affairs and Health, Research Department, 1980–86, *Housework Study*, Parts I to XIV, Special Social Studies, Official Statistics of Finland (Helsinki, 1980/86);
France: A. Chadeau and A. Fouquet, "Peut-on measurer le travail domestique?" *Economie et statistique* (Paris), No. 136 (1981); A. Chadeau, "Measuring household production, conceptual issues and results for France", report to the Second ECE/INSTRAW Joint Meeting on Statistics of Women, CES/AC.60/44 (Geneva, 1989);
India: M. Mukherjee, "Contributions and use of social product by women", in *Tyranny of the Household,* D. Jain and N. Banerjee, eds. (Delhi, Shakti Books/Vikas);

Japan: Economic Council, Net National Welfare Measurement Committee, *Measuring Net National Welfare in Japan* (Tokyo, 1973);
Norway: A. L. Brathaug and A. B. Dahle, 1989, "Verdiskapning i husholdningene", paper presented at the seminar "Kvinner og okonomi", held at Bergen 5–7 October 1989;
Pakistan: T. Alauddin, "Contribution of housewives to GNP: a case study of Pakistan", M.S. thesis (Vanderbilt University, Nashville, USA, 1980);
Philippines: National Commission on the Role of Filipino Women, "Quantification of housework", NCRFW monograph No. 4 (Manila, 1985);
United States of America: S. Kuznets, *National Income and Its Composition, 1919–1938,* Publication No. 40, 2 vols. (New York, National Bureau of Economic Research, 1941); M. Murphy, "The value of non-market household production: opportunity cost *vs* market cost estimates", *Review of Income and Wealth* (New Haven, USA, September 1978); M. Weinrobe, "Household production and national production: an improvement of the record", *Review of Income and Wealth* (New Haven, USA, March 1974); J. Peskin, "The value of household work in the 1980s", *in Proceedings* of the Social Statistics Section of the American Statistical Association Meeting, held at Toronto, Canada, 15–18 August 1983;
Venezuela: T. H. Valecillos et al., "División del trabajo, distribución personal del tiempo diario y valor económico del trabajo realizado en los hogares Venezolanos" (Caracas, Banco Central de Venezuela, 1983).

a   Data from one or a small number of major cities only.

6.18
Most women live in countries with very low per capita GDP and very low or declining economic growth in terms of US dollars

In 1987, two thirds of the world's women lived in countries with per capita GDP of less than $US1,000 per year

In the 1980s, per capita GDP was increasing less than $10 per year (or declining) in countries with 75 per cent of the world's women

Percentage distribution of population by level of countries' GDP (per capita GDP per year)

Average annual change in GDP per capita, 1980–1986 ($US) [b]

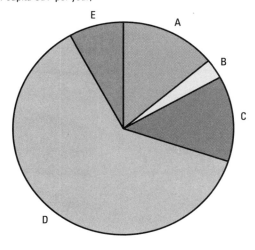

A   High GDP countries (more than $10,000), 14%
B   Middle GDP countries ($3,000 to 10,000), 3%
C   Low GDP countries ($1,000 to 3,000), 13%
D   Very low GDP countries (less than $1,000), 62%
E   GDP not available, 8% [a]

340 ●---------	High GDP countries (more than $10,000)
320	
300	
280	
260	
240	
220	
200	
180	
160	
140	
120	
100 ●---------	Middle GDP countries ($3,000 to 10,000)
80	
60	
40	
20 ●---------	Low GDP countries ($1,000 to 3,000)
0 ●------ ---	Very low GDP countries (less than $1,000)
−20	

Source: Calculated by the Statistical Office of the United Nations Secretariat from United Nations population and national accounts statistics databases.

a   Eastern Europe and USSR.
b   Excludes countries with high per capita oil income, which largely experienced declining GDP in the period due to declining oil prices, and eastern Europe and USSR, for which official GDP data are not available.

Indicators
Time use

Time-use statistics are unique because they measure what people do in the course of a day. This is especially important in determining what women do. Traditional methods of measuring economic activity are misleading in terms of looking at total work time. They ignore unpaid housework, child-bearing and child care, and they often overlook unpaid work in family enterprises, household food production and processing and doing one's own construction and repairs. Time-use statistics describe how peoples' time is distributed among various forms of activity according to a more or less detailed classification of activities. Thus, time-use statistics have aroused interest and can fill the gap when it comes to identifying and measuring women's real workload.

Since 1985 time-use studies have been carried out or planned by national statistical services in over 15 countries in the developed regions. In developing regions, however, time-use data are not generally available in official statistics. But some time-use studies have been done mainly at the community level in these regions and, while limited, show clearly the importance of these data in understanding women's daily lives.

Table 7 presents statistics and indicators on (a) time use of women and men in economic activity, unpaid housework and personal care and free time and (b) time allocation of women and men in unpaid housework, overall and broken down into meal preparation, child care, shopping and other housework. These data have been compiled and standardized to the extent possible from the published results of a large number of national and sub-national surveys taken between 1965 and 1986.

These surveys are listed in the source note to the table. More detailed descriptions of sources and methods for many of the time-use surveys consulted can be found in the United Nations study "Collection and compilation of time-use statistics to measure the participation of women in the informal sector".[28]

In part A of table 7, economic activity refers to time spent in income-earning activities and in unpaid work in family enterprises. It also includes commuting and educational activities. Unpaid housework includes household chores and child care. Household chores includes cooking, housecleaning, laundry, shopping, gardening, pet care and other housework. Child care refers to direct care of children, helping with homework or reading to or entertaining them. It does not include time during which an individual was responsible for children but not actually engaged in doing something for them. Personal care and free time includes bathing, sleeping, eating, time related to personal medical attention, resting, organizational participation, sports and games, socializing and media related activities (reading, television).

Part B of table 7 presents statistics on the division of work time between women and men in unpaid housework activities. In addition to meal preparation and the child care activities described above, time in shopping activities and other housework is shown. Shopping activities include marketing, errands or trips for services. Other housework includes housecleaning, laundry, mending and sewing, repairs, and animal, plant and yard care.

Economic activity and occupational groups

Table 8 presents statistics on the economically active population aged 15 years and over and on ratios of women to men in broad occupational groups.

Concepts and issues concerning statistics on women economically active are discussed in the special section "Counting economically active women" at the beginning of this chapter. As explained there, the standard concept of economically active population is defined to comprise all employed and unemployed persons, including those seeking work for the first time. It covers employers operating unincorporated enterprises, persons working on their own account, employees, unpaid family workers, members of producers co-operatives and members of the armed forces. In the internationally-recommended definition, production of primary products such as foodstuffs for own consumption and certain other non-monetary activities are considered economic activity and persons engaged in such production are to be con-

sidered economically active. In principle, any such work need only be for as little as one hour a week for a person to be considered economically active.

Specific elements of the standard concepts may, however, differ substantially from country to country and many of these differences may affect the measurement of women's participation in economic activity, such as the choice of time-reference period and the determination of minimum hours of work and unpaid family work, including production for own consumption. Moreover, the economic activity of women is often substantially understated because stereotypes held by census and survey interviewers and respondents lead to errors in the reporting and recording of the economic activity and because, in many countries, women account for the major portion of persons engaged in those economic activities that are the most difficult to measure.

Indicators concerning the total economically active population aged 15 years and over have been compiled mainly from estimates and projections prepared by ILO. [1] These are based primarily on population census results from the 1970 and 1980 world census rounds, adjusted by ILO to use common definitions and years. The size and economic activity rates of the total population and the size of the economically actively population are estimated and projected by age and sex for 10-year intervals from 1950 to 2020 and for 1985 and 2025. In addition, the numbers and percentage distributions of women and men employed in agriculture, industry, and services are estimated for each country for the years 1950, 1960, 1970 and 1980. The estimates and projections indicate significant changes over time in the pattern of participation of women in the labour force, as well as greater emphasis in data collection and methodology on more accurate and comprehensive measurement of unpaid family work, including production for own or household consumption, and own-account workers.

The indicators on occupational groups in table 8 are based on statistics compiled by the ILO based on the latest census or survey of the country concerned. [2] Occupations are classified according to the revised International Standard Classification of Occupations (ISCO) issued by ILO in 1968.

Unfortunately, the enumeration of women and persons under age 15 in the labour force is often biased and incomplete, censuses and surveys are seldom conducted regularly and the results in developing regions are often available only after many years. Furthermore, in many cases the data on economic activity of women fluctuate widely from one census or survey to the next.

6.19
Where GDP declined in the 1980s

Africa
Middle GDP per capita
Gabon
Low GDP per capita
Namibia
Very low GDP per capita
Chad
Guinea
Liberia
Mauritania
Mozambique
Nigeria
Sao Tome and Principe
Sierra Leone
Sudan
Togo
Zambia

Latin America and Caribbean
Middle GDP per capita
Trinidad and Tobago
Low GDP per capita
Argentina
French Guiana
Peru
Suriname
Uruguay
Venezuela
Very low GDP per capita
Bolivia
El Salvador
Guatemala
Guyana
Haiti

Asia and Pacific
Low GDP per capita
Iraq
Very low GDP per capita
Cambodia
Kiribati
Lebanon
Philippines

Note: Excludes countries of eastern Europe and USSR, for which official GDP data are not available, and oil-producing countries with GDP per capita higher than $US5000 per year.

Source: Statistical Office of the United Nations Secretariat.

The latest ILO estimates include retroactive adjustments of earlier estimates for some countries for 1950, 1960 and 1970, compared to previous estimates issued in 1977. These new estimates are substantially higher for women in some developing countries, especially in sub-Saharan Africa.

The ILO estimates correspond closely to census and survey enumerations in most cases where the latter are available, but depart significantly in others. For example, in Benin, ILO in 1977 estimated the total size of the agricultural labour force for 1970 as 655,000, among whom 14 per cent were women. In 1986 it adjusted the total retroactively to 1.2 million, among whom 50 per cent were women. The size of the labour force in industry and services for 1970 was simultaneously reduced in the new estimates from 662,000 to 277,000, and the female share from 75 to 39 per cent. African countries most seriously affected by the revised estimates include Angola, Benin, Guinea-Bissau, Libya, Mali, Mauritania, Mozambique, Niger, Sudan, and Tunisia; Asian countries include Afghanistan, Iraq and Syria.

In table 8, the first two columns show the numbers of women estimated by ILO to have been economically active in 1970 and projected to be economically active in 1990. The economic activity rates for both women and men in the next four columns show the estimated (for 1970) and projected (for 1990) percentages of women and men aged 15 and over economically active. The next two columns show the average growth rate in per cent per year for the total numbers of economically active women and men from 1970 to 1990. This rate is calculated according to the formula given in the notes for table 1, at the end of chap. 1 above. The final column on economically active population gives the percentage of the total estimated economically active population of both sexes in 1990 who are women.

The last four columns of table 8 show the number of women per 100 men in various broad groupings of occupations. The organization of the occupational groupings used is explained in the definitional note on page 86. The major group "professional, technical and related workers" is not shown here for lack of space. As can be see from chart 6.10, this major group has a high ratio of women to men in most areas, which is due mainly to large numbers of women teachers. These data have generally been compiled from the most recent population census data available since 1975 and issued in [2 and 10].

Gross domestic product and status in employment

Table 9 presents several series related to gross domestic product (GDP) or net material product (NMP) and series on the distribution of persons in the labour force according to their status in employment.

Indicators on GDP or NMP are based primarily on statistics of national accounts and balances compiled by the Statistical Office of the United Nations Secretariat for its National Accounts Database and yearbooks. They contain data available to the United Nations Secretariat up to March 1989. The general concept of gross domestic product is explained on page 94 above. For countries using the System of Material Product Balances (MPS) rather than the System of National Accounts (SNA) in the period shown, the principal aggregate measure is net material product (NMP).

Where no currency exchange rate controls are in effect, current market exchange rates are used to present GDP-NMP data in US dollars. Where multiple exchange rates are used in countries the official rate for business and investment transactions or the market rate is usually used. In a few countries where international transactions are limited, indicative estimates of the exchange rate made by the United Nations Secretariat are used for the conversion. As noted above, for purposes of international comparison, currency exchange rates applied to national accounts aggregates provide an important but highly approximate measure of national economic output.

The figures on average GDP-NMP growth rates are computed by the Statistical Office of the United Nations Secretariat as average annual geometric rates of growth expressed in percentages for the years and periods of years indicated. An exponential curve is fitted to the data by the least squares regression method. The growth rates for the individual countries are based on the estimates of gross domestic product and net material product at constant prices and selected components by type of expenditure (use) and by kind of economic activity.

In GDP, gross fixed capital formation consists of net outlays on new durable goods for addition to stocks of all fixed assets in a country. Included are all durable goods, work-in-progress on construction projects, capital repairs, improvement of land and the acquisition of breeding stock and the like. Excluded are acquisition of assets for military use and of land, mineral deposits, timber tracts and the like.

The series on debt service payments as a percentage of gross national product (GNP) refers to total service payments for long-term public and publicly guaranteed external debt and private nonguaranteed debt. These data are compiled by the World Bank and published in [34].[29]

The series on status of employment and the labour force are based on the status of employment classification used in population censuses and surveys in most countries. Using this classification, all economically active persons are classified in one of the following categories: employer, own-account worker, employee, unpaid family worker, member of producers' co-operative. An employer or own-account worker is defined as a person who operates his or her own economic enterprise or engages independently in a profession or trade. An employee is defined as a person who works for a public or private employer and receives remuneration in wages, salary, commission, tips, piece-rates or pay in kind. An unpaid family worker is a person who works without pay in an economic enterprise operated by a related person living in the same household.[30] For each of these categories, table 9 shows (a) the total number of persons of both sexes in that status as a percentage of the total labour force of both sexes, and (b) the percentage of all persons in the status category who are women.

These statistics have been compiled from [2].

Notes

1   Unless otherwise noted, statistics on time use have been compiled by Andrew Harvey as consultant to the United Nations Secretariat from national survey reports and studies (see source note to table 7). The geographical scope and population coverage of samples as well as concepts and definitions used in time-use surveys vary considerably among the surveys studied. In particular, they are more limited for earlier periods. The conclusions reported here may therefore be substantially modified in the light of future analysis and research.

2   *Engendering Adjustment for the 1980s: Report of the Commonwealth Expert Group on Women and Structural Adjustment* (London, Commonwealth Secretariat Publications, 1989); and *The Invisible Adjustment: Poor Women and the Economic Crisis* (Santiago, United Nations Children's Fund, Regional Office for the Americas and the Caribbean, 1989).

3   Iris Niemi and Hanni Pakkonen, *Time Use Changes in Finland in the 1980s* (Helsinki, Central Statistical Office of Finland, 1990).

4   *Engendering Adjustment...;* and Susan Joekes, "Gender and macro-economic policy", Association for Women in Development, Paper No. 4 (Blacksburg, Virginia, 1989).

5   *The Economic Role of Women in the ECE Region* (United Nations publication, Sales No. E.80.II.E.6), p. 39.

6   *Women and Men in Sweden: Equality of the Sexes 1990* (Stockholm, Statistics Sweden, 1990).

7   S. Bianchi and D. Spain, *American Women in Transition* (New York, Russell Sage Foundation, 1986); and W. Bielby and J. Baron, "A woman's place is with other women: sex segregation within organizations", in *Sex Segregation in the Workplace: Trends, Explanations, Remedies,* Barbara F. Reskin, ed. (Washington, D.C., National Academy Press, 1984).

8   Katherine Marshall, "Women in male-dominated professions", *Canadian Social Trends* (Ottawa, Statistics Canada), Winter, 1987.

9   Statistics compiled by the Statistical Office of the United Nations Secretariat from [2].

10   *Engendering Adjustment....*

11   Unless otherwise noted, statistics in this section have been compiled by the Statistical Office of the United Nations Secretariat from [1].

12   *Rural Women in Latin America: Rural Development, Migration, Land and Legislation* (Santiago, Food and Agriculture Organization of the United Nations, Regional Office for Latin America and the Caribbean, 1987); and "Data from censuses and household surveys for the analysis of female labour in Latin America and the Caribbean: appraisal of deficiencies and recommendations for dealing with them", Zulma Recchini de Lattes and Catalina H. Wainerman as consultants to the United Nations Secretariat (E/CEPAL/L.205, 1979).

13   *Effectiveness of Agricultural Extension Services in Reaching Rural Women in Africa,* vol. 1 (Rome, Food and Agriculture Organization of the United Nations, 1987); and *Engendering Adjustment....*

14   Calculated by Ruth Dixon as consultant to the United Nations Secretariat, from *Report on the 1980 World Census of Agriculture,* Bulletin Nos. 10 and 11 (1984), Nos. 14, 15, 16 and 20 (1985), and unpublished data of the Food and Agriculture Organization.

15   *Effectiveness of Agricultural Extension...,* and *Engendering Adjustment....*

16   "The current status of agriculture extension worldwide", paper prepared by the Food and Agriculture Organization for the Global Consultation on Agricultural Extension, convened by FAO in Rome, 4–8 December 1989.

17   *Engendering Adjustment....*

18   A. Evans, "The implications of economic reforms for women in Zambia: the case of the economic reform programme, 1983–1987" (London, Commonwealth Secretariat, 1989).

19   *Engendering Adjustment...;* and Joekes, op. cit.

20 "Collecting statistics on the participation of women in the informal sector: methods used in Latin America", in *Methods of Measuring Women's Participation and Production in the Informal Sector,* Series F, No. 46 (United Nations publication, Sales No. E.90.XVII.16); and D. Mazumdar, "The urban informal sector", *World Development* (Oxford) 1976.

21 Statistics compiled by Lourdes Urdaneta-Ferrán as consultant to INSTRAW and the United Nations Secretariat, from national population and census reports and unpublished tables provided by national statistical services. To be issued in *Compendium of Statistics on Women in the Informal Sector* (United Nations publication, forthcoming).

22 Unless otherwise noted, the statistics in this section have been compiled by the Statistical Office of the United Nations Secretariat from [17 and 23].

23 See United Nations Development Programme, *Human Development Report 1990* (New York and Oxford, Oxford University Press, 1990); and *The Feasibility of Welfare-oriented Measures to Supplement the National Accounts and Balances: A Technical Report,* Series F, No. 22 (United Nations publication, Sales No. E.77.XVII.12).

24 Some of the distortions in the use of GDP per capita as a measure of economic welfare can be removed by converting the series to a common currency, using statistics on comparative purchasing power rather than exchange rates. GDP comparisons based on purchasing power parities have been compiled by the Statistical Office of the United Nations Secretariat and issued in *World Comparisons of Purchasing Power and Real Product for 1980: Phase IV of the International Comparison Project,* Series F, No. 42, Part One: *Summary Results for 60 Countries* (United Nations publication, Sales No.E.86.XVII.9). See also *Compendium of Statistics and Indicators on the Situation of Women 1986,* Series K, No. 5 (United Nations publication, Sales No. E/F.88.XVII.6), table 16; and *Human Development Report 1990,* op. cit.

25 *Engendering Adjustment...; and The Invisible Adjustment....*

26 *Engendering Adjustment....*

27 Ibid.

28 Part Two of *Methods of Measuring Women's Participation....*

29 Gross national product (GNP), which is used by the World Bank in calculating this series, consists of GDP modified to add net income received by residents from abroad for labour and capital, and to subtract such payments made to nonresidents who contributed to the domestic economy.

30 *Principles and Recommendations for Population and Housing Censuses,* Series M, No. 67 (United Nations publication, Sales No. E.80.XVII.8), para. 2.205.

Table 7
Indicators on time use
A. Time use of women and men in selected country studies

Country or area	Year	Economic activity		Unpaid housework Household chores		Child care		Total		Personal care and free time	
		f	m	f	m	f	m	f	m	f	m
Northern America and Australia											
Australia	1987	16.9	35.5	27.2	13.8	5.8	1.6	33.0	15.3	118	117
Canada	1971	18.8	41.2	29.5	8.9	6.2	1.5	35.7	10.4	114	116
	1981	17.2	30.7	23.0	11.1	4.3	1.5	27.3	12.5	124	125
	1986	17.5	32.9	24.6	12.1	4.3	1.4	28.9	13.5	121	121
United States	1965	18.7	48.3	32.1	8.8	5.7	1.3	37.8	10.0	111	109
	1975	16.7	37.6	27.6	9.6	4.4	1.3	32.0	10.9	119	119
	1986	24.5	41.3	29.9	17.4	2.0	0.8	31.9	18.1	112	109
Western Europe											
Belgium	1966	19.3	50.8	34.7	6.0	3.6	0.8	38.4	6.9	110	111
Finland	1979	21.8	30.0	22.5	10.8	3.0	0.9	25.6	11.7	122	125
France	1965	21.7	51.8	35.0	9.9	7.6	1.3	42.6	11.3	104	105
Germany [a] Federal Rep. of Germany	1965	13.3	42.4	39.3	10.2	4.9	0.9	44.2	11.1	111	115
Netherlands	1975	5.8	27.3	27.1	7.1	5.3	1.6	32.4	8.7	130	132
	1980	7.1	23.9	27.9	7.4	5.5	1.5	33.4	8.8	130	135
Norway	1972	14.4	40.0	32.8	5.7	4.4	1.2	37.2	6.9	117	121
	1981	17.1	34.2	25.1	7.1	4.8	2.0	29.8	9.2	121	125
United Kingdom	1961	16.5	45.7	31.3	4.3	2.6	0.4	33.9	4.8	118	118
	1975	17.2	39.6	27.1	4.9	2.4	0.6	29.5	5.5	121	123
	1984	14.1	26.8	26.4	10.3	3.6	1.1	30.0	11.4	124	130
Eastern Europe and USSR											
Bulgaria	1965	42.6	52.9	25.6	11.1	2.9	1.4	28.6	12.5	97	103
	1988	37.7	46.9	29.3	14.3	4.3	1.1	33.7	15.3	97	106
Czechoslovakia	1965	29.8	44.4	36.0	12.7	4.7	2.5	40.7	15.1	97	109
Hungary	1965	34.0	56.6	36.3	5.5	4.7	2.5	41.0	7.9	93	103
	1976	26.7	41.5	30.2	10.9	3.0	1.4	33.3	12.3	108	114
Poland	1965	30.5	52.2	33.5	9.7	5.3	2.7	38.9	12.4	99	103
	1984	24.9	42.2	30.5	7.7	4.4	2.0	34.9	9.7	108	116
Yugoslavia	1965	19.5	49.5	37.0	8.1	3.8	1.4	40.7	9.5	108	109
USSR	1965	43.0	53.2	32.3	14.0	3.6	1.4	35.9	15.4	89	99
	1986	38.5	49.0	25.7	14.6	4.4	1.5	30.1	16.1	99	103
Latin America											
Guatemala	1977	29.4	56.7	39.9	6.3	9.8	4.6	49.7	10.9	89	101
Peru	1966	15.1	52.1	36.0	5.6	4.5	0.5	40.5	6.1	112	110
Venezuela	1983	15.5	42.2	28.2	3.0	4.0	0.7	32.2	3.7	120	122
Asia											
Indonesia (Java)	1973	41.3	55.3	28.9	3.0	7.2	2.6	36.1	5.6	..	..
Nepal	1979	32.3	40.7	38.5	10.8	4.8	1.1	43.3	11.9	..	..

Table 7. Indicators on time use [*cont.*]

B. Distribution between women and men of unpaid housework

Country or area	Year	Unpaid housework (% share of women and men)									
		Preparing meals		Child care		Shopping		Other housework		Total	
		Women %	Men %	Women %	Men %	Women %	Men %	Women %	Men %	Women %	Men %
Northern America and Australia											
Australia	1987	76	24	78	22	60	40	53	47	68	32
Canada	1971	87	13	80	20	58	42	78	22	77	23
	1981	74	26	75	25	61	39	66	34	69	31
	1986	81	19	76	24	58	42	67	33	68	32
United States	1965	90	10	82	18	66	34	78	22	79	21
	1975	87	13	77	23	62	38	69	31	75	25
	1986	78	22	73	28	60	40	61	39	64	36
Western Europe											
Belgium	1966	94	6	81	19	76	24	83	17	85	15
Finland	1979	82	18	77	23	57	43	54	46	69	31
France	1965	87	13	85	15	70	30	76	24	79	21
Germany[a]											
Federal Rep. of Germany	1965	94	6	84	16	75	25	74	26	80	20
Netherlands	1975	83	17	77	23	65	35	84	16	79	21
	1980	80	20	79	21	63	37	86	14	79	21
Norway	1972	89	11	79	21	67	33	86	14	84	16
	1981	81	19	70	30	57	43	82	18	76	24
United Kingdom	1961	90	10	86	14	79	21	89	11	88	12
	1975	89	11	81	19	69	31	87	13	84	16
	1984	74	26	76	24	60	40	76	24	72	28
Eastern Europe and USSR											
Bulgaria	1965	89	11	68	32	53	47	64	36	70	30
	1988	88	12	81	19	70	30	58	42	69	31
Czechoslovakia	1965	85	15	66	34	70	30	69	31	73	27
Germany[a]											
former German Dem. Rep.	1966	80	20	75	25	67	33	75	25	75	25
Hungary	1965	91	9	66	34	74	26	87	13	84	16
	1976	90	10	68	32	65	35	64	36	73	27
Poland	1965	86	14	66	34	75	25	73	27	76	24
	1984	90	10	69	31	70	30	76	24	78	22
Yugoslavia	1965	94	6	73	27	63	37	80	20	81	19
USSR	1965	87	13	72	28	50	50	67	33	70	30
	1986	75	25	75	25	62	38	59	41	65	35
Latin America											
Guatemala	1977	99	1	68	32	58	42	73	27	82	18
Peru	1966	94	6	90	10	69	31	86	14	87	13
Venezuela	1983	98	2	85	15	70	30	87	13	90	10
Asia											
Indonesia (Java)	1973	96	4	74	26	88	13	80	20	87	13
Nepal	1979	88	12	81	19	41	59	76	24	78	22

Sources for table 7 and charts 6.1, 6.2 and 6.3:
Compiled by Andrew Harvey as consultant to the United Nations Secretariat from national reports and studies on the following surveys—

Developed regions
Austria: Microcensus, 1981, Central Statistical Office;
Australia: Time Use Pilot Survey, 1987, Australian Bureau of Statistics;
Belgium: Multinational Time-Budget Project, 1965, Sociological Institute (Free University of Brussels);
Bulgaria: Multinational Time-Budget Project—Kazanlik and Surroundings, 1965, Scientific Research Group (Trade Union Council, Sofia); Time Use in Bulgaria, 1985, Institute of Sociology; Time Use in Bulgaria, 1988, Central Statistical Office;
Canada: Dimensions of Metropolitan Activity Study, 1971/72, Institute of Public Affairs, Dalhousie University; Canadian Time Use Pilot Study, 1981, Department of Employment and Immigration, Department of Communications; General Social Survey—Time Use Study, 1986, Statistics Canada;
Czechoslovakia: Multinational Time-Budget Project, 1965, Sociological Laboratory (Polytechnical Institute, Prague); Survey on Family Budget Statistics, 1967, Federal Statistical Office; Survey on the Use of Time, 1979/80, Federal Statistical Office;
Denmark: National Time Use Survey, 1964, National Institute of Social Research; National Time Budget Survey, 1975, National Institute of Social Research;
Finland: Time Use Study, 1979 and 1987, Central Statistical Office of Finland;
France: Multinational Time-Budget Project, 1965, National Institute of Statistics and Economic Studies (INSEE); 1985/86 Time Use Survey;
Germany: Multinational Time-Budget Project, 1965, Institute for Comparative Social Research (University of Cologne); Multinational Time-Budget Project—Osnabruck, 1965, Institute for Social Research (Dortmund); Multinational Time-Budget Project, 1965, Hoyerswerda, and Time-Budget Study, 1972, Institute for Living Standard and Consumption, University of Economic Sciences (Berlin); Time Use Study, 1974, 1980 and 1985, State Central Administration of Statistics (Berlin);
Hungary: Multinational Time-Budget Project, 1965, Sociological Research Group (Hungarian Academy of Sciences, Budapest); Time-Budget Survey, 1976/77, Central Statistical Office;
Italy: Time Use in Turin, 1979, University of Turin;
Japan: Time Use Survey, 1970, 1975, 1980, 1985, NHK Public Opinion Research Institute; Survey of Time Use and Leisure Activities, 1981, 1986, Statistics Bureau;
Netherlands: National Time Use Survey, 1975, 1980, Social and Cultural Planning Bureau;
Norway: Time Budget Survey, 1971/72, 1980/81, Central Bureau of Statistics;
Poland: Multinational Time-Budget Study, 1965, Institute of Philosophy and Sociology (Polish Academy of Science, Warsaw); Time-Budget Survey, 1969, Central Statistical Office; National Time Use Study, 1975/76, Central Statistical Office; Time-Budget Survey of Working People in Poland, 1984, Central Statistical Office;
Switzerland: Time Use in Switzerland, 1980, Federal Office of Statistics;
United Kingdom of Great Britain and Northern Ireland: National Time Use Study, 1961, 1975, British Broadcasting Corporation;
Union of Soviet Socialist Republics: Multinational Time Budget Project—Pskov, 1965, Institute of Economics, Siberian Section of the Academy of Sciences of the USSR (Novosibirsk); Time Use in a Latvian Town, 1972, Institute of Economics of the Academy of Science of Latvian SSR; Time Use in Pskov, 1986, USSR Academy of Sciences;
United States of America: Multinational Time-Budget Project—National Survey, 1965/66, Institute for Social Research (University of Michigan); Multinational Time-Budget Project, Jackson, Michigan, 1965/66, Institute for Social Research (University of Michigan); Study of Americans' Use of Time, 1975/76, Institute for Social Research (University of Michigan); Study of Americans' Use of Time, 1986, Survey Research Center (University of Maryland);

Yugoslavia: Multinational Time-Budget Project, 1965, Institute of Sociology (Belgrade); Multinational Time-Budget Project—Maribor and Surroundings, 1965, Institute of Philosophy and Sociology, University of Ljubljana;

Africa
Botswana: Rural Income Distribution Survey, 1974/75, Central Statistical Office;
Burkina Faso: Time Use among Women and Men in a Village in North-central Burkina Faso, 1975, Brenda McSweeny;
Central African Republic: Study of Time in Work in Two Villages, 1960, Bureau for the Development of Agricultural Productivity;
Côte d'Ivoire: Household Food Consumption and Budgetary Survey, 1979, Direction de la statistique;
Ghana: Time Allocation in a Farming Settlement in Northern Ghana, 1976/77, Robert Tripp;
Kenya: A Comparative Analysis of Decision Making in Rural Households in Embu and Buganda, 1967, Jane Hanger;
Malawi: National Agro-economic Survey, 1970/71, Barbara Cook;
Mozambique: Survey of Two Villages in Mueda Region, S. Caircross and J. L. Cliff, Mozambique Bureau of Water, 1982/83;
Senegal: Women's Time Budget in a Rural Village, 1977/78, E. E. Loose;

Latin America and the Caribbean
Columbia: Time Use in Bogota, 1983, J. C. Rodriguez-Gomez;
Guatemala: Family Time Use in Four Villages in Highland Guatemala, 1977, James Loucky;
Peru: Multinational Time-Budget Project, 1966, Political and Social Science Institute (Catholic University of Louvain), Rudolf Rezsohazy;
Venezuela: Division of Labour, Time Diary and Economic Value of Work Performed in Households in Venezuela, Central Bank of Venezuela, 1982;

Asia
Bangladesh: Use of Time in Rural and Urban Areas, 1974, A. Farouk, Agricultural Development Council; Time Use in Dacca and in Manikganj, 1976, J. C. Caldwell; Time Use in a Village, 1977, Mead Cain;
China: A Study of Time Spent in Housework by Workers in Two Cities in Heilongjian Province, 1980/81, Y. Wang and J. Li;
India: Women's Time Spent in Work in Baroda, 1981, International Labour Office;
Israel: A Comparison of Urban and Kibbutz Time Budget Data, 1973, Gurevitch and Brand;
Indonesia: Time Use of Adults and Children in 20 Households in Java, 1972/73, Moni Nag, B. N. F. White and R. C. Peet;
Republic of Korea: A Survey of Time Budgets of the Korean People, 1981, 1983, Institute of Mass Communications;
Nepal: Status of Women Project, 1978, Tribhuvan University; Time Use of Adults and Children in Rural Nepal, 1980, Moni Nag, B. N. F. White and R. C. Peet, Agricultural Development Council;
Pakistan: A Case Study of Attitudes, Environment and Activities of Rural Women in Jhok Sayal, 1976, S. Anwar and F. Bilquees;
Philippines: Laguna Household Studies, 1976, University of the Philippines in Quezon City, Agricultural Development Council.

a   Through the accession of the German Democratic Republic to the Federal Republic of Germany with effect from 3 October 1990, the two German States have united to form one sovereign State. As from the date of unification, the Federal Republic of Germany acts in the United Nations under the designation "Germany". All data shown for Germany pertain to end-June 1990 or earlier and are indicated separately for the Federal Republic of Germany and the former German Democratic Republic.

Table 8
Indicators on women's economic activity

Country or area	Economically active population aged 15 years and over										Occupational groups (F/ 100 M), 1980s			
	Women economically active (000s)		Estimated economic activity rate (%)				Average annual growth 1970–1990 (%)		Women as % of total	Admin., manage-rial workers	Clerical, sales, service workers	Product'n, transport workers, labourers	Agric., hunting, forestry workers
			f		m								
	1970	1990	1970	1990	1970	1990	f	m	1990				
Developed regions													
Albania	356	653	58	59	86	83	3.1	2.8	41	..	..	..	..
Australia	1666	3037	37	46	82	77	3.0	1.5	38	42	138	28	30
Austria	1199	1432	39	44	74	74	0.9	0.6	40	14	194	17	87
Belgium	1100	1400	29	33	71	70	1.2	0.5	34	15	102	16	28
Bulgaria	1951	2075	59	57	75	68	0.3	-0.1	46	41	352	54	117
Canada	2808	5313	37	49	79	78	3.2	1.6	40	54	178	17	25
Czechoslovakia	3224	3908	56	62	78	76	1.0	0.4	47	..	..	..	..
Denmark	857	1272	45	58	82	76	2.0	0.2	45	16	183	29	17
Finland	960	1200	53	57	75	70	1.1	0.4	47	24	282	24	56
France	7776	10132	39	45	75	71	1.3	0.5	40	10	164	18	48
Germany[a]													
Federal Rep. of Germany	9704	10915	39	41	79	75	0.6	0.4	37	20	140	18	82
former German Dem. Rep.	3953	4396	54	62	79	83	0.5	0.7	45	..	..	..	..
Greece	853	1024	25	25	78	73	0.9	0.6	27	18	72	21	80
Hungary	2179	2372	51	53	84	72	0.4	-0.6	45	..	..	..	..
Iceland	31	58	45	60	83	82	3.2	1.5	43	..	..	..	..
Ireland	294	435	29	32	81	77	2.0	1.2	29	19	103	17	7
Italy	5942	7450	28	30	76	69	1.1	0.3	32	60	45	60	4
Japan	20752	23557	51	46	84	79	0.6	0.9	38	8	99	41	91
Luxembourg	35	50	26	32	74	72	1.8	0.5	32	6	135	6	48
Malta	23	35	18	22	76	78	2.1	1.4	24	..	..	..	..
Netherlands	1235	1900	26	31	74	71	2.2	1.0	31	14	127	9	27
New Zealand	323	548	33	40	81	77	2.7	1.4	35	21	178	20	39
Norway	472	875	32	50	79	75	3.1	0.5	41	28	252	18	38
Poland	7853	8983	63	60	83	77	0.7	0.6	46	..	..	..	..
Portugal	802	1734	24	40	87	80	3.9	0.9	37	17	108	34	101
Romania	4806	5495	62	60	85	72	0.7	0.1	46	..	..	..	..
Spain	2267	3534	18	22	82	73	2.2	0.7	24	6	96	15	33
Sweden	1330	1927	41	55	76	71	1.9	0.0	45	191[b]	145[c]	23	34
Switzerland	975	1175	40	43	85	79	0.9	0.1	37	6	136	17	36
USSR	59308	70411	62	60	76	75	0.9	1.4	48	..	..	..	..
United Kingdom	9077	10724	41	46	82	77	0.8	0.2	39	29	225	18	18
United States	31727	50531	42	50	78	77	2.4	1.3	41	61	183	23	19
Yugoslavia	3295	4217	43	45	81	74	1.2	0.7	39	15	138	23	88
Africa													
Algeria	168	543	4	8	79	75	6.0	3.4	9	..	..	..	..
Angola	971	1462	59	52	90	87	2.1	2.6	39	..	..	..	..
Benin	649	986	83	77	93	89	2.1	2.2	48	..	..	..	..
Botswana	98	152	55	42	91	85	2.2	4.4	36	56	197	29	105
Burkina Faso	1251	1742	85	77	94	93	1.7	2.1	46	..	..	..	..
Burundi	904	1201	86	78	94	93	1.4	1.9	48	..	..	..	..
Cameroon	1048	1344	51	41	92	87	1.3	2.2	33	6	26	9	82
Cape Verde	21	40	27	33	93	90	3.3	2.0	31	..	..	..	..
Central African Rep.	473	584	80	68	92	88	1.1	1.8	46	..	..	..	..
Chad	293	387	27	23	92	90	1.4	2.0	21	..	..	..	..
Comoros	51	85	66	59	92	91	2.6	3.1	40	0	17	14	38
Congo	196	292	55	51	87	84	2.0	2.2	39	..	..	..	..
Côte d'Ivoire	947	1459	64	48	92	88	2.2	3.0	34	..	..	..	..
Djibouti	..	..	..	..	..	..	..	..	..	..	..	..	..
Egypt	554	1359	6	9	83	80	4.6	2.4	10	16	23	6	26
Equatorial Guinea	55	69	60	52	89	84	1.1	1.6	40	..	..	..	..
Ethiopia	5107	7188	59	52	91	89	1.7	2.3	37	..	..	..	..

Table 8. Indicators on women's economic activity [cont.]

Country or area	Economically active population aged 15 years and over									Occupational groups (F/ 100 M), 1980s			
	Women economically active (000s)		Estimated economic activity rate (%)				Average annual growth 1970–1990 (%)		Women as % of total	Admin., manage-rial workers	Clerical, sales, service workers	Product'n, transport workers, labourers	Agric., hunting, forestry workers
			f		m								
	1970	1990	1970	1990	1970	1990	f	m	1990				
Gabon	176	193	54	47	84	82	0.5	1.0	37	..	..	..	..
Gambia	92	121	65	58	92	90	1.4	1.9	40	17	48	7	118
Ghana	1411	2224	59	51	84	80	2.3	2.8	40	10	292	81	90
Guinea	830	1128	65	57	93	90	1.5	2.0	40	..	..	..	..
Guinea-Bissau	107	172	63	57	91	90	2.4	2.7	41	..	..	..	..
Kenya	1833	3527	65	58	92	90	3.3	3.9	40	..	..	..	..
Lesotho	253	340	76	65	89	91	1.5	2.5	44	..	..	..	..
Liberia	164	253	42	37	91	88	2.2	2.6	30	..	..	..	..
Libyan Arab Jamahiriya	30	95	6	9	81	77	5.9	3.6	9	..	..	..	..
Madagascar	1238	1799	63	55	92	89	1.9	2.3	39	..	..	..	..
Malawi	857	1303	68	57	93	89	2.1	2.9	41	..	..	..	..
Mali	283	408	17	16	92	90	1.8	2.2	16	..	..	..	..
Mauritania	83	140	24	24	93	87	2.6	2.4	22	..	..	..	..
Mauritius	51	117	21	29	85	84	4.2	2.4	27	17	53	55	45
Morocco	482	1480	12	19	84	81	5.8	3.1	20	34[b]	26[c]	30	19
Mozambique	2143	3655	89	79	93	91	2.7	3.3	48	..	..	..	..
Namibia	74	122	24	24	89	83	2.5	2.3	23	..	..	..	..
Niger	1046	1512	87	79	95	93	1.9	2.4	47	..	..	..	..
Nigeria	8099	13624	52	46	90	88	2.6	3.2	35	..	..	..	..
Reunion	26	80	22	38	77	77	5.8	2.3	34	..	..	..	..
Rwanda	873	1500	86	79	94	93	2.7	3.2	47	..	..	..	..
Sao Tome and Principe	..	..	..	..	..	..	..	..	..	10	85	7	56
Senegal	686	1112	60	53	88	86	2.4	2.9	39	..	..	..	..
Seychelles	7[d]	..	47[d]	..	81[d]	..	..	..	..	13	142	17	20
Sierra Leone	384	451	44	38	87	84	0.8	1.4	32	..	..	..	..
Somalia	467	762	60	53	90	88	2.5	3.0	39	..	..	..	..
South Africa	2728	4429	40	40	85	75	2.5	1.9	36	21	163	14	37
Sudan	866	1668	22	24	89	87	3.3	2.8	22	..	..	..	..
Swaziland	77	110	63	53	91	87	1.8	2.6	39	..	..	..	..
Togo	311	455	53	47	90	88	1.9	2.5	36	9	206	61	78
Tunisia	154	635	11	26	83	78	7.3	2.8	25	27[b]	22[c]	28	25
Uganda	1810	2974	68	62	94	92	2.5	3.0	41	..	..	..	..
United Rep. Tanzania	3260	5452	89	77	91	89	2.6	3.2	48	..	..	..	..
Western Sahara	..	..	..	..	..	..	..	..	..	..	..	..	..
Zaire	3308	4350	58	45	89	85	1.4	2.8	35	..	..	..	..
Zambia	354	699	31	33	90	87	3.5	3.0	28	12	44	6	69
Zimbabwe	736	1214	51	44	91	88	2.5	3.2	34	17	57	16	98

Latin America and Caribbean

Country or area	1970	1990	1970	1990	1970	1990	f	m	1990	Admin.	Clerical	Product'n	Agric.
Antigua and Barbuda	9	..	45	..	86	..	..	..	..	..	..	..	..
Argentina	2258	3233	27	28	81	75	1.8	0.9	28	..	..	..	..
Bahamas	28	..	57	..	90	..	..	..	..	..	..	..	..
Barbados	36	64	43	61	79	78	2.9	1.4	47	45	165	35	63
Belize	6	..	20	..	89	..	..	..	..	14	89	14	3
Bolivia	279	559	22	27	88	83	3.5	2.3	25	..	..	..	..
Brazil	6391	14886	23	30	85	81	4.3	2.6	28	..	..	..	..
Chile	652	1352	22	29	80	75	3.7	2.0	28	22	113	16	8
Colombia	1246	2249	22	22	84	79	3.0	2.7	22	27	117	26	20
Costa Rica	91	222	20	24	88	84	4.6	3.3	22	29	95	25	5
Cuba	486	1413	19	36	77	74	5.5	1.8	32	..	..	..	..
Dominica	8	..	..	..	..	..	..	..	..	32	184	18	22
Dominican Republic	121	322	11	15	88	85	5.0	3.1	15	27	112	16	11
Ecuador	287	623	17	19	90	82	4.0	2.9	19	18	79	13	8
El Salvador	229	531	24	29	90	86	4.3	3.0	25	19	188	32	22

Table 8. Indicators on women's economic activity [cont.]

Country or area	Economically active population aged 15 years and over									Occupational groups (F/ 100 M), 1980s			
	Women economically active (000s)		Estimated economic activity rate (%)				Average annual growth 1970–1990 (%)		Women as % of total	Admin., manage-rial workers	Clerical, sales, service workers	Product'n, transport workers, labourers	Agric., hunting, forestry workers
			f		m								
	1970	1990	1970	1990	1970	1990	f	m	1990				
French Guiana	4 e	..	36 e	..	81 e	..	..	..	..	21	151	13	55
Grenada	..	..	..	..	..	..	..	..	..	..	..	..	..
Guadeloupe	43	69	45	53	76	73	2.4	1.4	44	..	..	..	..
Guatemala	195	412	14	16	90	84	3.8	2.5	16	19	93	14	2
Guyana	42	96	22	28	86	84	4.2	3.0	25	15	75	10	10
Haiti	979	1208	72	56	90	83	1.1	2.1	41	50	542	46	34
Honduras	107	293	15	21	90	86	5.2	3.3	20	..	..	..	..
Jamaica	301	571	58	68	87	83	3.3	2.6	46	..	182	29	50
Martinique	39	68	39	52	77	73	2.8	1.2	44	..	..	..	..
Mexico	2463	8195	18	30	85	82	6.2	3.3	27	18	70	20	14
Netherlands Antilles	26 d	32 f	37 d	44 f	75 d	67 f	1.4	-0.4	42 f	16	135	5	11
Nicaragua	116	295	21	28	87	83	4.8	3.2	26	..	..	..	..
Panama	125	236	30	30	86	79	3.2	2.6	27	29	144	13	3
Paraguay	149	287	23	23	91	88	3.3	3.4	21	58 b	98 c	21	5
Peru	750	1702	20	25	82	79	4.2	2.9	24	9	60	13	17
Puerto Rico	214	365	24	26	71	69	2.7	2.1	29	34	119	32	3
St. Kitts and Nevis	5	..	39	..	79	..	..	..	..	16	167	34	43
St. Lucia	10	..	36	..	86	..	..	..	..	23	211	22	30
St. Vincent/Grenadines	9	..	..	..	..	..	..	..	..	25	152	24	30
Suriname	26	42	27	31	79	73	2.4	1.2	31	..	..	..	..
Trinidad and Tobago	95	151	33	34	82	81	2.3	2.3	30	196 b	105 c	13	28
Uruguay	289	378	28	32	81	75	1.4	0.2	31	33	111	22	7
US Virgin Islands	10	..	50	..	80	..	..	..	..	64	203	20	4
Venezuela	622	1893	22	31	82	81	5.7	3.7	28	17	86	11	4
Asia and Pacific													
Afghanistan	245	502	6	8	90	86	3.7	2.1	9	..	..	..	..
Bahrain	2	23	4	18	81	88	13.0	6.5	11	4	20	0.5	0.2
Bangladesh	941	2206	5	7	91	87	4.4	2.5	7	2	29	20	1
Bhutan	147	197	48	43	91	89	1.5	2.1	31	..	..	..	..
Brunei Darussalam	7 d	..	20 d	..	80 d	..	..	..	..	6	60	4	23
Cambodia	1163	1409	59	52	86	86	1.0	1.5	38	..	..	..	..
China	162390	283433	67	70	90	87	2.8	2.4	43	12	71	55	88
Cyprus	85	115	39	44	83	82	1.5	1.1	35	7	84	35	86
East Timor	20	36	12	15	92	89	3.0	1.4	14	..	..	..	..
Fiji	17	52	12	22	87	86	5.7	2.2	20	10	71	10	13
French Polynesia	10 d	..	34 d	..	78 d	..	..	..	..	8	101	20	26
Guam	7	15 g	33	50 g	83	76 g	4.2	-0.8	41 g	..	..	..	..
Hong Kong	552	1037	45	48	85	84	3.2	3.4	33	13	78	43	51
India	60008	76570	38	29	87	84	1.2	2.3	25	2	11	15	31
Indonesia	12825	21628	36	37	88	83	2.6	2.3	31	7	86	36	55
Iran (Islamic Rep. of)	947	2589	12	17	85	80	5.2	3.2	18	..	..	..	..
Iraq	147	1043	6	21	83	77	10.3	3.3	21	..	..	..	..
Israel	326	608	33	37	77	75	3.2	2.3	34	16	125	16	19
Jordan	36	99	6	9	83	77	5.2	2.6	10	..	..	..	..
Kiribati	..	..	..	..	..	..	..	..	..	..	..	..	..
Korea, D. People's R.	2614	4787	65	64	85	81	3.1	2.9	46	..	..	..	..
Korea, Republic of	3590	6303	38	40	81	78	2.9	2.6	34	3	92	45	83
Kuwait	18	120	11	24	87	85	10.0	5.9	14	4	43	0.2	0.4
Lao People's Dem. Rep.	693	955	80	71	91	88	1.6	2.0	44	..	..	..	..
Lebanon	117	249	17	25	76	72	3.8	1.2	27	..	..	..	..
Macau	..	..	..	..	..	..	..	..	..	..	..	..	..
Malaysia	1092	2463	37	44	83	82	4.2	3.1	35	9	49	28	61
Maldives	..	..	..	..	..	..	..	..	..	11	19	57	11
Mongolia	258	468	73	72	91	87	3.0	2.9	46	..	..	..	..

Table 8. Indicators on women's economic activity [cont.]

Country or area	Economically active population aged 15 years and over									Occupational groups (F/ 100 M), 1980s			
	Women economically active (000s)		Estimated economic activity rate (%)				Average annual growth 1970–1990 (%)		Women as % of total	Admin., managerial workers	Clerical, sales, service workers	Product'n, transport workers, labourers	Agric., hunting, forestry workers
			f		m								
	1970	1990	1970	1990	1970	1990	f	m	1990				
Myanmar	4319	6375	54	48	87	85	2.0	2.4	36	..	..	..	..
Nepal	1589	2253	47	43	91	87	1.8	2.2	32	..	..	..	..
New Caledonia	12 [h]	..	42 [h]	..	82 [h]	..	..	..	..	..	..	..	..
Oman	11	34	6	9	89	84	5.8	4.1	9	..	..	..	..
Pacific Islands	3	..	13	..	43	..	..	..	..	..	..	..	..
Pakistan	1583	3983	9	13	88	86	4.7	2.9	12	..	..	..	..
Papua New Guinea	463	663	69	58	90	87	1.8	2.4	38	..	..	..	..
Philippines	4250	6843	42	36	84	81	2.4	2.8	31	34	163	28	33
Qatar	1	13	5	17	93	93	13.7	6.6	7	..	..	..	..
Samoa	4 [d]	..	11 [d]	..	86 [d]	..	..	..	..	24	81	10	3
Saudi Arabia	74	282	5	9	88	84	6.9	4.8	7	..	..	..	..
Singapore	185	417	30	40	82	83	4.1	2.5	32	28	114	40	23
Solomon Islands	..	..	..	..	..	..	..	..	..	..	..	..	..
Sri Lanka	1054	1691	31	29	83	80	2.4	1.9	27	7	35	31	51
Syrian Arab Republic	157	488	10	15	81	78	5.8	3.4	16	49	7	4	34
Thailand	7601	12754	75	68	87	85	2.6	3.1	45	26	126	43	93
Tonga	1 [e]	5 [f]	5 [e]	18 [f]	85 [e]	69 [f]	8.1	0.3	21 [f]	16	96	14	1
Turkey	5564	7762	54	45	88	84	1.7	2.6	34	3	14	9	109
United Arab Emirates	4	48	9	18	93	92	13.2	11.0	6	1	9	0.1	0.1
Vanuatu	16 [e]	..	83 [e]	..	85 [e]	..	..	..	..	..	..	..	..
Viet Nam	9006	15040	71	70	88	86	2.6	2.8	47	..	..	..	..
Yemen	109	303	6	10	89	84	5.2	1.7	12	..	..	..	..

Sources:

International Labour Office, *Economically Active Population—Estimates, 1950–1980, Projections, 1985–2025,* six volumes (Geneva, 1986); International Labour Office, *Year Book of Labour Statistics* (Geneva, various years).

a   Through the accession of the German Democratic Republic to the Federal Republic of Germany with effect from 3 October 1990, the two German States have united to form one sovereign State. As from the date of unification, the Federal Republic of Germany acts in the United Nations under the designation "Germany". All data shown for Germany pertain to end-June 1990 or earlier and are indicated separately for the Federal Republic of Germany and the former German Democratic Republic.

b   Administative and managerial workers and clerical and related workers combined.
c   Sales and service workers only.
d   1971.
e   1966/67.
f   1986.
g   1988.
h   1969.

Table 9
Indicators on the economy and women's work

	Gross domestic product or net material product							Labour force by status in employment, 1980/87					
				Average growth (% per year)			1987 debt service (% GNP)	Employers/own-acc't		Employees		Unpaid family	
Country or area	$US 1987	$US per cap. 1987	Capital formation 1985 (%)	1970-75	1975-80	1980-86		% of total	% f	% of total	% f	% of total	% f
Developed regions													
Albania	..	..	..	6.1	6.4	3.0	..	..	..	..	..	..	..
Australia	210739	13038	25	3.6	2.7	3.2	..	14	30	77	41	0.8	59
Austria	117584	15688	22	4.2	3.3	1.6	..	10	31	86	39	4	77
Belgium	142708	14387	16	4.0	2.7	1.1	..	12	26	72	38	3	78
Bulgaria	..	..	..	7.8	5.2	3.8	..	0.3	27	98	47	0	..
Canada	419122	16200	20	5.5	4.0	2.9	..	9	33	90	44	0.7	78
Czechoslovakia	..	..	17	5.4	3.7	2.0	..	0.1	39	91	47	8	48
Denmark	101813	19881	18	2.2	2.4	2.8	..	9	17	89	47	2	97
Finland	89428	18110	24	4.6	3.0	3.0	..	14	37	85	49	1	39
France	881450	15854	19	3.7	3.2	1.5	..	11	22	75	43	3	82
Germany[a]													
Federal Rep. of Germany	1116161	18354	20	2.4	3.3	1.5	..	9	21	88	40	3	87
former German Dem. Rep.	..	..	..	5.5	4.2	4.5	..	..	..	..	..	..	..
Greece	47190	4722	19	4.9	4.5	1.4	7.6	33	17	46	32	14	79
Hungary	..	..	22	6.6	3.2	1.2	12.9	4	34	81	46	2	89
Iceland	5361	21617	20	6.0	6.6	2.0	..	14[b]	..	85[b]	..	0[b]	..
Ireland	28250	7808	20	4.7	5.0	1.5	..	18	10	71	37	2	35
Italy	755865	13205	21	3.1	3.6	1.8	..	21	23	62	35	4	65
Japan	2373707	19471	28	4.6	5.0	3.8	..	15	31	73	36	9	83
Luxembourg	5993	16285	18	4.1	2.5	3.2	..	9	27	85	34	2	85
Malta	1831	5292	26	3.7	11.5	1.7	0.8	16	15	80	29	0	..
Netherlands	215910	14792	19	3.4	2.6	1.3	..	9	29	79	35	2	83
New Zealand	34857	10553	25	3.8	0.0	3.0	..	16	25	76	43	1	75
Norway	83123	19895	22	4.7	4.7	3.8	..	9	20	87	46	2	67
Poland	..	..	18	10.0	1.4	1.2	3.0	13[b]	32[b]	74[b]	43[b]	12[b]	76[b]
Portugal	36828	3601	22	5.2	5.2	1.2	14.3	25	43	64	39	5	58
Romania	..	..	..	11.2	7.2	5.0	..	..	..	..	..	..	..
Spain	289186	7432	19	5.7	1.7	1.7	..	18	24	65	30	5	59
Sweden	159560	19109	19	2.8	1.3	2.0	..	9	25	89	50	0.4	74
Switzerland	170087	26155	24	1.3	1.7	1.5	..	10	14	90	39	0	..
USSR	..	..	26	7.1	3.9	3.3	..	..	..	..	..	..	..
United Kingdom	688727	12096	17	2.5	1.9	2.2	..	10	25	79	45	0	..
United States	4472910	18374	18	2.5	3.4	3.1	..	8	31	91	45	0.3	76
Yugoslavia	71018	3032	22	5.8	6.4	0.7	5.1	17	30	66	35	10	72
Africa													
Algeria	65271	2825	32[b]	6.1	8.4	5.0	7.5	17[b]	1[b]	47[b]	8[b]	2[b]	2[b]
Angola	5843	633	..	-5.7	1.4	3.4	..	..	..	..	..	..	..
Benin	1608	373	15	4.8	-0.8	0.5	2.1	..	..	..	..	..	..
Botswana	1923	1661	..	9.7	12.6	11.3	6.4	2	63	33	40	39	57
Burkina Faso	1672	201	25	4.9	4.3	1.2	1.6	..	..	..	..	..	..
Burundi	1137	227	14	0.6	5.0	4.2	3.5	36[b]	28[b]	6[b]	9[b]	59[b]	73[b]
Cameroon	15564	1496	..	3.5	7.7	7.2	4.8	60	37	15	9	18	68
Cape Verde	178	510	..	-2.5	2.1	7.8	4.0	..	..	..	..	..	..
Central African Rep.	1298	480	..	-0.2	1.9	1.5	2.1	..	..	..	..	..	..
Chad	1137	216	..	2.6	-5.1	-3.2	0.7	..	..	..	..	..	..
Comoros	205	433	..	2.4	1.6	4.0	0.6	48	25	26	24	0	..
Congo	2153	1171	..	4.4	2.0	7.8	10.3	..	..	..	..	..	..
Côte d'Ivoire	10165	912	11	6.4	6.4	0.8	15.6	..	..	..	..	..	..
Djibouti	437	1172	..	3.8	-1.9	2.0	..	..	..	..	..	..	..
Egypt	93143	1857	..	5.1	9.2	6.7	5.1	27	10	51	14	17	41
Equatorial Guinea	139	338	15	-7.1	-11.7	2.5	..	..	..	..	..	..	..
Ethiopia	5302	121	11	2.8	2.1	0.2	3.6	..	..	..	..	..	..

Table 9. Indicators on the economy and women's work [*cont.*]

Country or area	Gross domestic product or net material product							Labour force by status in employment, 1980/87					
				Average growth (% per year)			1987 debt service	Employers/own-acc't		Employees		Unpaid family	
	$US 1987	$US per cap. 1987	Capital formation 1985 (%)	1970-75	1975-80	1980-86	(% GNP)	% of total	% f	% of total	% f	% of total	% f
Gabon	4321	4080	..	20.6	-5.6	-0.9	2.3	..	..	..	..	..	..
Gambia	206	261	..	8.5	2.0	1.2	7.2	..	..	..	..	..	..
Ghana	5225	381	10	1.2	1.6	0.5	3.5	68	56	16	24	12	63
Guinea	2140	335	..	2.5	2.8	-3.6	5.4	..	..	..	..	..	..
Guinea-Bissau	165	178	..	2.6	0.1	2.5	7.2	..	..	..	..	..	..
Kenya	8268	373	18	4.5	6.6	2.3	7.6	..	..	..	..	..	..
Lesotho	363	223	32	9.1	9.5	1.7	2.3	8[b]	38[b]	50[b]	15[b]	37[b]	52[b]
Liberia	1085	467	12	2.7	2.5	-1.5	1.0	..	..	..	..	..	..
Libyan Arab Jamahiriya	22790	5580	..	7.8	8.1	-3.1	..	..	..	..	..	..	..
Madagascar	1824	168	..	0.2	1.7	0.0	8.0	..	..	..	..	..	..
Malawi	1236	162	13	8.7	6.9	2.6	5.7	80[b]	55[b]	18[b]	9[b]	0.3[b]	50[b]
Mali	1894	221	..	1.9	4.7	1.4	1.7	46[b]	5[b]	4[b]	11[b]	43[b]	30[b]
Mauritania	844	453	..	3.2	1.1	-0.4	9.9	..	..	..	..	..	..
Mauritius	1782	1673	19	9.3	3.9	4.8	4.6	..	..	..	..	..	..
Morocco	18929	812	21	4.9	6.8	3.4	8.4	27	11	41	18	18	31
Mozambique	506	35	..	-1.5	0.4	-9.3	..	..	..	..	..	..	..
Namibia	1710	1002	..	4.0	5.6	-1.9	..	..	..	..	..	..	..
Niger	2163	333	..	0.0	8.8	0.8	7.2	..	..	..	..	..	..
Nigeria	20927	205	..	6.8	1.6	-3.5	3.9	56	37	28	18	9	42
Reunion	3394	5996	20	5.3	6.6	4.1	..	10	13	56	39	1	35
Rwanda	2089	320	17	9.0	7.9	2.2	1.0	39[b]	33[b]	7[b]	15[b]	54[b]	70[b]
Sao Tome and Principe	40	385	..	..	..	..	15.3	16	26	79	32	0.1	54
Senegal	4616	680	14	1.9	0.6	3.2	6.3	..	..	..	..	..	..
Seychelles	263	3868	24	4.2	8.2	1.4	4.6	11	15	77	38	0.3	60
Sierra Leone	1778	462	9	1.8	3.7	-1.8	0.6	..	..	..	..	..	..
Somalia	1612	235	..	2.2	2.1	0.7	..	..	..	..	..	..	..
South Africa	65126	1972	24	4.1	2.5	0.8	..	4	18	89	31	0	..
Sudan	9197	398	..	1.8	2.6	-0.5	0.6	..	..	..	..	..	..
Swaziland	561	787	..	15.3	3.8	2.4	5.2	..	..	..	..	..	..
Togo	1252	398	..	1.6	4.4	-1.2	5.5	70	48	10	15	11	54
Tunisia	9919	1301	25	8.0	6.1	3.8	10.8	22	26	58	14	6	77
Uganda	2460	148	..	0.1	-4.0	0.8	1.9	..	..	..	..	..	..
United Rep. Tanzania	3544	145	14	4.3	2.9	0.9	2.9	..	..	..	..	..	..
Western Sahara	..	..	..	..	..	..	..	..	..	..	..	..	..
Zaire	1991	61	22	3.1	-2.1	1.6	4.7	..	..	..	..	..	..
Zambia	1903	252	10	2.9	-0.6	-0.1	6.7	23	34	43	24	4	72
Zimbabwe	5721	647	17	4.6	0.1	3.6	6.8	..	..	..	..	..	..

Latin America and Caribbean

Country or area	$US 1987	$US per cap. 1987	Capital formation 1985 (%)	1970-75	1975-80	1980-86	(% GNP)	% of total	% f	% of total	% f	% of total	% f
Antigua and Barbuda	269	3202	28	0.1	4.5	5.9	..	..	..	..	..	..	..
Argentina	82433	2647	..	3.1	2.4	-0.7	5.8	25	..	71	..	3	..
Bahamas	2257	8992	17	-5.0	4.4	7.2	1.9	10	33	81	44	0.5	68
Barbados	1457	5669	15	1.9	5.1	0.4	5.3	9	34	75	45	1	23
Belize	223	1304	18	5.3	4.4	1.5	..	..	..	..	..	..	..
Bolivia	3958	588	12	5.9	2.5	-2.5	3.3	49[b]	19[b]	38[b]	24[b]	9[b]	38[b]
Brazil	326250	2306	18	10.7	6.6	2.7	3.0	26	17	65	31	7	35
Chile	18951	1511	14	-2.3	7.9	0.1	10.0	24	21	64	33	4	33
Colombia	36189	1209	17	6.0	5.6	2.5	7.6	28	31	61	43	2	70
Costa Rica	4534	1624	19	6.4	5.6	1.4	5.3	23	18	71	31	5	18
Cuba	15253	1514	22	7.3	3.7	6.3	..	5	7	94	33	0.2	5
Dominica	117	1481	..	-3.7	1.7	4.6	..	29	23	50	38	2	34
Dominican Republic	5713	851	19	9.3	4.5	1.4	4.1	36	20	51	35	3	43
Ecuador	10606	1069	16	12.7	6.4	2.0	5.4	37	15	48	25	6	20
El Salvador	4662	946	12	5.5	1.8	-0.9	4.2	28	43	59	32	11	25

Table 9. Indicators on the economy and women's work [*cont.*]

| | Gross domestic product or net material product | | | | | | | Labour force by status in employment, 1980/87 | | | | | |
| | | | | Average growth (% per year) | | | 1987 debt service | Employers/own-acc't | | Employees | | Unpaid family | |
Country or area	$US 1987	$US per cap. 1987	Capital formation 1985 (%)	1970-75	1975-80	1980-86	(% GNP)	% of total	% f	% of total	% f	% of total	% f
French Guiana	238	2736	..	8.5	-2.7	-0.6	..	15	24	61	36	3	72
Grenada	139	1390	31	-4.3	5.3	4.9	4.1	..	..	..	..	..	..
Guadeloupe	1864	5515	23	5.4	5.0	1.3	..	19	25	54	46	0.5	52
Guatemala	7038	834	11	5.9	5.7	-1.1	4.4	31	25	47	24	16	22
Guyana	343	346	21	3.2	-1.3	-3.4	10.1	..	..	..	..	..	..
Haiti	1994	324	..	3.8	5.3	-0.6	1.0	52	36	14	42	9	35
Honduras	4022	859	18	3.9	7.6	1.2	6.8	..	..	..	..	..	..
Jamaica	2858	1186	22	1.8	-2.6	0.2	17.9	..	..	..	..	..	..
Martinique	2600	7879	17	4.1	3.7	4.3	..	12	22	57	49	0.3	53
Mexico	139991	1686	19	6.9	6.8	0.7	8.2	27	25	44	27	5	35
Netherlands Antilles	1591	8508	..	1.9	5.0	-1.3	..	..	..	..	..	..	..
Nicaragua	3036	867	21	5.7	-5.8	0.3	1.1	..	..	..	..	..	..
Panama	5317	2337	16	4.6	6.1	2.5	7.5	26	14	65	38	4	15
Paraguay	4534	1155	21	7.2	10.7	1.4	5.1	43	15	38	20	9	11
Peru	45248	2183	22	4.5	1.2	0.0	1.0	49	17	45	20	6	55
Puerto Rico	24372	6856	11	2.6	4.7	3.6	..	13	13	85	41	0.8	75
St. Kitts and Nevis	88	1544	..	3.7	2.3	4.4	..	..	..	..	..	..	..
St. Lucia	197	1492	..	1.2	8.9	4.3	..	..	..	..	..	..	..
St. Vincent/Grenadines	132	1234	..	-0.6	6.2	4.9	2.4	..	..	..	..	..	..
Suriname	1068	2760	17	7.2	2.3	-1.0	..	11	19	78	29	2	56
Trinidad and Tobago	4603	3761	21	3.0	7.9	-4.7	9.2	19	25	73	33	5	50
Uruguay	7501	2452	7	1.3	4.4	-2.5	5.9	23	25	71	35	2	40
US Virgin Islands	1157	10615	..	7.5	-1.4	0.5	..	7	25	86	47	0.3	66
Venezuela	49615	2716	15	5.0	3.3	-0.9	10.6	26	19	63	32	3	30

Asia and Pacific

Country or area	$US 1987	$US per cap. 1987	Capital formation 1985 (%)	1970-75	1975-80	1980-86	(% GNP)	% of total	% f	% of total	% f	% of total	% f
Afghanistan	3587	244	..	3.5	0.6	2.0	..	..	..	..	..	..	..
Bahrain	3896	8378	31	1.6	7.0	2.5	..	9	1	86	12	0.1	8
Bangladesh	19227	180	10	4.8	4.1	3.7	1.8	38	4	44	14	16	6
Bhutan	277	195	..	5.2	9.3	5.1	0.2	..	..	..	..	..	..
Brunei Darussalam	2374	9810	..	6.9	10.8	-2.7	..	7	19	88	23	0.6	55
Cambodia	625	81	..	-8.5	-7.3	-3.2	..	..	..	..	..	..	..
China	251919	236	..	5.2	6.6	10.5	1.0	..	..	..	..	..	..
Cyprus	3557	5223	27	-3.3	11.2	5.6	7.0	24	31	71	35	2	83
East Timor	..	..	..	..	..	..	..	..	..	..	..	..	..
Fiji	1183	1652	17	6.5	4.4	1.5	5.6	34	10	42	26	16	20
French Polynesia	2586	15123	..	5.7	5.1	4.3	..	15	22	72	33	5	47
Guam	..	..	..	..	..	..	..	..	..	..	..	..	..
Hong Kong	46537	8289	21	7.2	11.9	6.1	..	12	20	85	38	2	90
India	254203	317	21	2.6	3.4	5.3	1.7	9	9	17	12	4	23
Indonesia	69667	405	21	8.5	7.8	4.2	9.8	44	26	25	30	28	67
Iran (Islamic Rep. of)	197702	3853	17	10.0	-5.0	4.3	..	31[b]	5[b]	48[b]	12[b]	10[b]	49[b]
Iraq	50669	2971	21	8.6	13.0	-8.1	..	25[b]	7[b]	60[b]	8[b]	11[b]	88[b]
Israel	37571	8592	18	7.7	3.3	2.2	10.4	18	24	74	42	1	74
Jordan	4216	1112	30	0.1	12.3	5.4	11.1	23[b]	1[b]	67[b]	9[b]	0.8[b]	4[b]
Kiribati	24	358	..	17.9	-15.0	-2.1	..	..	..	..	..	..	..
Korea, D. People's R.	17100	799	..	12.0	11.6	9.9	..	33[b]	27[b]	40[b]	29[b]	24[b]	69[b]
Korea, Republic of	121310	2880	30	9.4	8.3	8.2	13.1	30	30	54	36	13	83
Kuwait	18147	9751	22	-4.8	1.5	-1.8	..	6	1	92	21	0.1	4
Lao People's Dem. Rep.	660	175	..	1.6	-1.2	7.3	1.9	..	..	..	..	..	..
Lebanon	1866	675	..	2.8	3.6	-14.4	..	..	..	..	..	..	..
Macau	..	..	..	..	..	..	..	..	..	..	..	..	..
Malaysia	32244	1991	30	10.3	8.3	4.7	14.3	29	29	54	31	10	54
Maldives	80	408	..	13.5	13.5	6.1	12.2	49	26	39	14	6	37
Mongolia	1629	803	..	6.8	5.8	6.2	..	..	..	..	..	..	..

Table 9. Indicators on the economy and women's work [*cont.*]

Country or area	Gross domestic product or net material product							Labour force by status in employment, 1980/87					
	$US 1987	$US per cap. 1987	Capital formation 1985 (%)	Average growth (% per year) 1970-75	1975-80	1980-86	1987 debt service (% GNP)	Employers/own-acc't % of total	% f	Employees % of total	% f	Unpaid family % of total	% f
Myanmar	9054	231	15	2.1	6.2	5.0	2.0	..	..	..	..	..	..
Nepal	2684	151	19	2.0	2.6	3.9	1.2	86	36	9	15	3	55
New Caledonia	1381	8686	..	2.3	-0.2	-1.2	..	15	22	72	33	5	47
Oman	7523	5635	28	4.0	3.1	13.7	8.6	..	..	..	..	..	..
Pacific Islands	..	..	..	..	..	..	..	..	..	..	..	..	..
Pakistan	39418	355	15	4.5	6.6	6.8	3.5	45	2	26	5	26	7
Papua New Guinea	3071	829	20	3.2	0.5	2.3	18.3	..	..	..	..	..	..
Philippines	34387	593	15	6.2	6.1	-0.9	6.9	36	29	40	37	15	52
Qatar	5161	15783	..	5.0	3.5	-3.0	..	..	..	..	..	..	..
Samoa	121	725	..	3.1	3.1	0.0	4.5	21	5	43	30	35	3
Saudi Arabia	72335	5757	26	14.0	8.4	-7.7	..	..	..	..	..	..	..
Singapore	19952	7624	42	9.8	8.5	5.6	4.3	13	19	80	40	2	68
Solomon Islands	147	502	..	5.7	10.8	3.3	7.3	..	..	..	..	..	..
Sri Lanka	6423	388	24	3.3	5.6	5.0	5.4	24	20	50	30	11	52
Syrian Arab Republic	32391	2884	24	13.1	4.7	2.9	1.7	33	4	55	12	10	54
Thailand	47596	893	22	6.4	7.7	4.8	6.3	30	27	24	38	43	65
Tonga	95	826	..	2.6	4.3	5.3	..	33[b]	1[b]	33[b]	24[b]	13[b]	4[b]
Turkey	68007	1295	20	7.1	2.6	5.0	7.5	23	7	32	15	41	70
United Arab Emirates	23119	15889	25	63.8	14.4	-4.4	..	7	1	93	5	0.1	9
Vanuatu	120	789	..	11.8	3.4	4.8	..	..	..	..	..	..	..
Viet Nam	7085	113	..	-1.7	0.9	6.5	..	..	..	..	..	..	..
Yemen [c]	4229[d]	579[e]	15	9.8[f]	6.1[f]	8.0[f]	3.2[g]	45[b]	..	34[b]	..	19[b]	..

Sources:
National Accounts Statistics: Analysis of Main Aggregates, 1987 (United Nations publication, Sales No. E.90.XVII.8); National Accounts Database of the Statistical Office of the United Nations Secretariat; International Labour Office, *Year Book of Labour Statistics* (Geneva, various years); World Bank, *World Debt Tables: External Debt of Developing Countries, 1988–89 edition,* vol. II, *Country Tables* (Washington, D.C., 1988).

a   Through the accession of the German Democratic Republic to the Federal Republic of Germany with effect from 3 October 1990, the two German States have united to form one sovereign State. As from the date of unification, the Federal Republic of Germany acts in the United Nations under the designation "Germany". All data shown for Germany pertain to end-June 1990 or earlier and are indicated separately for the Federal Republic of Germany and the former German Democratic Republic.

b   1975/79.
c   Data refer to the former Yemen Arab Republic only.
d   For the former Democratic Yemen, corresponding figure is 1165.
e   For the former Democratic Yemen, corresponding figure is 513.
f   For the former Democratic Yemen, corresponding figures are -7.8 for 1970–1975, 14.6 for 1975–1980 and 4.0 for 1980–1986.
g   For the former Democratic Yemen, corresponding figure is 7.6.

Annex I

Nairobi Forward-looking Strategies for the Advancement of Women

The Nairobi Forward-looking Strategies for the Advancement of Women were adopted by the World Conference to Review and Appraise the Achievements of the United Nations Decade for Women: Equality, Development and Peace, held in Nairobi, Kenya, 15–26 July 1985,[1] and endorsed by the General Assembly in its resolution 40/108 on 13 December 1985. They call for:

Sexual equality [2]
- the elimination of all forms of discrimination against women
- equal rights under the law
- equal rights to marriage and divorce
- the establishment, in every country, of a high-level governmental body to monitor and implement progress towards equality.

Women's autonomy and power [3]
- the right of all women—irrespective or marital status—to buy, sell, own and administer property and other resources independently
- the protection of women's rights to land, credit, training, investment and income as an integral part of all agrarian reform and agricultural development
- the equal involvement of women, at every stage and level of development
- the promotion of women to positions of power at every level within all political and legislative bodies in order to achieve parity with men
- measures to promote equal distribution of productive resources and reduce mass poverty among women, particularly in times of economic recession.

Recognition of women's unpaid work [4]
- recognition of the extent and value of women's unpaid work, inside and outside the home
- inclusion of women's paid and unpaid work in national accounts and economic statistics
- the sharing of domestic responsibilities
- the development of services, to reduce women's child-care and domestic workload, including introduction of incentives to encourage employers to provide child-care facilities for working parents
- the establishment of flexible working hours to encourage the sharing of child-care and domestic work between parents.

Advances in women's paid work [5]
- equal employment opportunities
- equal pay for work of equal value
- recognition of the extent and value of women's work in the informal sector
- measures to encourage women to work in male-dominated occupations and vice versa, in order to desegregate the work place
- preferential treatment in hiring of women so long as they are a disproportionate share of the unemployed
- adequate social security and unemployment benefits.

Health services and family planning [6]
- equal access to health services
- adequate health facilities for mothers and children
- every woman's right to decide on the number and spacing of her children, and access to family planning for every woman
- discouragement of child-bearing at too early an age.

Better educational opportunities [7]
- equal access to education and training
- efforts to have more girls study subjects usually selected by boys, and vice versa, in order to desegregate curricula
- efforts to ensure that girls don't drop out of school
- the provision of adult education for women.

Promotion of peace [8]
- the involvement of women, in promoting peace and disarmament.

Minimum targets for the year 2000 [9]
- enforcement of laws guaranteeing implementation of women's equality
- an increase in the life expectancy of women to at least 65 years in all countries
- the reduction of maternal mortality
- the elimination of women's illiteracy
- the expansion of employment opportunities.

Notes

1 See *Report of the Conference to Review and Appraise the Achievements of the United Nations Decade for Women: Equality, Development and Peace* (United Nations publication, Sales No. E.85.IV.10).

2 Ibid., paras. 43, 54, 74, 57.

3 Ibid., paras. 74, 62, 111, 86, 19.

4 Ibid., paras. 59, 120, 59, 228, 136 and 228.

5 Ibid., paras. 54; 137; 59 and 120; 137, 133 and 138; 144 and 145; 140.

6 Ibid., paras. 54, 155, 156, 158.

7 Ibid., paras. 54 and 189, 171, 165.

8 Ibid., para. 240.

9 Ibid., paras. 35, 155, 35, 132.

Annex II

Convention on the Elimination of All Forms of Discrimination against Women

On 18 December 1979, the Convention on the Elimination of All Forms of Discrimination against Women was adopted by the General Assembly. It became an international treaty on 3 September 1981 after the twentieth country had ratified it.

Bringing the female half of humanity into the focus of human rights concerns, the Convention establishes not only an international bill of rights for women but also an agenda for action by countries to guarantee those rights.

Governments are committed to:
- creating conditions within which women can exercise and employ basic rights and freedoms.
- affirmative action for women until parity with men is achieved.
- abolishing all forms of slavery and prostitution of women.
- securing women's right to vote, stand for election and hold public or political office.
- providing equal opportunity for women to represent their countries internationally.
- allowing women the right to change or retain their nationality and that of their children, regardless of marital status.
- ensuring girls' and women's equal access to quality education in all subjects and at all levels, including continuing and vocational programmes for women.
- ensuring equal employment opportunities, promotion, vocational training, job security benefits and equal pay for work of equal value. In addition, they must ensure that women who are married, pregnant or have children have the right to work and the right to maternity leave and other benefits; they must also ensure that child care is available and that pregnant women are protected from work that may be hazardous to their health.
- providing adequate health services, including family planning where necessary, and pre-natal and post-natal care, including nutrition for pregnant and lactating mothers.
- ensuring access to financial credit and family benefits, and the right to participate in recreational, cultural and athletic activities.
- giving special attention to all the provisions of the Convention to women living in rural areas.
- ensuring equal rights to choose a spouse, name or occupation; marry and divorce; own, buy, sell and administer property; share parenting, regardless of marital status; and choose the number and spacing of their children, including adoption or guardianship. In addition, governments are committed to establishing a minimum age for marriage and to ensuring that all marriages are entered into freely, by mutual consent.

States which have ratified or acceded to the Convention
(102 as of 1 June 1990)

Developed regions (32)
Australia, Austria, Belgium, Bulgaria, Byelorussian Soviet Socialist Republic, Canada, Cyprus, Czechoslovakia, Denmark, Finland, France, German Democratic Republic,[1] Germany, Federal Republic of,[1] Greece, Hungary, Iceland, Ireland, Italy, Japan, Luxembourg, New Zealand, Norway, Poland, Portugal, Romania, Spain, Sweden, Turkey, Ukrainian Soviet Socialist Republic, Union of Soviet Socialist Republics, United Kingdom of Great Britain and Northern Ireland, Yugoslavia

Africa (28)
Angola, Burkina Faso, Cape Verde, Congo, Egypt, Equatorial Guinea, Ethiopia, Gabon, Ghana, Guinea, Guinea-Bissau, Kenya, Liberia, Libyan Arab Jamahiriya, Madagascar, Malawi, Mali, Mauritius, Nigeria, Rwanda, Senegal, Sierra Leone, Togo, Tunisia, United Republic of Tanzania, Uganda, Zaire, Zambia

Latin America and the Caribbean (30)
Antigua and Barbuda, Argentina, Barbados, Belize, Bolivia, Brazil, Chile, Colombia, Costa Rica, Cuba, Dominica, Dominican Republic, Ecuador, El Salvador, Guatemala, Guyana, Haiti, Honduras, Jamaica, Mexico, Nicaragua, Panama, Paraguay, Peru, St. Kitts and Nevis, St. Lucia, St. Vincent, Trinidad and Tobago, Uruguay, Venezuela

Asia and the Pacific (12)
Bangladesh, Bhutan, China, Indonesia, Iraq, Lao Peoples Democratic Republic, Philippines, Republic of Korea, Mongolia, Sri Lanka, Thailand, Viet Nam

States which have signed but not ratified the Convention (14)

Developed regions (3)
Netherlands, Switzerland, United States of America

Africa (5)
Benin, Cameroon, Gambia, Côte d'Ivoire, Sierra Leone

Latin America and the Caribbean (1)
Grenada

Asia and the Pacific (5)
Afghanistan, Cambodia, India, Israel, Jordan

States which have neither signed nor acceded to the Convention (45)

Developed regions (3)
Albania, Holy See, Malta

Africa (16)
Algeria, Botswana, Central African Republic, Chad, Comoros, Lesotho, Mali, Mauritania, Morocco, Mozambique, Namibia, Seychelles, South Africa, Sudan, Swaziland, Zimbabwe

Latin America and the Caribbean (2)
Bahamas, Suriname

Asia and the Pacific (24)
Bahrain, Brunei Darussalam, Burma, Fiji, Iran, Kiribati, Democratic People's Republic of Korea, Kuwait, Malaysia, Nauru, Nepal, Oman, Pakistan, Papua New Guinea, Qatar, Samoa, Saudi Arabia, Solomon Islands, Syria, Tonga, Tuvalu, United Arab Emirates, Vanuatu, Yemen

Note

1   Through the accession of the German Democratic Republic to the Federal Republic of Germany with effect from 3 October 1990, the two German States have united to form one sovereign State. As from the date of unification, the Federal Republic of Germany acts in the United Nations under the designation "Germany".

Annex III
Geographical groupings of countries and areas

Developed regions [1]
Albania
Australia
Austria
Belgium
Bulgaria
Canada
Czechoslovakia
Denmark
Finland
France
Germany [2]
    Federal Republic of Germany
    former German Democratic Republic
Greece
Hungary
Iceland
Ireland
Italy
Japan
Luxembourg
Malta
Netherlands
New Zealand
Norway
Poland
Portugal
Romania
Spain
Sweden
Switzerland
United Kingdom of Britain and
    Northern Ireland
United States of America
Union of Soviet Socialist Republics
Yugoslavia

Africa
Northern Africa
Algeria
Egypt
Libyan Arab Jamahiriya
Morocco
Sudan
Tunisia
Western Sahara

Sub-Saharan Africa
Angola
Benin
Botswana
Burkina Faso
Burundi
Cameroon
Cape Verde
Central African Republic
Chad
Comoros
Congo
Côte d'Ivoire
Djibouti
Equatorial Guinea
Ethiopia
Gabon
Gambia
Ghana
Guinea
Guinea-Bissau
Kenya
Lesotho
Liberia
Madagascar
Malawi
Mali
Mauritania
Mauritius
Mozambique
Namibia
Niger
Nigeria
Reunion
Rwanda
Sao Tome and Principe
Senegal
Seychelles
Sierra Leone
Somalia
South Africa
Swaziland
Togo
Uganda
United Republic of Tanzania
Zaire
Zambia
Zimbabwe

Latin America and Caribbean
Antigua and Barbuda
Argentina
Bahamas
Barbados
Belize
Bolivia
Brazil
Chile
Colombia
Costa Rica
Cuba
Dominica
Dominican Republic
Ecuador
El Salvador
French Guiana
Grenada
Guadeloupe
Guatemala
Guyana
Haiti

Honduras
Jamaica
Martinique
Mexico
Netherlands Antilles
Nicaragua
Panama
Paraguay
Peru
Puerto Rico
St. Kitts and Nevis
St. Lucia
St. Vincent/Grenadines
Suriname
Trinidad and Tobago
Uruguay
United States Virgin Islands
Venezuela

Asia and Pacific

Eastern Asia
China
Hong Kong
Korea, Democratic
    People's Republic of
Korea, Republic of
Macau
Mongolia

South-eastern Asia
Brunei Darussalam
Cambodia
East Timor
Indonesia
Lao People's Democratic Republic
Malaysia
Myanmar
Philippines
Singapore
Thailand
Viet Nam

Southern Asia
Afghanistan
Bangladesh
Bhutan
India
Iran (Islamic Republic of)
Maldives
Nepal
Pakistan
Sri Lanka

Western Asia
Bahrain
Cyprus
Iraq
Israel
Jordan
Kuwait
Lebanon
Oman
Qatar
Saudi Arabia
Syrian Arab Republic
Turkey
United Arab Emirates
Yemen

Oceania
Fiji
French Polynesia
Guam
Kiribati
New Caledonia
Pacific Islands
Papua New Guinea
Samoa
Solomon Islands
Tonga
Vanuatu

Notes

1   Comprising Europe and the USSR, northern America, Australia, Japan and New Zealand. Where used in the present publication, "eastern Europe" refers to Albania, Bulgaria, Czechoslovakia, Germany: former German Democratic Republic (see note 2 below), Hungary, Poland and Romania.

2   Through the accession of the German Democratic Republic to the Federal Republic of Germany with effect from 3 October 1990, the two German States have united to form one sovereign State. As from the date of unification, the Federal Republic of Germany acts in the United Nations under the designation "Germany". All data shown for Germany in the present publication pertain to end-June 1990 or earlier and are indicated separately for the Federal Republic of Germany and the former German Democratic Republic.

Statistical sources

1 International Labour Organisation, *Economically Active Population—Estimates, 1950–1980; Projections, 1985–2025,* six volumes (Geneva, 1986).

2 _____, *Year Book of Labour Statistics* (Geneva, various years up to 1988).

3 Inter-Parliamentary Union, "Distribution of seats between men and women in national assemblies", Reports and Documents, No. 14 (Geneva, 1987).

4 National Standards Association, *World-wide Government Directory of 1987–1988* (Bethesda, Maryland, 1987).

5 Sivard, R.L., *World Military and Social Expenditures 1989,* 13th edition (Washington, D.C., 1989).

6 United Nations, "Age and sex structure of urban and rural populations, 1970–2000: the 1980 assessment" (ESA/P/WP.81).

7 _____, *Compendium of Human Settlements Statistics 1983* (United Nations publication, Sales No. E/F.84.XVII.5).

8 _____, *Compendium of Statistics and Indicators on the Situation of Women 1986* (United Nations publication, Sales No. E/F.88.XVII.6).

9 _____, "Composition of the Secretariat", annual reports of the Secretary-General to the General Assembly.

10 _____, *Demographic Yearbook:*
1973, special topic, population census statistics (United Nations publication, Sales No. E/F.74.XIII.1);
1974, special topic, mortality statistics (United Nations publication, Sales No. E/F.75.XIII.1);
1976, special topic, marriage and divorce statistics (United Nations publication, Sales No. E/F.77.XIII.1);
1977, special topic, international migration statistics (United Nations publication, Sales No. E/F.78.XIII.1);
1978, Historical Supplement (United Nations publication, Sales No. E/F.79.XIII.8);
1979, special topic, population census statistics (United Nations publication, Sales No. E/F.80.XIII.1);
1980, special topic, mortality statistics (United Nations publication, Sales No. E/F.81.XIII.1);
1982, special topic, marriage and divorce statistics (United Nations publication, Sales No. E/F.83.XIII.1);
1983, special topic, population census statistics I (United Nations publication, Sales No. E/F.84.XIII.1);
1984, special topic, population census statistics II (United Nations publication, Sales No. E/F.85.XIII.1);
1985, special topic, mortality statistics (United Nations publication, Sales No. E/F.86.XIII.1);
1987, special topic, household composition (United Nations publication, Sales No. E/F.88.XIII.1);
1988, special topic, population census statistics (United Nations publication, Sales No. E/F.89.XIII.1).

11 _____, Demographic Statistics Database, Economic Commission for Europe, unpublished statistics compiled from national reports.

12 _____, *Disability Statistics Compendium* (United Nations publication, Sales No. E.90.XVII.17).

13 _____, *Fertility Behaviour in the Context of Development: Evidence from the World Fertility Survey,* Population Studies No. 100 (United Nations publication, Sales No. E.86.XIII.5).

14 _____, *First Marriage: Patterns and Determinants* (United Nations publication, ST/ESA/SER.R/76).

15 _____, *Global Estimates and Projections of Population by Sex and Age: The 1988 Revision* (United Nations publication, ST/ESA/SER.R/93).

16 _____, *Levels and Trends of Contraceptive Use as Assessed in 1988,* Population Studies No. 110 (United Nations publication, Sales No. E.89.XIII.4).

17 _____, National Accounts Statistics Database of the Statistical Office, Department of International Economic and Social Affairs.

18 _____, *Population and Vital Statistics Report, 1984 Special Supplement* (United Nations publication, Sales No. E/F.84.III.2).

19 _____, *Prospects of World Urbanization 1988,* Population Studies No. 112 (United Nations publication, Sales No. E.89.XIII.8).

20 _____, Second United Nations Survey of Crime Trends, Operations of Criminal Justice Systems and Crime Prevention Strategies, Centre for Social Development and Humanitarian Affairs, unpublished data.

21 _____, Women's Indicators and Statistics Database (Wistat), version 1 (diskette database issued by the Statistical Office, Department of International Economic and Social Affairs, 1988).

22 _____, "World Migrant Populations: The Foreign-born" (wall chart) (United Nations publication, Sales No. E.89.XIII.7A).

23 _____, *World Population Prospects 1988,* Population Studies No. 106 (United Nations publication, Sales No. E.88.XIII.7).

24 _____, *World Population Trends and Policies, 1987 Monitoring Report,* Population Studies No. 103 (United Nations publication, Sales No. E.88.XIII.3).

25 _____, *World Population Trends and Policies, 1989 Monitoring Report,* Population Studies No. 113 (United Nations publication, Sales No. E.89.XIII.12).

26 _____, *World Population Trends and Policies, 1991 Monitoring Report,* Population Studies (United Nations publication, forthcoming).

27 United Nations Children's Fund, *The State of the World's Children 1990* (New York and Oxford, Oxford University Press, 1990).

28 United Nations Development Programme, *Human Development Report 1990* (New York and Oxford, Oxford University Press, 1990).

29 United Nations Educational, Scientific and Cultural Organization, *Compendium of Statistics on Illiteracy,* Statistical Reports and Studies No. 31 (Paris, 1990).

30 _____, Education Statistics Database.

31 _____, *Statistical Yearbook* (Paris, various years up to 1988).

32 _____, *Statistics of Educational Attainment and Illiteracy 1970–1980,* CSR-E-44 (Paris, 1983).

33 United States Department of Commerce, Bureau of the Census, *Women of the World,* Nos. 1–4 (Washington, D.C., 1984/85).

34 World Bank, *World Debt Tables: External Debt of Developing Countries, 1988–89 edition,* vol. II *Country Tables* (Washington, D.C., 1988).

35 World Health Organization, "Coverage of maternity care; a tabulation of available information (second edition)" (Geneva, WHO/FHE/89.2).

36 _____, "Evaluation of the Strategy for Health for All, 1985–1986; detailed analysis of global indicators" (Geneva, WHO/HST/87.2).

37 _____, "Maternal mortality rates; a tabulation of available information (second edition)" (Geneva, WHO/FHE/86.3).

38 _____, "The prevalance of anaemia in the world", by E. DeMaeyer and M. Adiels-Tegman, *World Health Statistics Quarterly,* 38 (Geneva, 1985).

39 _____, Statistics Database on AIDS compiled from national reports to WHO, and WHO estimates, updated to August 1990.

40 _____, "Tendances et effets du tabagisme dans le monde", by R. Masironi and K. Rothwell, *World Health Statistics Quarterly,* 41 (Geneva, 1988).

41 _____, *World Health Statistics Annual 1988* (Geneva, 1988).